William Russell

Russell on Scientific Horseshoeing

For Leveling and Balancing the Action and Gait of Horses and Remedying and

Curing the Different Diseases of the Foot

William Russell

Russell on Scientific Horseshoeing

For Leveling and Balancing the Action and Gait of Horses and Remedying and Curing the Different Diseases of the Foot

ISBN/EAN: 9783337168599

Printed in Europe, USA, Canada, Australia, Japan

Cover: Foto ©Lupo / pixelio.de

More available books at **www.hansebooks.com**

RUSSELL

ON

SCIENTIFIC HORSESHOEING

FOR

LEVELING AND BALANCING THE ACTION
AND GAIT OF HORSES

AND

REMEDYING AND CURING THE DIFFERENT
DISEASES OF THE FOOT

FOURTH EDITION REVISED AND ENLARGED

WITH 450 ILLUSTRATIONS

BY

PROF. WILLIAM RUSSELL
PRACTICAL HORSESHOER

CINCINNATI
THE ROBERT CLARKE COMPANY
1899

COPYRIGHTED, 1899
BY GEORGE B. RUSSELL

[*Copy.*]

"The United States of America, by act of their Congress, have authorized The World's Columbian Commission, at the International Exhibition held in the City of Chicago, State of Illinois, in the year 1893, to decree a medal for specific merit which is set forth below, over the name of an individual judge acting as an examiner, upon the finding of a board of International Judges, to WILLIAM RUSSELL, Cincinnati, Ohio. Exhibit: Horseshoes and Horseshoers' Tools. Award; Horseshoes—for extent and comprehensiveness of Exhibit of Hand-made Horseshoes, of special design, intended to remedy defects in horses' feet, both natural and as the results of improper shoeing, and also to increase the speed of trotting and driving horses. Horseshoers' Tools—for Great Merit especially in the Foot Adjuster, which is very effective and simple, and enables the operator to so adjust the shoe as to perfectly equalize its pressure to all parts of the foot."

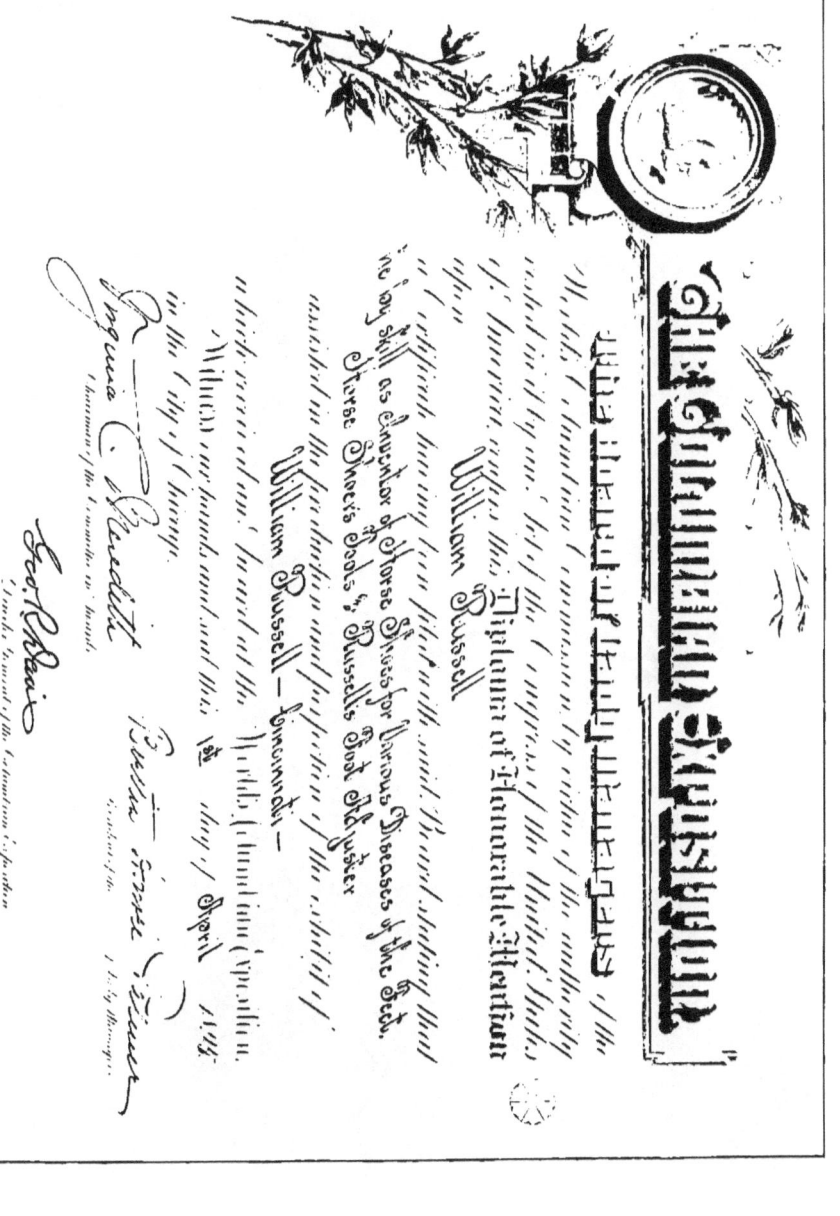

Cincinnati · Industrial · Exposition.

THE FIRST PREMIUM
AWARDED TO
WILLIAM RUSSELL AND SONS

For Best Display of Hand-made Horseshoes,
Remedying Defects in Horses' Feet,
For Improvement in Horseshoe Iron,
And for Morbid Specimens of Horses' Feet,
Showing Injuries sustained from Improper Shoeing.

CHAS. F. WILSTACH, President,
ABNER L. FRAZER, Secretary.

The First Premium Medals and Certificates

At the Cincinnati Expositions have been awarded to Prof. Russell, as above, for the successive years of 1870, 1871, 1872, 1873, 1874, 1875, 1879, 1880, 1881, and 1883.

· · · First Premiums · · ·

Have also been awarded to Prof. Russell's displays wherever exhibited, notably at the

TEXAS STATE FAIRS AND DALLAS EXPOSITIONS,
IN 1889 AND 1890, FOR

Best System of Scientific Horseshoeing.
Best Display of Hand-made Horseshoes,
And Best Display of Morbid Anatomical Specimens.

INTERNATIONAL EXHIBITION,
PHILADELPHIA, 1876.

The United States Centennial Commission has examined the report of the Judges, and accepted the following reasons, and decreed an award in conformity therewith.

Philadelphia, December 14, 1876.

REPORT ON AWARDS.

Product: HORSESHOES (Hand and Machine Made); also, HORSESHOE IRON.
Name and Address of Exhibitor: WILLIAM RUSSELL, CINCINNATI, OHIO.

The undersigned, having examined the product herein described, respectfully recommends the same to the United States Centennial Commission, for Award, for the following reasons, viz.,

A variety of shoes remedying defects in hoofs; also, patented rolled iron, for hand-shoe making. All highly meritorious.

J. D. IMBODEN,
[Signature of the Judge.]

Approval of Group Judges.

DANIEL STEINMETZ, CHAS. STAPLES, JULIUS DIEFENBACH,
G. L. REED,   DAV. McHARDY,   J. BAIN.

A true copy of the record.
FRANCIS A. WALKER, Chief of the Bureau of Awards.

Given by authority of the United States Centennial Commission.

A. T. GOSHORN,
Director General.

J. L. CAMPBELL,   J. R. HAWLEY,
Secretary.   President.

Tennessee · Centennial · Exposition.

AT NASHVILLE, 1897.

AWARDED TO

WILLIAM RUSSELL, CINCINNATI, OHIO.

The Highest and only Premium Given for
The Best Exhibit of Hand-made Horseshoes
And Horseshoers' Tools and Paraphernalia,
Including a Most Complete Anatomical Museum
Of the Horse's Feet and Legs, with Special Reference to the Diseases Caused
From Unbalanced Feet and Improper Shoeing.

INTRODUCTION TO THE FOURTH EDITION.

Modern farriery has become one of the most progressive of the sciences. For many years the standard works of the English, French and German authors were reprinted and followed as if the subject had been exhausted by them. But this view has given place in America to the most rigid examination into the wants of the American trotting horse, the latest development of the high bred and swift trotting horse; so that instead of American farriery being confined to the proper dressing of the foot and shoeing of the sound and the unsound horse, investigation has been extended to the action or gait, and many invaluable shoeing devices have been invented by the ingenious American mind to regulate, as well as to control the action of the horse both at the walk and at full speed. This is so great a step in advance that European works are no longer regarded as the highest standard of authority, but the American treatises have largely taken their place both in Europe and America.

The author has been impressed with this conviction for more than a decade. For forty years he has been a practical blacksmith, and has shod all grades of horses from the ponderous Norman to the fleet-footed thoroughbred race horse. His place of business has been headquarters for the treatment of every species of lameness and abnormal condition of the foot, as well as the smithy for perfecting the gait and developing the speed, by the introduction of such shoes as each individual horse under treatment demanded.

Moreover, he has patiently studied the anatomy, pathology and mechanical action of the foot, limb and body, so that by this dual mastery of the theoretical and practical science of modern farriery he might leave, as a monument, a life work that would prove both instructive and useful to the horse community. When the third edition of the present treatise was published he believed that he would not issue still another revised edition; but his constant study of the subject and his interviews with the leading trainers and shoers and horse owners of this country have evolved so many valuable inventions and so much improvement in the treatment of chronic disorders that another edition has become absolutely imperative.

The author trusts that the fourth edition will meet all requirements of being the latest standard authority on modern farriery. Prof. William Russell.

PREFACE TO FOURTH EDITION.

Since the publication of the third edition of my treatise on Scientific Horseshoeing, so many additional cases have come to my attention of the results of neglect of the horse's foot, that I have concluded to embody them, with copious illustration, in a complete final work to embrace all the important matter contained in the first, second and third editions, as well as the additional contents comprised in the fourth edition.

After a practical experience of over a half century at the forge and anvil, I trust that I have herein demonstrated my theory, by the most indubitable proofs, that the cause of most of the foot and leg diseases of the horse is to be attributed to the failure to properly balance the feet in shoeing. And I am upheld in my opinion by the best and most experienced trainers and horseshoers in the country. Readers of this, the fourth edition of Scientific Horseshoeing, therefore, will understand my theory; upon this I believe that the horseshoeing craft can rely faithfully, and I thus confidently proclaim it, so that the inquiring reader, who necessarily must be either a practical horseshoer, trainer, owner, or interested in the horse, may understand as he reads the reasons for the remedies and treatments for the disorders to the foot and leg herein described.

Some diseases are recognizable at once and can be assigned to known causes; others appear only after a shorter or longer course of treatment and experiment, while many do not respond to the most exhaustive diagnosis. In the present instance I believe a very comprehensive field has been covered, and that a study of this book and the cases cited will enable the farrier to prescribe the proper treatment from his own diagnosis of cases.

But it is not to diseases mainly this edition is devoted. The few remarks here relative to proper care of the feet are equally applicable to the sound horse, and make more emphatic the necessity for the care and preservation of the sound foot.

It is my good fortune to number on my list of friends many of the most prominent horsemen and farriers in almost all parts of the country, and for the many courtesies received from them, at various times and places, my thanks are due. Particularly, it should be stated here, that I am indebted to Mr. S. T. Harris, of Cincinnati, the well-known authority on all subjects relating to the welfare of the horse, for his valuable assistance and suggestions opportunely given while I was pursuing the investigation of the principles of this work, and continuing through an association of more than thirty-five years. WM. RUSSELL.

No. 1722 Freeman avenue, Cincinnati, O.

TABLE OF CONTENTS.

	PAGE.
Portrait of Author	ii
Diploma, Cincinnati Industrial Exposition	v
Medals and Report on Awards, Centennial Commission	vii
Medals and Awards, World's Columbian Exposition	viii
Tennessee Centennial Exposition	x
Introduction to Fourth Edition	xi
Preface to Fourth Edition	xiii
List of Illustrations	xxi

CHAPTER I.
THE HORSE IN GENERAL.

Judging the Useful Qualities of Horses	25
The Ideal Horse	26
Light Horses	26
Symmetrical Qualities	27
Judging Action	28
Structural Examination	29
Muscular Development	29
Front Limbs	30
Feet and Legs	31
The Trunk	31
Hind Limbs	32

CHAPTER II.
BONES OF THE HORSE.

The Trunk	33
The Limbs	33
The Bones in Detail	34
The Bones Enumerated	35
The Skeleton Described	37

CHAPTER III.
THE FOOT AND LOCOMOTORY APPARATUS.

The Subject Defined	38
Motion in General	38
The Limbs in General	39
The Foot in General	39
Bones at the Foot	40

	PAGE.
The Pedal or Coffin-bone	40
Bones and their Articulations	41
Ligaments and Lubricants	41
Muscles of the Foot and Leg	42
Soft Tissues	43
Sensitive Tissues	44
Circulation of the Foot	45
Nerve Supply	46
Horny Tissues	46
The Wall, the Sole, the Frog	47
Development of the Hoof	48
Importance of the Subject	49
Colored Plates, with Anatomical Sections, described	50
Queries and Answers, Outlining the Anatomy of the Foot	63

CHAPTER IV.

Practical Horseshoeing—Science, Art and Common Sense.

Prof. Russell in His Study	67
Necessity of Shoeing	68
Past and Present	69
Important to Horsemen	70
Essential Knowledge	71
Condensed Anatomy	72
The Center of Gravity	73
Emphasizing the Facts	74
Variation of Feet	75
The Angle of Incidence	75
What Rule to go by	75
How to get on in the Work	76
Farriers' Tools	76
Russell's Scientific Foot Adjuster	77
The Adjuster Applied—for Leveling and Balancing the Foot	77
Other Mechanical Aids	77
Method of Procedure	78
Different Kinds of Feet	81
The Natural Model	81
Rational Shoeing	82
Fundamental Principles	82
Securing the Levels	83
Maintaining the Balance	83
Preparing the Foot for the Shoe	83
"Opening up the Heels"	84
Indefensible Practices	85
Thinning out the Sole	85
Trimming the Frog	85
Weight of the Shoe	86
Form of the Shoe	88
Setting the Shoe	88

Hot and Cold Fitting	88
Adaptation of the Shoe	90
Fullering and Punching	91
Concerning the Nails	91
Driving the Nails	92
The Finished Work	92
Sizes and Uses of Nails	93

CHAPTER V.
Shoeing Young Horses—Action and Gait.

Practical Balance of Foot and Leg	103a
A Cause of Unbalanced Feet	103f
Condition of Action	104
Care Bestowed in Colthood	105
First Trial of Shoes	105
Modifications of Action	106
Care of Horses' Mouths	107
Handling Young Horses	108
Determining the Gait	109
Regulating the Gait	110
Balancing the Action	110
The Useful Gait	112

CHAPTER VI.
Special and General Shoeing.

Different Kinds of Feet	114
The Running or Galloping Horse	115
The Trotting Horse	117
Records of Champion Trotters from 1806 to 1894	118
The Pacing Horse	121
The Racking Horse	121
The General Purpose Horse	122
The Draft Horse	123
Frog Pressure	127
Proportions of the Hoof	128
Resetting the Shoes	129
Gait of Speed Horses	130

CHAPTER VII.
Lameness and Diseases of the Foot.

Pathological Shoeing	131
Causation of Diseases	132
Locating the Lameness	134
Laminitis or Founder	136
Primary or Passive Stage	137
Acute Stage—Villitis	137
Chronic or Violent Stage	138
Complications of Laminitis—Dropped Sole	141
Pediitis, Periostitis, Suppuration	142
Seedy Toe	143

TABLE OF CONTENTS.

	PAGE.
Complications of Laminitis—Dropped Sole	141
Poditis, Periostitis, Suppuration	142
Seedy Toe	143
Dished Foot	146
Side Bones (Ossified Cartilages)	147
Parallel of Normal and Abnormal Leg Bones	148
Hot Fitting, Clips and Spurs	151
Contraction	154
Toe Cracks	159
Quarter Cracks	161
Corns	163
Navicular Disease	165
Raised or Twisted Coronet	168
Another Example of Peditic Disorganization	170
Dished-wheel Foot	170
Wheeled Foot	173
Defective Ankle Joints or Knuckling	174
Knee Sprung	176
Curb	178
Bone Spavin	180
Bog Spavin	181
Canker	181
Foot Rot or Seedy Toe	182
Broken Bars	185
Lameness and Diseases of the Foot	186
Abnormal Feet	188

CHAPTER VIII.

FAULTS OF STRUCTURE AND ACTION.

Regulated or Restricted by Shoeing	198
Faulty Positions of the Limbs and Feet	200
Care of the Foot from Colthood	204
Splay Foot—Knee Hitting	205
Forging or Clicking	208
Speedy Cutting	211
Ankle, Shin and Knee Cutting	212
Sprains of the Tendons	213
Elbow and Arm Cutting	214
Adjustable Toe Weight	214
More about Ankle, Shin and Knee Hitting	216
Speed Shoes	217
Shoes for Quarter Crack	221
Rate of Speed of Trotters and Pacers	225

CHAPTER IX.

Specific and Remedial Shoeing.

	PAGE.
Its Purpose and Scope Delineated	227
Centennial Shoe, No. 1	229
Centennial Shoe, No. 2	230
Centennial Shoe, No. 3	230
Raised Spring Shoe	231
Scooped Toe Rolling-Motion Shoe	232
"Goldsmith Maid" Bar Shoe	233
Shoe to Prevent Forging, etc.	233
Non-paddling Shoe	234
Rolling Motion Shoe, No. 1	235
Rolling Motion Shoe, No. 2	236
Shoe to Prevent Stumbling	236
Toe Weight Shoe	238
Improved Toe Weight Shoe	238
Turn-Table Shoe	239
Common-Sense Shoe	240
Side Weight Shoe	242
Rolling-Motion Shoe on Foot	242
Shoes for Draft Horses	243
Shoe to Prevent Paddling, Cutting, etc.	244
Shoe for Bruised Heels, Corns, etc.	244
Shoe to Balance and Slow Action of Trotting Horses	245
Shoe for Track and Road Horses	246
Shoe for Ankle Hitting	246
Shoe to Widen Action	247
Side-Weight Shoe to Equalize the Wearing	248
Shoe to Prevent Ankle Cutting	248
Shoe for Curb, Spavin and Sore Tendons	249
Shoe to Prevent Bruising and Calking	250
Shoe to Prevent Twisting	250
Shoe for Wheeled Foot	251
Scooped-Toe Rolling Motion Shoe	252
Shoe for Line Trotters, to Prevent Scalping	252
Bar Shoe, for Line Trotters	253
Rasp-Cut Shoe to Prevent Slipping	253
Rasp-Cut Shoe to Prevent Slipping	254
Raised Split-Bar Shoe for Contraction, etc.	254
Scooped-Toe Grab Shoe	255
Center Bearing Double Rolling-Motion Bar Shoe	255
Scooped-Toe Grab Shoe for Speedy Cutting	256
Scooped Grab-Toe Bar Shoe	256
Three-quarter Shoe	257
Shoes for Sprained Tendons (five views)	258
Spreading Shoe (two views)	260
Shoe to Prevent Dragging and Forging	261
Shoe to Prevent Ankle Hitting	261

	PAGE.
Use and Abuse of Tips	262
Sharpening or Winter Shoeing	263
All About Calks	264
Bracing or Crutch Shoes	264
Knuckling Shoes	269
Hitching, its Cause and Cure	274

CHAPTER X.

A Tableau of Horse Shoes and Tools.

No. 1, Case and Description of Farriers' Tools		278
No. 2, Case and Description of Shoes	280	Showing a progressive series of 170 different patterns of old and new styles for all purposes.
No. 3, Case and Description of Shoes	282	
No. 4, Case and Description of Shoes	284	
No. 5, Case and Description of Shoes	286	
A Case of Fine Horseshoes, Made by Prof. Wm. Russell		288
Russell's Scientific Foot and Heel Adjusters		289
Russell's Hand Vise for Hot Filing and Foot Testers		290

CHAPTER XI.

Useful Prescriptions.

Cleansing the Feet	292
Foot Salve, for Various Diseases, Wounds, etc.	292
Liniment for Inflammations	294
Caustic Wash for General Purposes	294
Witch Hazel Wash	295

LIST OF ILLUSTRATIONS.

1. Model Light Horse.. 24
2. Skeleton of the Horse... 36
3. Bones of the Foot... 50
4. Muscles, Tendons, Ligaments and Joints of Leg and Foot............ 51
5. Median Section of Leg and Foot from Base to Knee.................. 52
6. Side of Foot with Hoof removed showing the Laminæ................ 53
7. Front of Foot with Hoof removed showing the Laminæ............... 54
8. Internal Structures of Left Fore Foot—outer side.................. 55
9. Internal Structures of Left Fore Foot—inner side.................. 56
10. Internal Structures of Left Fore Foot—front...................... 57
11. Internal Structures of Left Fore Foot—back....................... 58
12. Plantar Face of Coffin-bone and Insertion of Tendon.............. 59
13. Plantar Reticulum—with Veins, Nerves, etc....................... 60
14. Velvety Tissue or Sensitive Sole and Plantar Cushion............. 61
15. Inside View of Perfect Hoof..................................... 62
16. Bed Plate of Russell's Foot Adjuster............................ 94
17. Side View of Adjuster... 94
18. Front View of Adjuster.. 94
19. Back View of Adjuster... 95
20. Russell's Leveling Plate.. 95
21. Compass for Spanning the Hoof, etc.............................. 95
22. Position of Foot for Examination................................ 96
23. Sole or Lower Face of Perfect Foot Leveled, etc................. 97
24. Upper Face of Perfect Foot...................................... 98
25. Side of Perfect Leg and Foot Leveled and Balanced............... 99
26. Transverse Section of Foot and Leg.............................. 100
27. Front Foot Shoe for General Purposes............................ 101
28. Side of Perfect Foot Properly Shod as directed.................. 102
29. Full Size Section of Perfect Hoof—showing Natural Proportions—with Shoe Properly Nailed in Position.................................. 103
30. Racing Plate for Running Horses................................. 116
31. English Seated Shoe for Saddle Horses........................... 122
32. Front Foot Shoe for Draft Horses................................ 126
33. Hind Foot Shoe for Draft Horses................................. 126
34. Median Section of a "Foundered" Foot............................ 139
35. Front Foot Shoe for Dropped Flat or Weak-Soled Feet............. 140
36. Side of Hoof with Shoe Sprung off the Heel...................... 141
37. Bottom View of same Hoof.. 141
38. Coffin-bone Distorted by Laminitis and Peditis.................. 142
39. Specimen of Seedy Toe... 143

LIST OF ILLUSTRATIONS.

	PAGE.
40. Another Example of Seedy Toe	144
41. The Same Hoof Straightened on One Side	145
42. Dished Foot and Dropped Sole	146
43. Side Bone or Ossified Cartilage	147
44. Hoof from which Fig. 43 was taken	147
45. Normal Position of Foot and Leg Bones	148
46. Abnormal Position of same	148
47. Outside Appearance of Side Bones	150
48. Hoof of Draft Horse with Spur Inside	151
49. Bottom of same Hoof showing Contraction, etc.	152
50. Median Section of Hoof showing Spurs, etc.	152
51. Upper Face of Coffin-bone worn by Spur, etc.	153
52. Contracted Hoof	155
53. Lower Face of Same Hoof	155
54. Median Section of Foot showing Effects of Contraction	156
55. Mule's Hoof Overgrown and Contracted	158
56. Mule Shoe	158
57. Toe Crack in Hoof Properly Dressed	159
58. Quarter Crack in Hoof Properly Dressed and Shod	161
59. Bottom of Hoof Properly Shod for Quarter Crack	162
60. Inside of Hoof showing Toe Corns	164
61. Navicular Disease as Indicated by the Hoof	166
62. Navicular Bone Diseased (one half size)	166
63. Bar Shoe for Navicular Disease	167
64. Raised Coronet as seen from Back of Hoof	169
65. Peditis, or Chronic Laminitis shown by Abnormal Hoof	170
66. Median Section of same Hoof showing Structural Changes	171
67. Back View of Hoof showing Dished Quarter and Curled Heel	172
68. Side View of Another Dished Foot	173
69. Side View of Wheeled Foot	174
70. Knuckling or Defective Ankle Joint	174
71. Shoe to Prevent and Cure Knuckling	175
72. Position of Leg when Knee Sprung	176
73. Hind Leg, Showing Curb	179
74. Same, Bandaged and Shod	179
75. Hoof with Seedy Toe, Shod	184
76. Section of Hoof Affected with Seedy Toe	184
77. Disease of Coronet	186
78. Healthy Foot Covered by Swab	187
79. Felt Swab	188
80. Perfect Front Foot	188
81. Coffin Bone—Lateral View of Correct Position	189
82. High Toe	190
83. Coffin Bone in Case of High Toe	190
84. High Heels	191
85. Coffin Bone in Case of High Heels	191
86. Coffin Bone—Vertical	192
87. Coffin Bone—out of Vertical	192

LIST OF ILLUSTRATIONS. xxiii

	PAGE.
88. Perfect Front Limb and Foot	193
89. Front Limb and Toe—Pointing	193
90. Result of High Heel	194
91. Foot Properly Pared	195
92. Foot after Being Bandaged and Shod	196
93. Soaking Tub	197
94. Faulty Positions of Hind Legs (side view)	200
95. Faulty Positions of Hind Legs (back view)	201
96. Correct Positions of Hind Legs (side view)	202
97. Faulty Positions of Fore Legs (front view)	202
98. Faulty Positions of Fore Legs (front view)	203
99. Correct Positions of Fore Legs (front and side)	203
100. Shoe for Splay Foot and Chronic Knee Hitters	208
101. Shoe for the Relief of Sore Tendons, etc	213
102. Adjustable Toe Weight (side view)	215
103. Adjustable Toe Weight (ground tread)	215
104. Front Foot Shoe, for Ankle or Shin Hitting	216
105. Hind Foot Shoe, for ankle or Shin Hitting	216
106. Bar Shoe for Wide Movement	217
107. Record Breaker Front Shoe	218
108. Record Breaker Hind Shoe	218
109. Record Breaker—Grab Shoe	219
110. Improved Grab Shoe	220
111. Shoe for Quarter Crack Set on Well-balanced Foot	221
112-113. Variations of same	222
114. Quarter Crack Shoe Set on Foot	223
115. Side View of Foot Shod for Quarter Crack	224
116. Shoe for Quarter Crack	225
117. Centennial Shoe, No. 1	229
118. Centennial Shoe, No. 2	230
119. Centennial Shoe, No. 3	231
120. Raised Spring Bar Shoe	231
121. Scooped-Toe Rolling-Motion Shoe	232
122. "Goldsmith Maid" Bar Shoe	233
123. Shoe to Lessen Knee Action, Prevent Forging, etc	233
124. Non-Paddling Shoe	234
125. Rolling-Motion Shoe, No. 1, for Knee Sprung, Sore Tendons, etc	235
126. Rolling-Motion Shoe, No. 2	236
127. Front Foot Shoe to Prevent Stumbling, etc	236
128. Front Foot Toe-Weight Shoe to Balance Action	238
129. Improved Toe-Weight Shoe	238
130. Front Foot Turn-Table Shoe, for Various Diseases	239
131. Double Roller Shoe	240
132. Common-Sense Four-Calk Shoe, for Faulty Movements	241
133. Front Foot Side-Weight Shoe, for Ankle or Knee Hitting	242
134. Side of Foot with Roller Motion Shoe	242
135. Front Foot Shoe for Draft Horse	243
136. Front Foot Shoe for Draft Horse	243

LIST OF ILLUSTRATIONS.

	PAGE.
137. Non-paddling Shoe, Ankle and Shin Cutting	244
138. Shoe for Bruised and Ulcered Heels, Corns, etc.	244
139. Shoe to Balance and Slow Action of Trotters	245
140. Shoe for Track and Road Horses	246
141. Shoe for Extreme Cases of Ankle and Knee Hitting	246
142. Shoe to Widen the Action Behind	247
143. Hind Foot Side-Weight Shoe	248
144. Hind Foot Shoe for Ankle Cutting	248
145. Shoe for Curb, Spavin and Sore Tendons	249
146. Shoe to Prevent Bruising or Calking the Coronet	250
147. Shoe with Calkins to Prevent Twisting	250
148. Shoe for Wheeled Foot	251
149. Scooped-Toe Rolling Motion Shoe	252
150. Shoe for Line Trotters to Prevent Scalping	252
151. Bar Shoe for Line Trotters	253
152. Rasp-Cut Bar Shoe to Prevent Slipping	253
153. Rasp-Cut Scooped-Toe Grab Shoe	254
154. Raised Split-Bar Shoe for Contraction, etc.	254
155. Scoop-Toe Grab Shoe	255
156. Center-Bearing Double Rolling-Motion Bar Shoe	255
157. Scooped-Toe Grab Shoe to Prevent Speedy Cutting	256
158. Scooped Grab-Toe Bar Shoe to Prevent Slipping	256
159. Three-quarter Spring Tongue Shoe for Sand Cracks, etc.	257
160. Shoe on Hoof for Sprained Tendons, Wounds, etc.	258
161. Modified Form of Same Shoe	258
162. Ground Surface of Shoe, Fig. 160	259
163. Ground Surface of Shoe, Fig. 161	259
164. Foot Bearing Surface of Shoe, Figs. 161 and 163	259
165. Ground Surface of Spreading Shoe	260
166. Foot Bearing Surface of Same Shoe	260
167. Shoe to Prevent Dragging and Forging	261
168. Shoe to Prevent Ankle Hitting	261
169. Right Front Bracing Shoe	264
170. Left Front Bracing Shoe	265
171. Split Bar Shoe	265
172. Broad Bar Beveled Shoe	266
173. Left Hind Shoe	266
174. Shoe to Correct Cutting Inside Point of Toe	267
175. Shoe to Prevent Ankle Hitting	268
176. Same	268
177. Illustration of Knuckling	269
178–179. Shoe to Prevent Knuckling	270
180–181. Shoes for Inner and Outer Contraction	271
182–183. Anti-dragging Shoe Set on Foot	272
184. Half Bar Shoe for Contraction of Outside Heels and Quarters	273
186. Case No. 1. Improved Tools for Scientific Horseshoeing	278
187. Case No. 2. Description of Shoes	280
188. Case No. 3. Description of Shoes	282

LIST OF ILLUSTRATIONS.

	PAGE.
189. Case No. 4. Description of Shoes	284
190. Case No. 5. Description of Shoes	286
191. A Case of Fine Horseshoes, by Prof. Wm. Russell	288
192. Russell's Foot Adjuster	289
193. Russell's Heel Adjuster	289
194. Russell's Foot Testers	290
195. Russell's Hand Vise for Hot Rasping Shoes	290

Fig. 1. Model Light Harness Horse.
Properly shod so as to equalize the pressure on all parts of the foot and leg.

SCIENTIFIC HORSESHOEING.

CHAPTER I.

THE HORSE IN GENERAL.

JUDGING THE USEFUL QUALITIES OF LIGHT HORSES.

At the present day, when the horse is so universally employed, and when, as a rule, each description of work is performed by an animal having qualities especially adapted for it, most men claim to be familiar with the general characteristics that distinguish or mark the several types of horses, but few are really qualified to make an accurate discrimination between them, or have the ability to recognize or to judge knowingly of the "points" of a horse when it confronts them. This demands a close study of the useful qualities of a horse in all his spheres of labor, as well as a close knowledge of his vices, defects, and relative soundness in all parts, and implies the possession of ripe experience, extensive observation, and intimate acquaintance with the ideals that guide breeders in the countless shiftings of their work to suit the varying dictates of utility and fashion. These attainments are rare and difficult possessions. Previous, therefore, to making a critical examination of the organs and functions of locomotion, in their relation to shoeing, which is intended to be the main theme of this book, it is best to take a preliminary view of the horse at large, that will, by a natural and easy process, lead to a discussion of the details of the subject.

Ideal Horse.—The ideal type of horse is the blending together of a great many, and this may account for the divergence of opinion respecting it, for it is only ideal in the minds of some; each see in part and contribute their observation, and the ideal type becomes evolved; and it is in knowing this type that the skill of the judge is displayed.

Light Horses.—It is by patient labor that great works are accomplished, and this applies with much force and truth to the American method of breeding and training young horses to-day. The trotting horse is distinctively America's national horse and par excellence the light roadster of the world, and has been evolved from the thoroughbred and draft horse in a period of less than one hundred years, until now he stands the product of the highest and most perfect development of grace, speed, and nervous animal force. The light horses of America may be said to be included mostly under three heads—the roadster, carriage, and cob; and basing this division on the sphere in which each of the types act, we find the trotter the pure bred prototype of the roadster, the coach breeds of Europe bearing the same relation to the carriage horse of every-day occupation, and the hackney the progenitor of the cob.

The qualities that have the highest value in the roadster are speed, stamina, and style; speed at the trotting gait, and the talent of making a pleasing display. Such a horse must have a free and easy way of going, with a spirited and graceful movement. The typical roadster has a well-balanced stride and a high-headed straight movement that wastes no effort or time. He is not a light horse, nor a heavy one, but has the deep chest, round barrel and long-drawn quarters, chiseled limbs, tense muscles, dense clean bone, lean tendons, and refined appearance observable among the best turf campaigners.

The prominent peculiarities of the carriage horse may be grouped as style, size, and substance. The sphere of the carriage horse is different from the roadster, and the type is tall, with a muscular, large-boned, up and outstanding attitude, having the appearance of style and a comparatively slow movement.

The cob is the counterpart of the hackney in the common current of horse life, distinguished by the series of beautiful curves that define the outline. The rotundity of the rib and the plump muscular quarters and arched molding of the neck are influential features in producing the appearance. In movement, the spirit, dash, and striking muscular action of the knees and hocks impress the beholder with the style it displays and the appearance of graceful effort without corresponding speed.

These different types embrace also what might be said here in description of the different forms, and include in a general way the three points of size, symmetry, and substance.

The carriage horse should be sixteen hands, the cob fifteen hands two inches, and the roadster has no recognized limits. It is hard to say to what degree size adds to a horse's value. Speed does not seem to be always an associate of size, but as the market runs it would be advisable to give it some consideration in the roadster classes.

Symmetrical Qualities.—The proportions of a horse for symmetry should be such as to make a well-balanced whole. The trotter has a proportion of parts peculiarly its own, and likewise the other types, and any deviation from these should be considered. The substance of a horse is not solely related to weight. It is a consideration bearing on power and endurance; the density of bone, curve of muscle, and development of the vital organs are the chief concern, and durability as connected with these qualities is of prime importance to all horses. The term, good or high quality, as applied to horses, is understood to refer to clean-cut features, glove-like skin, silky hair, and firm, clean bone and tendons; these are evidences of good healthy organization and valuable indications of power under hard strains of usage.

Judging Action.—To form a correct idea of the action of a horse, it is necessary to observe it from the front, at the sides, and behind. As he squares away from you, the width and straightness of the movement may be noticed. An outward swing to the hind limbs, as well as a dishing in of the front action, is to be discountenanced. As the horse comes toward you, the smoothness of action is made apparent. A wide chest is usually connected with a rolling motion that gives a horse an awkward method of moving. From a side view, it is easy to observe if the action is balanced, and the knee action can be noted. A stiff knee action may indicate speed when it is rapid and gliding, but it is hard on the fore legs. The front action should be such as to give the limbs the appearance of unfolding gradually and steadily reaching out to cover as much ground as possible. Many horses have an easy, pleasant knee action, but the fault lies in the slowness of recovery. In the action of the hind limbs, the style and hock movement should be observed. Horses that are long-backed or weak-loined have a dwelling action behind that is unpleasing and detracts from their speed. If there is any thing the matter with the joints of a horse, it is quickly disclosed by the irregularity of their action. Most infirmities have a distinct influence on the regularity of the movement. The walk is also of great importance in considering the action. The horse should carry his head well up and his step should be lightly measured and deliberate, his feet being lifted clear of the ground and placed down evenly. The hind and fore limbs should work in unison, with an elastic, nervy movement that lifts some of the soil with every step. The flexion of the hocks should be free and straight, throwing the hind feet well under the body.

Structural Examination.—The chief aim of a critical structural examination is to discover blemishes and any unsoundness of "wind or limb."

It is of equal importance to recognize the conformation that gives rise to these diseases. The conformation favorable to the various diseases should be as familiar to the horse critic as the appearance of the diseases. The structural examination should begin at the head and extend over all regions systematically, so that no parts may be overlooked. The shape of the head and the expression of the countenance add to the beauty and tell much of the mind and disposition of a horse. When the line from the poll to the point of the nose is almost straight, it contributes greatly to the beauty of a horse's head. The nostrils should be widely expanded, as indicating well-developed respiratory organs. The features of the face should be distinct, the muzzle fine, with breadth enough between the eyes to give a pleasing, docile, sensible appearance, and to mark the indication of brain development. A large, bright, clear, full eye reflects a kind, courageous disposition, with plenty of staying power or stamina at the bottom. Active and slightly pointed ears are indicative of unimpaired hearing and an energetic disposition. A lithe, distinctly-lined neck is one of the most pleasing and taking features of a handsome horse. It begins with a light throttle and swells smoothly into the shoulders. The wind-pipe stands out large and distinct below, while above, the crest gives a fuller curve and more muscular development to the part. The chest should be deep rather than broad, as giving equal capacity while permitting the free play of the shoulder-blade on the body. The floor of the chest should be low between the fore legs, and of good length from the point of the chest to that of the elbow.

Muscular Development.—The formation of the shoulders has much to do with the elasticity and quickness of the front action. The length and obliquity of the shoulder-blades are the influential features. A long shoulder-blade implies long muscles, and these possess the greatest elasticity. Short and heavy muscles are productive of power at the expense of speed. Upright shoulders result in a short, stilted front action, while sloping shoulders give the leg a far-reaching motion. Horses of this conformation carry their heads well and legs well under the body, that adds much to their appearance.

Front Limbs.—As a whole, the front legs should be rather flat and cordy, due to properly attached tendons. In their proportions, the limbs should be long from the elbow to the knee and relatively short from thence to the ground. It is the upper part that is muscular, the lower portion being controlled by tendons, and it is desirable to have these muscles long and the distance over which the tendons move short, that there may be no waste of energy and a better control over the lower extremities.

Breadth and depth are very desirable in the knee, that concussion may be better distributed and carried off. The pisiform-bone should be sharp and prominent, for to it is attached one of the important muscles of the fore limb. The cannon should be short, flat, and clean of any thickness of tendon or bone disease. A pastern of the proper proportions not only adds to the gracefulness and elasticity of the action, but to its reach as well. A slope of forty-five to fifty degrees seems to be about right to give the required degree of strength and suppleness. When the pastern is too long, weakness follows; but when right in length and slope, there is a combination of strength, elasticity, and gracefulness beautiful to observe.

When the foot leaves the ground the pastern is bent back, but when it again touches the ground, it is extended fully and brings the foot down on its heels. There is no other part of the mechanism of a horse that does more work and does it with less friction than a sound and perfectly proportioned pastern.

Feet and Legs.—It is unnecessary for me to say that the feet should receive the most rigorous and careful criticism. The old maxim, "no foot, no horse," is to all intents and purposes more applicable to-day than when it was first expressed.

The perfect foot is of firm texture, fair size, and, of course, thoroughly sound in all its parts. The general healthiness of it is denoted by the natural waxy appearance of the horny fibers, the well-formed, cup-like sole, and the marks of natural usage of the spongy frog as a buffer.

Flatness of sole, dessicated or brittle walls, and contracted heels owing to mutilation of the frog, are defections commonly met with, not to say any thing of the abnormal variations that occur in the direction of the axis of the foot. A skillful judge may well spend one-half of his allotted time on the feet of the horses undergoing examination, to detect or give tokens of recognition to any defects of the wall, to see that the horn is dense and free from cracks; the sole, to observe the absence of any disease and the presence of the natural concavity and connections; the heel to see that the feet are medium size and of proper shape, the frog large and wide, and the bars strong and high.

The Trunk.—Passing onward the ribs claim attention. Round ribs that spring out from the spine may give the horse the appearance of being too long in the legs, but they are nevertheless good in point of giving the greatest amount of space to the vital organs. Close coupling to the hip is strength, and so is a broad loin thick with layers of muscles. Considering the proportions of the body, it is evident that the shorter it is above and the longer it is beneath, the better for the action. This formation gives rise to the approving term that "he stands over a deal of ground," and is associated with sloping shoulders. In such a conformation the legs have free play, and there is no loss of strength.

Hind Limbs.—The hind quarters should be scrutinized as to muscular development. From the construction of the hind quarters, it is observable that most of the propelling power comes from this source, and though the fore hand contributes in a degree, yet it chiefly supports the weight and carries the body; in fact, we may almost compare the hind and fore legs of the horse to the drivers and forward trucks of a locomotive. The shoulder-blade of the fore leg, attached only by muscles, plays upon the body loosely, while the hind limb is connected to it by a powerful ball- and socket-joint. The muscular development of the hind legs should be such as to cover any ranginess of the hips, which should also be wide and level. The croup from hip to tail requires length, width, and muscle to give it proportion and service. Long and muscular thighs, well spread and open-angled, provide for a long, quick stride. The quarters require an abundance of muscle extending well down on the legs. Below this the gaskin, or lower thigh, should be long so as to let the hock well down, and it should also be muscular and wide. For the hock to do its work to the best advantage and remain free from disease, it is necessary for it to be straight, broad in front, sharp behind, and free from any gumminess. Experience, knowledge and observation are essentials to the accurate judgment of these various points, as I have already indicated. And much more might be written on the subject, but the foundation of facts which I have thus far prepared will be found sufficiently broad, I trust, to include whatever may be necessary to insure a ready comprehension of the essential matters involved in judging light horses as most commonly pursued, the primary object being to show that scrupulous care must be constantly employed in the selection to secure a good representative of the equine kind.

CHAPTER II.

BONES OF THE HORSE.

THE SKELETON.

In the animal body, the bones form an internal framework, consolidating the whole structure and giving it general form and dimensions. In their connection and natural assemblage they constitute the skeleton, and before undertaking a particular description of the foot, it is advantageous that a summary indication of the general principles of the skeleton of a horse should be known, in order to better understand the details of the special parts with which we are afterward to have most to do. The skeleton is divided into the trunk and limbs. The trunk consists of the spine, a series of distinct bones, jointed one to another in the middle upper part of the trunk of which it is the essential portion, forming a flexible support to the entire body from the head to the tail; and the ribs attached to the spine above and the sternum below, inclosing the thorax or chest and viscera.

The Limbs.—The limbs, four in number, distinguished as the two anterior (or fore) and the two posterior (or hind), are the supports of the trunk, and are each divided into several parts, resting one upon another. Each limb has four principal regions, those of the front limbs being the shoulder, resting against the front part of the chest; the arm, next below the shoulder; the forearm, succeeding the arm; and the foot, the end of the limb. Those of the hind limbs are the haunch or pelvis, connected with the hind part of the spine, and the thigh, leg, and foot.

Bones Detailed.—The various bones entering into the composition of the skeleton of an adult horse are apportioned to the regions of the trunk and limbs, as follows:

The spine or vertebral column consists of bones more or less regular in their form, divided into five regions.

The cervical, 7 vertebræ, serving as a base for the neck.—The dorsal, 18 vertebræ, to which the ribs connect.—The lumbar, 6 vertebræ, supporting the loins.—The sacral, 5 vertebræ, in age fusing into one bone—the sacrum.—The coccygeal, 16 vertebræ, decreasing in size to form the tail.

The first cervical is called the atlas, being elevated above the others, and supports the head. The second cervical is the axis, being the center upon which the atlas turns. The fourteenth dorsal is the center to which all motions and weights are referred.

The thorax consists of the eighteen ribs on each side, placed against the dorsal vertebræ as mentioned, and resting by their lower ends on the sternum, or breast-bone, 37 bones in all.

The head is divided into two regions, the cranium and face. It is formed of 28 bones, which are distinct only in young colts, for when matured the majority of these bones are united and can not be separated.

The shoulder has for its base a single bone on each side—the scapula or collar-bone—making 2 bones for double region.—The arm has also only one bone to each limb—the humerus—or 2 for double region.—The forearm has 2 bones—the radius and ulna—4 for double region.—The forefoot, from knee down, has 16 bones, or 32 for double region—that is, the pisiform, cuneiform, lunar, scaphoid, unciform, magnum, and trapezoid bones form the carpus or knee, and the cannon-bone and two splints form the metacarpus, while the phalangeal or digital region is formed of the two sessamoids, upper and lower pastern-bones, navicular-bone, and coffin- or pedal-bone.

The pelvis of the back limbs is formed by the union of the sacrum and the two ossa innominata or coxæ, making for the double region 2 bones. The thigh has for its base one bone—the femur—2 for the double region.—The leg has for its base 3 bones—the tibia, fibula, and patella—making 6 for the double region.—The hindfoot bears a great resemblance to the same region in front: 6 bones form the tarsus or hock—the astragalus, calcis, cuboid, scaphoid, great cuneiform, and small cuneiform—making 12 for the double region.—The bones of the metatarsus or shank are three in number—the cannon and two splints—making 6 for the double region.—The bones of the foot or digital region behind are the same in number and name as those described for this region before—two sesamoids, two pasterns, navicular, and coffin- or pedal-bone—making 12 for the double region.

There are four bones in each ear, and the tongue is made up in five sections. Summing up, therefore, we find the bones of the horse distributed in the manner indicated in the following table:

Bones Enumerated.—Spine or vertebral column (entire length, but counting the sacral as one bone—the sacrum), ... 48
Thorax or chest, ... 37
Head—cranium, face, ears, and tongue, . . 41
Shoulders, forearm and foot—double regions, . . 40
Pelvis, thigh, hindleg and foot—double regions, . 40
Teeth, ... 40

    Total, .   . 246

Fig. 2 shows the skeleton of the horse with the bones in their totality and natural relation to each other enumerated and described.

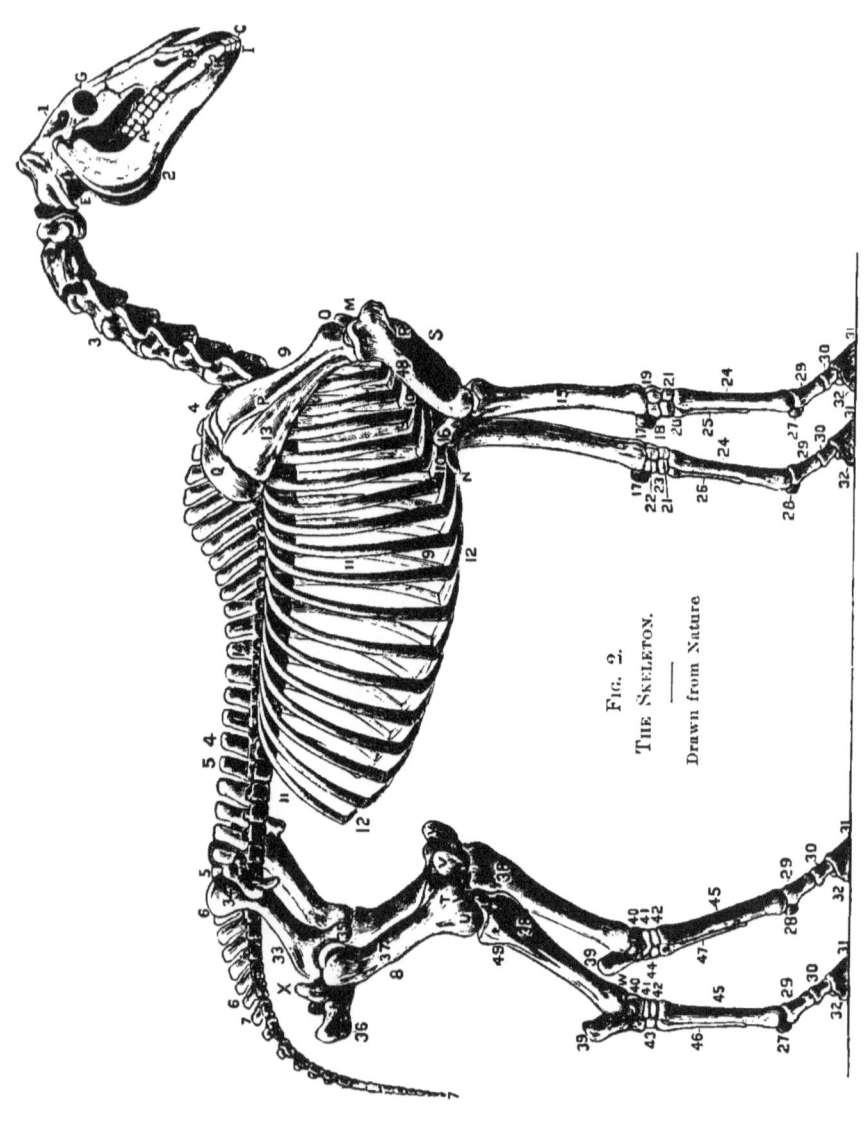

Fig. 2.
THE SKELETON.
Drawn from Nature

DESCRIPTION—ARTIFICIAL SKELETON OF THE HORSE.

1. Cranium and upper jaw.
2. Lower jaw.
3. Cervical vertebræ—Jointed process of the neck.
4-4. Dorsal vertebræ—Jointed process of the back.
5-5. Lumbar vertebræ—Jointed process of the loins.
6-6. Sacrum. A consolidation of the five sacral vertebræ, articulated, or jointed in front with the last lumbar, or loin, vertebræ, and behind with the first coccygeal bone; and on the sides with the coxæ, the bones which, with the sacrum, form the pelvis or haunch.
7-7. Coccygeal vertebræ—Jointed process extending from sacrum backward.
8. Sub-trochanterian crest.
9-9. Sternal or true ribs.
10-10. Cartilages of true ribs.
11-11. Asternal, or false ribs.
12-12. Cartilages of false ribs.
13. Scapula, or collar bone.
14. **Fourteenth Dorsal Vertebra**—The axis upon which the carcass is hung.
15. Radius—Forearm.
16. Ulna, or elbow.
17. Pisiform, or pea-shaped bone.
18. Cuneiform, or wedge-shaped bone.
19. Lunar bone.
20. Trapezoid, or table bone.
21. Magnum, or large bone.
22. Scaphoid, or cradle bone.
23. Unciform. This, with the last six named, make up the carpus or knee of the front limb.
24. Metacarpal, or cannon bone.
25-26. Splint bones, two on each leg.
27-28. Sesamoid bones, two on each leg.
29. Large, or upper pastern bone.
30. Small, or lower pastern bone.
31. Pedal, coffin, or foot bone.
32. Wings of coffin, or foot bone.

33-36 and 34-35. Coxæ—these bones with the sacrum form the pelvis.
37. Femur, or thigh bone.
38. Tibia, large leg bone.
39. Calcis.
40. Astralagus.
41. Scaphoid or cradle bone.
42. Cuneiform, or large wedge-shaped bone.
43. Cuboid, or cube bone.
44. Little cuneiform, or wedge-shaped bone. This, with the last five named, form the tarsus, or hock, of the hind limbs.
45. Metatarsal, or cannon bone.
46-47. External and internal splint bones.
48. Humerus, or arm bone.
49. Fibula annexed to tibia (38).
A. Molars.
B. Canine teeth, or tusks.
C. Incisors.
E. Atlas—First vertebra, or joint of neck, articulating or jointing immediately with the occipital or head bone, and sustaining the head. Hence its name.
G. Orbit—Cavity in which the eye is situated.
M. Cariniform cartilage of head of humerus (48).
N. Ensiform or sword-shaped cartilage of ulna (16).
O. Coracoid process of scapula (13).
P. Spine, or ridge of scapula (13).
Q. Cartilage of prolongation of scapula (13).
R. External trochanter of humerus (48).
S. Sternum, or breast bone supporting the ribs.
T. Trochlea, a pulley-like process of femur (37).
U. External condyle of femur (37).
V. Patella, or stifle annexed to femur (37).
W. Hock joint.
X. Major trochanter of femur (37).

CHAPTER III.

THE FOOT OF THE HORSE.

LOCOMOTORY APPARATUS.

The Subject Defined.—The object of this chapter is to pass in concise review, the organs or apparatus controlling or ministering to the function of locomotion in the horse, certainly one of the most important in the economy of the animal, by the necessary co-operation it affords the other organs and apparatuses in the performance of their natural properties and functions, and similarly one of primary importance in approaching the study of its conditions in health and disease. For these reasons, then, a clear understanding of the foot in general is absolutely essential to every horseman and farrier, if they would profit by its harmonious action and acquire practical working ideas of the relation of its parts and the mode of their co-operation, to be remembered, applied and utilized.

Motion in General.—The locomotory apparatus is composed of two kinds or systems of organs—the bones and muscles. The bones are the hard, passive portions, with joints and movable articulating surfaces providing for the necessary play in their relative positions. The muscles, grouped around the bones, are the active portions of the movement—the motor engines of the limbs, in fact—being firmly attached to the bones at certain determinate points, either directly or by tendons, which contract upon the organs to be moved, and produce the different postures and various gaits of the living animal.

The Limbs in General.—The bony sections which compose the limbs are destined both for the support of the trunk and for its transport during progression. This double purpose marks a distinction between the fore and hind members. The front limbs, being nearest the center of gravity, have to sustain most of the body weight, and are therefore specially organized for this service. Thus, the scapula, or shoulder-bone, is attached only by muscles to the trunk, and the weight transmitted through them passes to the vertical bones of the leg below, which sustain the pressure without muscular assistance, but when it is finally thrown on the oblique bones of the foot, at the angle of the fetlock, nature has provided strong muscular bands for their support and maintenance.

The hind limbs more especially play the part of propelling agents in the locomotory acts, and are joined in an angular manner to the different regions and by direct bony connection of the pelvis with the vertebral column, as may be seen by glancing at the skeleton, Fig. 2. Muscular agency is therefore necessary to support these columns, but notwithstanding the difference in functions assigned these limbs, they offer striking resemblances to each other, and what remains to be said of one is to be considered applicable alike to all.

The Foot in General.—The limits of this region are customarily held to extend from the lower end of the cannon or shank-bone, to the coffin- or pedal-bone, inclusive, possessing the elements of a single digit inclosed in one hoof. Approaching a little nearer, we will proceed with the subject, from within to without, by first glancing at the parts contained in the hoof, returning afterward to a description of the horny case itself.

The parts contained in the hoof may be given thus: 1. The pedal- or coffin-bone, and the navicular-bone, and the lower end of the small pastern, forming the articulation of the foot. 2.

The ligaments binding this joint. 3. The terminations of the tendons that flex and extend the foot from their insertions in the coffin-bone. 4. The soft structures of the foot. 5. The sensitive structures, including the vessels and nerves of this region.

Bones of the Foot.—In addition to the foregoing, it is customary to include in each complete digit the ankle, and fetlock, as constituting the apparent foot of a horse. The bones of this region are then divided into three sections—reckoning from above to below—placed end to end one upon another, which are termed the phalanges. The first comprises the large or upper pastern-bone and the two sesamoids, which unite with the lower head of the cannon-bone in forming the pastern-joint. The second phalanx is composed of the small or lower pastern and by its contact with the upper pastern makes the pastern-joint. The third and last phalanx, terminating the limb, consists of the pedal- or coffin-bone and the navicular-bone, which unite with the lower end of the small pastern in forming the pedal- or coffin-joint. These bones are situated in an oblique direction downward and forward, and form the extremity of the digit upon which the soft structures of the foot are built, as shown in Fig. 3 and 5.

The Pedal- or Coffin-bone.—The third phalanx of the foot has, from the earliest times, most occupied the attention of observers, owing to its greater liability than any bone of the extremities to injury from casualties natural to its peculiar situation and uses. It is the base upon which the entire foot is constructed, sustaining the hoof that incloses it as it fixes itself on the ground, and acting as the point of leverage in receiving and applying the power involved in the movement of the limb. It is a very hard bone, very finely poroused with numerous perforations and channels for the penetration of blood-vessels and nerves supplying the enveloping tissues. Its lower border swells forward in a half-circle and obliquely upward to a pyramidal eminence in its middle, on the front face of which is inserted the attachments of the principal extensor tendon of the foot, as shown in Fig. 4 and colored plates.

The under face is hollowed out like an arch, corresponding to the sole of the hoof, and here the terminal tendon of the deep flexor of the foot—the flexor perforans—is inserted into the semi-lunar crest, widening in a remarkable manner over the median imprints, as shown in Fig. 12.

There are two lateral wings to this bone directed backward, on the summit of which the lateral cartilages of the foot are implanted.

Bones and their Articulations.—In all those situations which have to sustain violent efforts, the substance of the bones is found to be very compact, formed of a proper tissue, covered outside with a tough, elastic membrane—the periosteum—and are abundantly supplied with blood-vessels and nerves for their nutritive movement. On their articular surfaces—between the opposing heads or facets combining in the joints—they are covered with layers of elastic cartilage, which are of the greatest importance in the smooth gliding movements of the bones and in the reduction of shocks and articular friction. When they are worn or transformed into bone, in consequence of certain articular maladies, the movements become painful and very difficult.

Ligaments and Lubricants.—The structures whose office is to brace and maintain the joints in contact and unite the movable surfaces are the ligaments. These are powerful auxiliaries of the muscular forces, give permanent equilibrium to the weight, and secure the firm and effective working of the articular surfaces. A serous membrane covers the internal face of the ligaments, which secretes the synovia, a kind of animal oil that facilitates the gliding of the articular surfaces and tendons. It is the vital lubricant of the living machine, and its use in the animal economy is identical with that of other greasy substances employed to lubricate mechanical bearings. See colored plates.

Muscles of the Foot and Leg.—Following the indication given of the passive organs of locomotion, the bony levers and their joints, comes a reference to the active agents whose function it is to move them. These are the muscles, and form, generally speaking, the fleshy covering surrounding the bony frame-work and grouped around and attached to the bones of the extremities.

The situation and direction of the muscles are important features to be acquired with regard to their arrangement and use in communicating motion to the leg and foot, for it allows the determination of the angle of incidence of a muscle on its arm of the lever, the relation of its principal axis to the vertical line, and its comparison with the axis of the bony lever which it moves. If the direction of the muscles be compared with that of the bones of the limb that they move, it will be found that they are parallel to these levers, and the proper direction of the bones being known to be rectilinear, that is, their principal axis being straight or parallel to the median plane of the body, it is sufficient to indicate that of the muscles to clearly establish this comparison. Undoubtedly the most essential part of the study of the muscles is their attachments or insertions, for with this knowledge we may determine their extent and direction, and even their relations and uses. The principal muscles of the extremities have fixed insertions of a cordy structure known as tendon or sinew. The superficial muscles are only related to the bones by their extremities, while the deep muscles are applied by their bodies directly against the bones of the skeleton. Three principal tendons serve to move the bones of the foot.

Two of these flex or bend the joints while the other straightens the column of bones thus displaced. The superficial flexor of the foot is the flexor perforatus, which is attached to the sides of the lower pastern-bone and flexes the ankle at the fetlock. The deep flexor of the foot is the flexor perforans, inserted into the bottom of the coffin-bone, whence it bends the coffin-joint and with it the whole foot. The front extensor tendon of the foot is attached to the pyramidal process of the coffin-bone. There are many other minor muscles, fixed and movable, connected with the cannon, splints, and other bones of the limb, which assist in the various movements and in their degree relieve the controlling muscles of a share of the stress of weight, as well as of whatever force or stain is brought to bear upon them. See Fig. 4 and colored plates.

Soft Tissues.—The bones, ligaments and muscles of the foot are covered by a loose connective tissue, which gives symmetry to the parts, and all are protected by the external covering of skin and horn tissues. I have already mentioned that in connection with the coffin-bone there is a supplementary apparatus of cartilage formation. This is composed of two lateral pieces, representing a thin flat plate on each side, of a fibrous elastic substance, pierced with openings for the passage of veins and nerves of the digital region. They are united behind and below to the plantar cushion, and in front cover the articulation of the coffin-joint and synovial sac, blending into the ligaments at that point. These cartilages are adapted to act as pads in easing shocks caused by exertions of the foot, but it often happens that they undergo changes and are invaded by an ossifying process which converts them into bone, as explained in a subsequent chapter.

The coronary cushion is a continuation of the skin and forms an intermediate juncture between it and the wall of the hoof, of which it is the matrix. It occupies a groove, called the cutigeral cavity, at the upper border of the horny wall, and forms a rounded prominence of dense, thick fibers, and assists in the elastic action of the cartilages and laminar tissues. Its surface is tufted with villi and shows a considerable number of nerves and blood-vessels which branch through its substance and secrete the horny tissue of the wall. Around its upper border is a narrow, lip-like margin called the perioplic ring, from which exudes the periople—the natural horny varnish of the wall. The coronary cushion mingles with the internal tissues of the foot and becomes continuous with the bulbs of the sensitive frog. See colored plates.

Sensitive Tissues.—The sensitive frog, or plantar cushion, is a thick, wedge-shaped mass of fibrous structure of fine elastic pulp situated beneath and behind the foot bones (to which it is attached) and between the back tendons (which it supports) and the lower part of the hoof. It is lodged in the fissures of the horny frog, receiving the spur or frog stay in the middle of its pyramidal body, which thus divides it into two diverging bulbs exactly like that of the outer frog to which it corresponds. At the point, or apex in front, it becomes continuous with the sensitive sole, and at the sides is attached to the lower edges of the cartilages. The base, formed by the bulbs behind, is inclined upward, and mixes its fibers with the cartilages and coronary cushion. Numerous blood-vessels and nerves complete this structure. See colored plates.

The sensitive sole, or velvety tissue, is the formative organ of the horny sole and frog. It is much thinner than the plantar cushion, and extends over or under the entire plantar region as well as the plantar cushion, which it covers by adapting itself to the inequalities of this elastic mass. This tissue shows the same structure as the coronary cushion, with the extremities of which it unites on the bulbs of the frog continuing above the laminæ on the bars. The surface of this tissue is studded with villi, similar to those on the coronary cushion, which penetrate into and supply the horny sole and frog, and in its meshes are sustained the veins of the lower surface of the foot. See colored plates.

Continuous with the sensitive sole (and resembling it in structure), and spreading over the entire outer or upper face of the coffin-bone until it is merged into the projecting substance of the coronary cushion, is a villous sheath, called the keratogenous membrane or laminal tissue, which completes the sensitive envelopes of the extremity of the digit. This laminal tissue exhibits on the external face of the coffin-bone a series of fine elastic leaves, called the sensitive laminæ, which lie in parallel rows, to the number of five or six hundred, running from above to below, separated by narrow, somewhat deep channels, into which are dovetailed similar horny leaves from the wall and bars of the hoof. This leafy tissue is intimately attached to the coffin-bone through the medium of the reticulum, which also supports the veins that supply its secretion. Like the other vascular tissues, it is very richly supplied with blood-vessels and nerves, and is at once the seat of acute sensation and the point where the active changes of inflammation—villitis and laminitis—are especially concentrated, becoming morbidly increased through the effects of bad shoeing, hard pulling, or driving and other like abuses. These parts are, in fact, the principal instruments concerned in the sensory apparatuses of the horse's foot, and the sensitive laminæ play a most important mechanical part in concurring, by their dovetailing with the horny laminæ, in securing the solidity of the hoof with the living parts as well as in supporting the weight of the animal, which is distributed through them upon the base of the wall. See colored plates.

Circulation of the Foot.—As we have indicated in the foregoing analysis, all the soft or sensitive tissues of the foot are freely supplied with blood, in greater or less quantities, depending upon the function which the tissue has to perform. If this is great, as in the more sensitive parts of the foot, a large amount of blood is required, if the labor is a less exciting one, as in the cartilages, and ligaments or membranes, the nutrition is furnished by imbibing the fluids brought to the surface by blood-vessels. The blood is carried from the heart to the various organs by the arteries or their small terminations, and is named red or arterial blood. The veins of general circulation bring the nutritive fluid back to the heart, and, according to its tint, it is named dark colored or venous blood. Both systems present at their extremities innumerable branches, which finally join each other, so that the fluid they carry passes from one to the other in a constant or circular direction. Between the two are small delicate networks of vessels called capillaries, which subdivide into a regular lacework so as to reach the neighborhood of every element.

Nerve Supply.—The amount of blood, under normal conditions is governed by nerves of the sympathetic system which regulate the conditions of repose and activity. The nerves issue from the cranium and branch into all the organs like the arteries which they generally accompany. They furnish the stimulus to animal life, and in the digits are the essential instruments of touch or sensation. Three branches of the internal and external plantar nerves furnish the foot on each side, and accompany the digital artery and vein, which at some points they cover with their divisions. The order of their distribution and termination, together with that relating to the circulatory system of the foot generally, will be clearly comprehended by a glance at the several colored plates illustrating this section.

Horny Tissues.—The hoof of the horse—considered as a whole—represents the horny outer covering, completing the extremity of the digit. It answers to the same natural purpose as the nail in man, by protecting the sensitive parts beneath. It is united most intimately with the internal tissues by the interlocking processes of the surfaces in contact, and is made up of three portions—the wall, sole and frog.

The Wall.—The wall is that portion visible when the foot rests on the ground, the middle of which is termed the toe, the adjoining fronts of face are the inside and outside toes, while the side regions are the quarters, the back extremities are the heels, which fold underneath and terminate in the bars. These parts are all continuous, diminishing in height and thickness from toe to heels, and all are lined with the horny leaves referred to. The bars are separated from the frog by lateral excavations called commissures, until they gradually fuse into sole. They form a lateral brace to the heels, limiting expansion and opposing contraction in these parts. The outside of the upper border is hollowed out, forming the cutigeral cavity of the coronary cushion and perioplic ring.

The Sole.—The sole incloses the hoof on the ground surface, between the wall and bars, with which it is united throughout its extent. Its upper surface corresponds with the sensitive sole, showing the pores receiving the velvety tufts, and its external face is more or less concave according to circumstances. It is a thick horny plate, scaling off after a certain natural growth, and is designed to cover and protect the internal foot.

The Frog.—Between the ∧ shaped angle formed by the inflection of the bars at the heels, the frog—a prominent mass of spongy horn—is lodged. It is wedge-shaped, with its point near the center of the sole, to which it closely adheres along its lines as they diverge backward, where it becomes continuous with the coronary band. The frog is separated into two external branches by a median cleft, each branch forming a rounded elastic eminence at the heels where they cover the angles of inflection of the wall. The internal face of the frog is indented with pores like the sole, and is molded to conform to the body of the sensitive frog, having a triangular fissure divided into two channels by a spine or ridge-like spur, called the frog-stay, into and over which the sensitive frog is bedded. The frog, like the sole, exfoliates or scales off by usage and growth, and is the natural buffer of a healthy foot when allowed to come in contact with the ground.

Development of the Hoof.—The horny substance constituting the hoof of a horse is of a fibrous nature, formed of minute hair-like tubes, cemented together by a tenacious opaque matter, taking its general color from the skin of the limb to which it adjoins; the inner face of the wall, however, is always of a light tint. The horny tissue of the hoof, being a dependency of the skin, is developed like it; that is, by cells in rows and layers. The perioplic ring forms the beriople; the coronary cushion, the wall, and the velvety tissue, the sole and frog. The consistence of the horn in the wall is dense, solid and compact, while that of the sole and frog is of a scaly, spongy nature. The growth of the wall of the hoof is constant or indefinite, but the sole and frog, after attaining a certain thickness, exfoliate and fall off, unless prevented by shoes from maintaining their natural flexibility. See colored plates.

It may here be noted that the angle of wall of the hoof in front varies from forty-five to fifty-six degrees. The inner face of the wall at the middle of the toe is in line with the frog-stay, and in mules frequently shows a more or less prominence of base toward the lower margin of wall, which corresponds to a vertical depression in the coffin-bone, and it is not improbable that it serves the same purpose as the frog-stay—to maintain the position of the coffin-bone, and prevent its rotation within the hoof.

Importance of the Subject.—The foot of the horse is an extremely important study because of the numerous diseases which affect this region, but what I have said, in thus reviewing the structure and normal condition of the essential organs of locomotion, will probably be sufficient to include whatever may be necessary to insure a ready comprehension of the other essential matters which are to follow, and facilitate a clear understanding of the requirements necessary to that perfection and regularity which characterize the natural performance of the various movements of the horse.

So long as the bones muscles and tendons; the joints with their ligaments, cartilages and their synovial structure; the nerves and the controlling influences which they exercise over all, with the blood-vessels which distribute to every part the vitalizing fluid which sustains the whole in being and activity— so long as these various constituents and adjuncts of animal life preserve their physiological functions, locomotion will continue to be performed with perfection and efficiency. Other points of pathological interest, relating to obstruction or misdirection and lack of balance in certain portions of the locomotory apparatus, will receive due attention as we proceed with the illustration of our subject and examine the matters which it most concerns us to bring under consideration.

Fig. 3. SIDE VIEW OF THE PHALANGIAL SECTIONS OF THE FOOT, SHOWING THE BONES OF THE DIGITAL REGION IN THEIR NORMAL RELATIONS TO EACH OTHER.

A, Pedal- or coffin-bone—third phalanx terminating the foot.

B, Extremity of navicular bone.

C, Small or lower pastern bone—second phalanx.

D, Large or upper pastern bone first phalanx.

E, Pyramidal process on coffin-bone, which gives insertion to the tendon of the front extensor of the foot, and which braces the joint by preventing the pastern from slipping too far forward.

F, Basilar process of wing to which the lateral cartilage is attached.

G, Irregular ridge above the retrorsal process or preplantar fissure, through which passes the lateral laminal and preplantar ungual arteries and their satellite nerves.

The lower face of this bone is arched, and into its crest is fixed the insertion of the deep flexor of the foot. The articulations of these bones with each other, and with the lower extremity of the cannon-bone, form the ankle and fetlock joints. The line through their central axis defines the natural incidence of the weight in its descent from the body, and indicates that the natural inclination of the coffin-bone is in direct line with the pasterns.

A, Flexor perforatus (attached to lower pastern bone).
B, Flexor perforans (inserted under coffin-bone).
C, Metacarpal or check ligament of the perforans tendon.
D, Suspensory ligament of the fetlock.
E, Front extensor tendon (inserted into front of coffin-bone).
F, Splint bone on outer side of the cannon.
G, Branching of the suspensory.
H, Branch of same passing forward to join the extensor tendon.
I, J, K, Periosteum membrane covering the surfaces of the cannon and pastern bones.
L, Fibrous reticulum covering the face of the coffin-bone and forming the reticular tissue leaves, or sensitive laminae, which dovetail into the horny leaves of the wall, completing the union of these regions.
M, The pastern-supporting or check ligament. This has never before been shown in anatomical drawings. It binds the upper head of the lower pastern to the lower head of the upper pastern, and is located midway between the flexor tendon and upper pastern bone. Its office is plainly duplex it holds the ankle and pastern joint firmly in position, and divides the strain with the flexor tendon in its severe downward action.

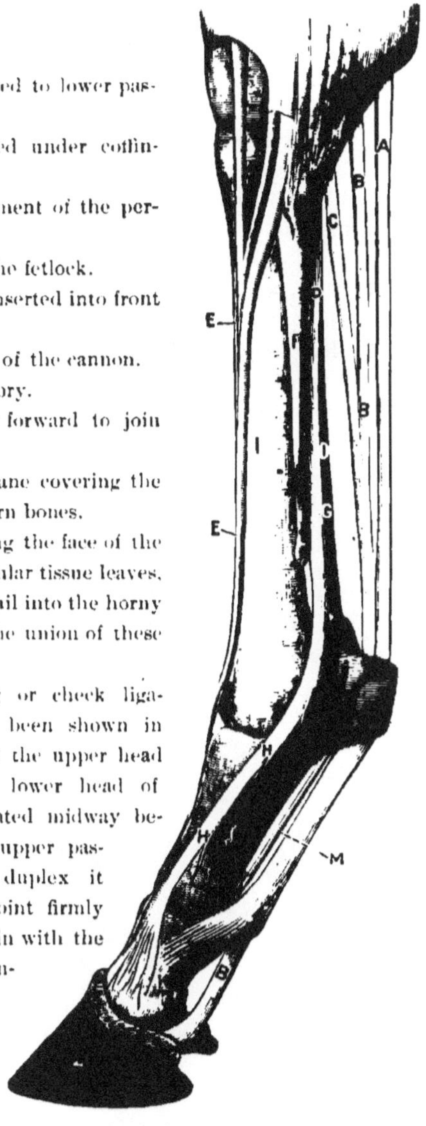

FIG. 4. EXTERNAL SIDE VIEW OF LEFT FRONT LIMB, SHOWING THE ARTICULATIONS, TENDONS, AND LIGAMENTS OF THE KNEE, FETLOCK, AND FOOT.

A, Coffin-bone.
B, Navicular-bone.
C, Lower pastern-bone.
D, Upper pastern-bone.
E, Cannon-bone.
F, Velvety tissue or sensitive sole.
G, Horny wall.
H, Horny sole.
I, Horny frog.
K, Plantar-cushion or sensitive sole.
L, Horny laminae.
M, Sensitive laminae.
N, Front extensor tendon.
O, Perforatus (superficial flexor).
P, Perforans (deep flexor of the foot inserted under the coffin-bone.
Q, Metacarpal ligament (joining the perforans tendons.
R, Suspensory ligament of the fetlock.
S, Sesamoid-bone (dotted line).
T, Branch of perforatus tendon attached to lower pastern-bone.

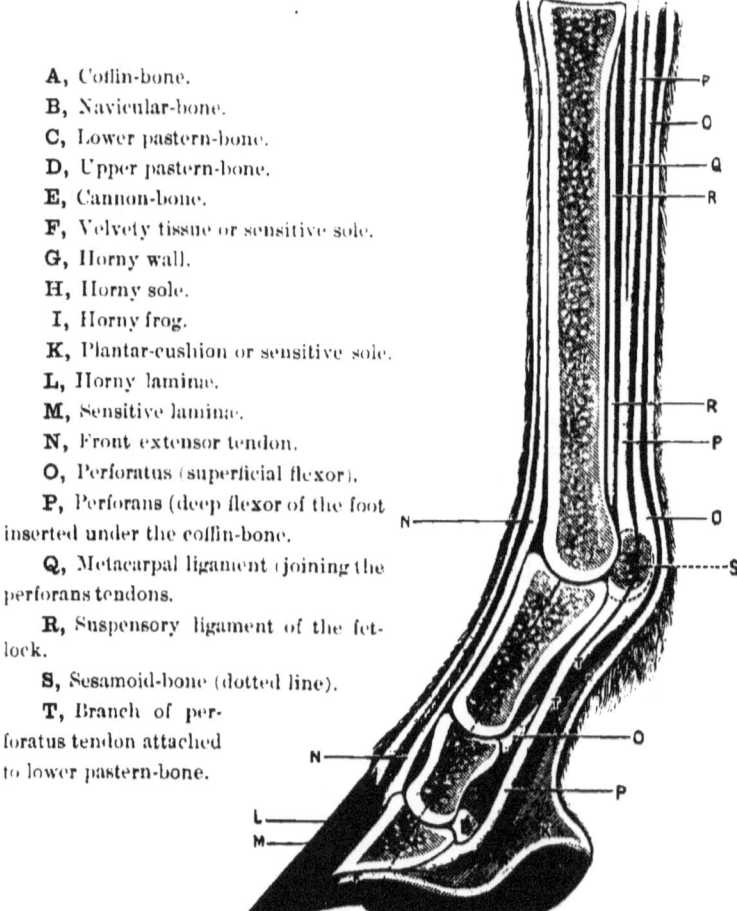

FIG. 5. MEDIAN SECTION OF FRONT DIGIT, FROM BASE OF FOOT TO HEAD OF CANNON BONE, SHOWING ARRANGEMENT OF THE ARTICULAR AND MUSCULAR APPARATUS.

The dotted line through center of digital bones shows the line of action of weight from above to below, and marks the normal angle of the foot.

THE FOOT OF THE HORSE. 53

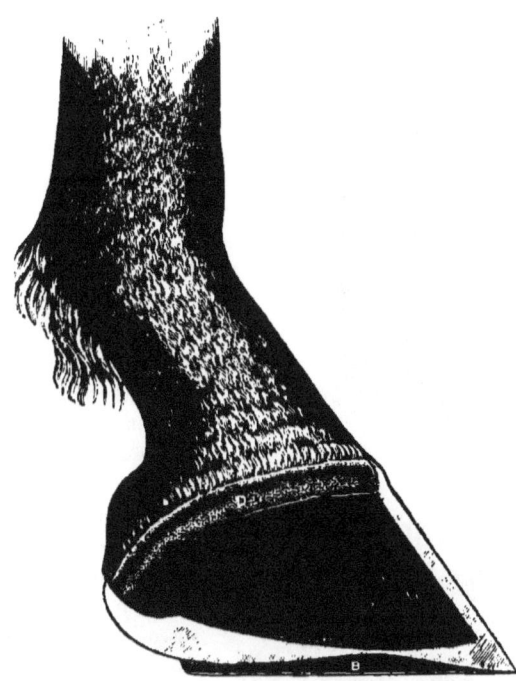

FIG. 6. SIDE VIEW OF THE OUTSIDE HALF OF THE RIGHT FRONT FOOT WITH WALL OF THE HOOF REMOVED, SHOWING NUMEROUS LEAVES OF THE SENSITIVE LAMINAL TISSUE.

A, Median section of the hoof, continued through wall, sole and frog. **B,** Base of hoof on opposite side. **C,** The keratogenous membrane or sensitive laminæ, covering the upper face of the pedal-bone, consisting of vascular leaves, designed to interlock with the horny laminæ on the inner face of the wall of the hoof. **D,** The coronary-cushion, showing its continuance to the bulbs of the plantar-cushion at the heel and the perioplic ring around its upper border

To the great vascularity of these sensitive tissues is due the bright red color they show on the surface. They form in their connection with the plantar surface of the velvety tissue, the essential apparatus of touch and feeling in the foot. They are, in addition, highly elastic and assist in the springy action so necessary to the ease of the foot when exerted in speed or in the severe strains of drawing heavy loads.

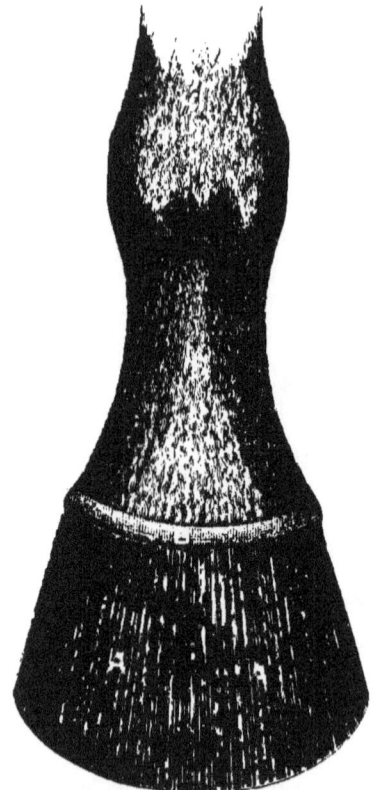

A, Numerous leaves of the sensitive laminæ (podophyllous tissue) formed by the reticulum covering the external face of the coffin-bone, and which interlock with the horny leaves (keraphyllous tissue) of the surrounding wall.

B, Coronary-cushion, the organ which develops the horny wall, and acts in reciprocal relation between it and the skin above, as an elastic medium of connection. It also unites in the same manner with the vascular laminæ, and is prolonged downward at the back, into the bulbs of the plantar-cushion and the villous tunic of the velvety tissue.

FIG. 7. FRONT VIEW OF THE HORSE'S FOOT, SHOWING THE SUPERFICIAL APPEARANCE OF THE KERATOGENOUS MEMBRANE, OR LAMINAL TISSUE, AFTER REMOVAL OF THE HOOF.

The villi of the coronary-cushion and velvety tissue determine the structure and maintain the elasticity of the entire hoof. The laminal tissue has the property of throwing out a temporary horn, whether exposed by stripping off the hoof or by the active changes of inflammation, but this must be replaced by that from the coronet when the foot returns to its normal condition.

THE FOOT OF THE HORSE.

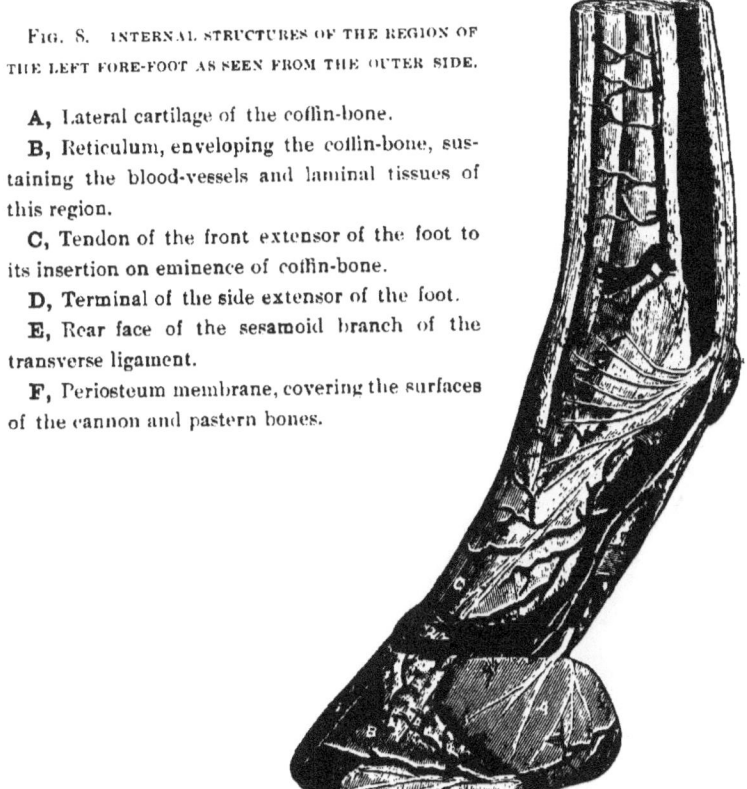

Fig. 8. INTERNAL STRUCTURES OF THE REGION OF THE LEFT FORE-FOOT AS SEEN FROM THE OUTER SIDE.

A, Lateral cartilage of the coffin-bone.

B, Reticulum, enveloping the coffin-bone, sustaining the blood-vessels and laminal tissues of this region.

C, Tendon of the front extensor of the foot to its insertion on eminence of coffin-bone.

D, Terminal of the side extensor of the foot.

E, Rear face of the sesamoid branch of the transverse ligament.

F, Periosteum membrane, covering the surfaces of the cannon and pastern bones.

These plates represent the arteries in red, the veins in blue, and the nerves in white. Each of these systems maintains the most intimate relations with the others and meets in the extremities in various forms of branches, collaterals, and ganglionic enlargements, remarkable alike for their large volume, intricate reticulation and extreme delicacy.

The divisions shown in this plate are the digital and ungual arteries and veins of the plantar region, the veins of the coronary plexus, and the median circumflex artery of the foot together with the digital branches of the median or cubic plantar nerve.

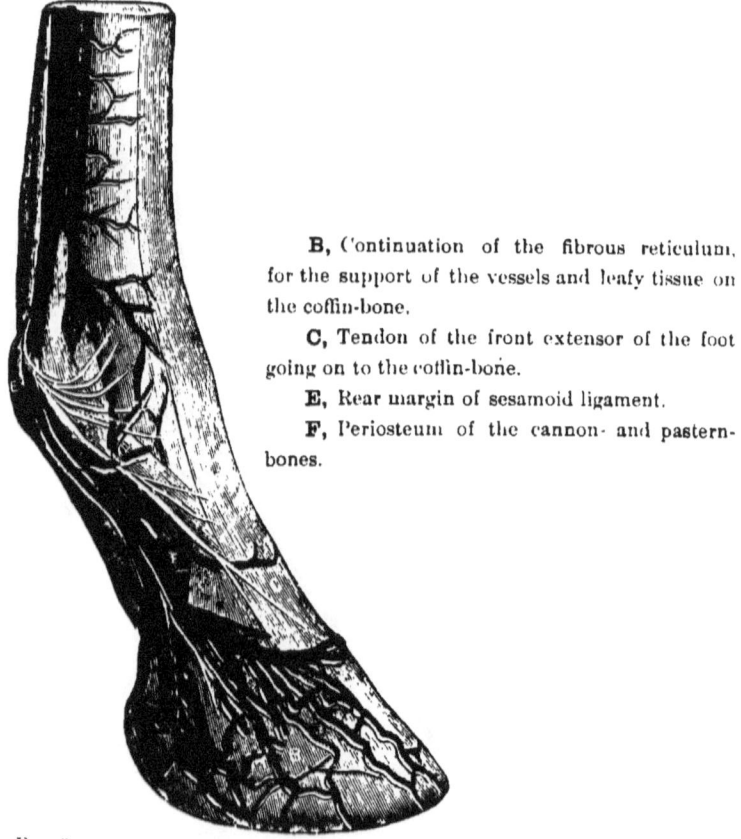

B, Continuation of the fibrous reticulum, for the support of the vessels and leafy tissue on the coffin-bone.

C, Tendon of the front extensor of the foot going on to the coffin-bone.

E, Rear margin of sesamoid ligament.

F, Periosteum of the cannon- and pastern-bones.

FIG. 9. INTERNAL STRUCTURES OF THE REGION OF THE LEFT FORE FOOT, AS SEEN FROM THE INNER SIDE.

The digital arteries and veins course almost immediately beneath the skin. Descending from above the fetlock joint they follow the course of the flexor tendon and throw out innumerable twigs and divergant ramifications to supply the surfaces, as well as the deeper tissue substances of the foot. Those shown in this plate are the perpendicular artery, circumflex coronary, artery of the plantar cushion, preplantar ungual, venous network of the laminal tissue, coronary plexus, and the deep cartilaginous layer —all flanked by the plantar nerve, which interlaces them with numerous filaments.

THE FOOT OF THE HORSE. 57

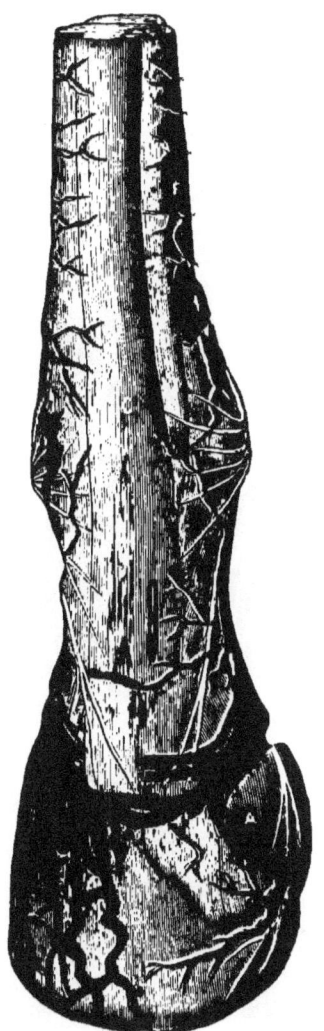

Fig. 10. FRONT VIEW OF THE FOOT REGION, SHOWING THE ARRANGEMENT OF THE INTERNAL STRUCTURES.

A, Front border of the lateral cartilage of the coffin-bone (the corresponding piece on the other side having been removed).

B, Continuation of the reticulum, forming the membraneous net, which holds in its meshes the dependent vessels and laminal tissues on the coffin-bone.

C, Tendon of the front extensor of the foot to its insertion in the coffin-bone.

D, Terminal of the side extensor of the foot.

F, Inner and outer borders of the cannon-bone.

The external and collateral branches of the perpendicular artery and satellite veins and nerves are here shown by their anterior branches, which concur in forming the articular branch of the phalanx, veiny plexus of the coronary crown circle, and net of the reticular tissue, accompanied by the vasa motor nerves belonging to the plantar system.

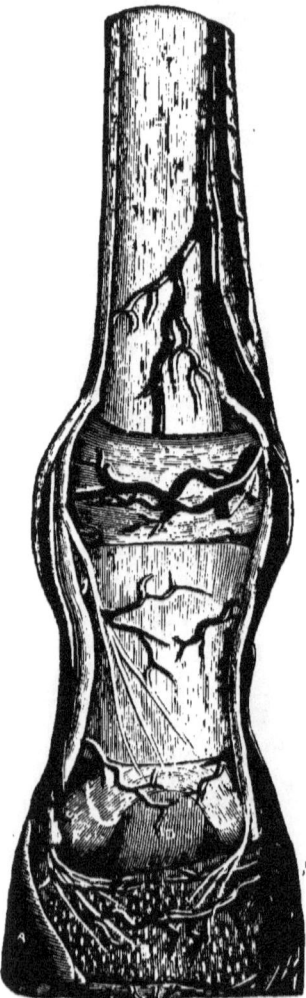

A, Rear border of the lateral cartilage (the other being omitted).

B, Pyramidal base or bulbs of the plantar cushion or sensitive frog, interposed between the perforans tendon and the horny hoof.

C, Reinforcing phalangeal sheath covering the perforans tendon and the suspensory ligament with a fibrous expansion and attaching itself to the larger part of the pastern-bones.

D, Flexor perforans at its exit from between the two branches of the perforatus.

E, Superficial bundle or ring of the sesamoid ligament.

F, Flexor perforatus, giving off two branches toward the bottom, which become attached to the lower pastern-bone.

FIG. 11. BACK OF THE FOOT REGION, SHOWING THE INTERNAL ARRANGEMENT OF THE PHALANGES.

The arteries, veins and nerves are the posterior offshoots of the internal and external collaterals, furnishing this region same as previously referred to.

THE FOOT OF THE HORSE. 59

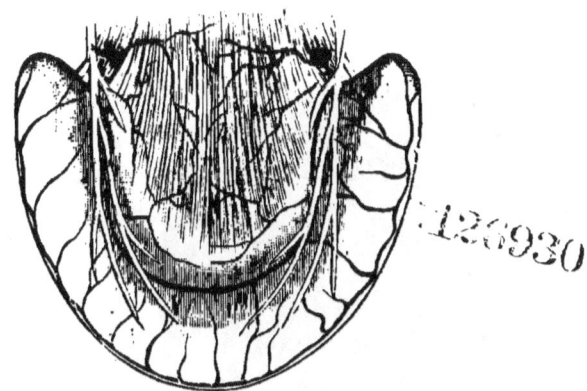

FIG. 12. PLANTAR SURFACE AT LOWER FACE OF THE THIRD OR UNGUAL PHALANX OF THE FOOT, THE PEDAL, OR COFFIN-BONE, UPON WHICH THE DIGIT IS BASED

This view represents the sole of the bone covered by the plantar reticulum and shows the origin of the preplantar ungual artery as it emerges at the retrossal process of the wings and loops into the semi-lunar anastomotic arch, communicating in the bone. The radiating branches from this arch and from the outer border correspond with the affluents of Figs. 13 and 14. The nerves shown are the descending posterior branches of the preplantar nerve, accompanying the digital artery on the retrossal process, traversing the cartilages and laminal tissues, and terminating around the plantar ungual artery in the plantar fissure.

The attachment of the deep flexor of the foot—the perforans—is shown as covering the semi-lunar crest and the median imprints of this bone; widening into a large expansion designated the plantar aponeurosis. This terminal expansion is covered by the plantar cushion which adheres to it most intimately. This muscle flexes the phalanges on one another, and it also concurs in flexing the entire foot on the fore-arm.

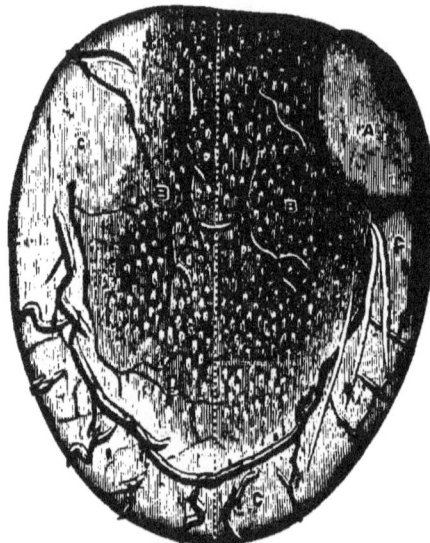

FIG. 13. THE PLANTAR RETICULUM OR KERATOGENOUS MEMBRANE COVERING THE LOWER FACE OF THE COFFIN-BONE, AND SUSTAINING IN ITS MESHES THE VEINS OF THE SOLAR PLEXUS.

A, Lower border of the lateral cartilage of the coffin-bone (the part corresponding to this on the other side being detached for this illustration.)

B, The proper tissue, or villous tunic of the reticulum, which is correlated to the upper surface of the velvety tissue, and answers to the periosteum on the coffin-bone, which it envelopes like a villous sheath.

C, The periphery of the reticular tissue, conspicuous for the divisions of arteries and vessels which it sustains and which prevail so largely throughout the whole extent of the plantar surface.

The venous apparatus of the digital region is remarkable for the number, distribution and interlaced disposition of the vessels composing it. They are extended over and molded on the two last phalanges of the foot, discharging themselves by numerous descending and ascending branches, converging in flexiform nets and arches, and communicating with each other, or traversing every element, by an intricate system of arterioles or venules, analogous to the capillary system.

THE FOOT OF THE HORSE. 61

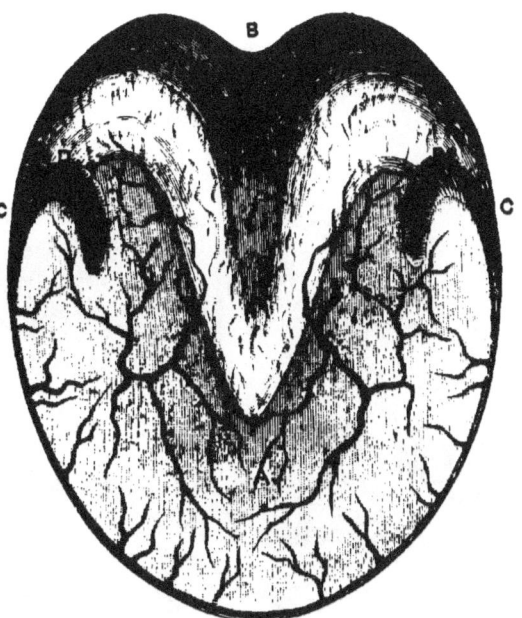

A, Lower face of the velvety tissue, or sensitive sole immediately overlying the horny sole, which it secretes.

B, Base, or bulbs of the plantar cushion, separated by the depression or cleft (median lacuna), on the inside of which the spur or stay of the horny frog reaches.

C, Return of the bars to their junction with the wall.

D, Arch, or spring of the bars, formed by their angle of inflection at the heels, also showing the laminal leaves covering them.

Fig. 14. THE LOWER FACE OF THE HORSE'S FOOT, AFTER REMOVAL OF THE HORNY HOOF.

The arteries forming the plexus or network furnishing this region of the foot are similar to those shown on the other plates, and like them proceed from the parent trunk, descending on the side of the digit, terminating in the plantar ungual branch from which the inferior communicating arteries pass through the foramina just above the edge of the coffin-bone, branching closely over the laminal tissue and uniting below to form the large circumflex, or peripheral artery, which runs around the toe. They also help to form the inferior circumflex artery and finally join the coronary plexus—collectively forming the circulatory apparatus of the entire digital region.

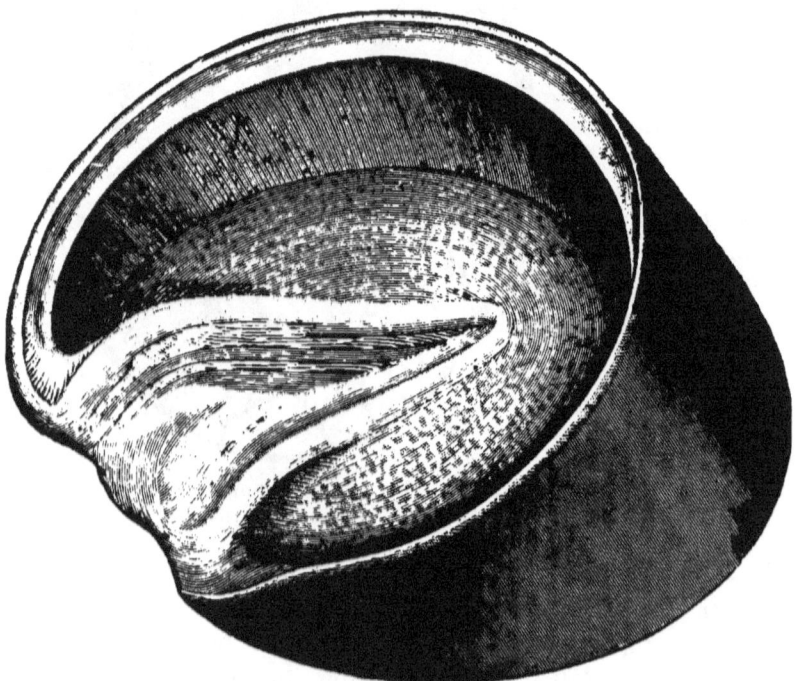

FIG. 15. A PERFECT HOOF, REMOVED FROM THE FOOT, SHOWING A LATERAL POSTERIOR VIEW OF A SOUND NATURAL AND HEALTHY DEVELOPMENT OF WALL— HORNY LAMINÆ—CORONARY CHAMBER—SOLE, FROG-STAY, FISSURES AND BARS.

BRIEF OUTLINE OF ANATOMY OF THE FOOT.

Adapted from the Subject-matter of this Chapter.

It should be studied by all who wish to get a brief, connected view of the principal parts and practical workings of the locomotory apparatus of the horse.

Q. 1. What constitutes the apparatus of locomotion?

A. The bones and muscles co-operating with the vital organism.

Q. 2. What does the " foot" or " digital region" imply?

A. It includes the ankle from the fetlock down, comprised in a single hoof.

Q. 3. What bones enter into its formation?

A. The lower end of the cannon, the two sesamoids, upper and lower pasterns; navicular and coffin-bones form the skeleton on which the other structures are built.

Q. 4. How do these co-operate?

A. They concur to form joints, which provide for the necessary motion. (For details, see Figs. 3 to 5.)

Q. 5. Name the joints of the foot or digit.

A. There are three of them—the fetlock, pastern, and coffin joints, made by the union of two or more bones moving one upon the other.

Q. 6. What completes the jointed processes?

A. They are held together by ligaments, and are lubricated by the synovial fluid secreted by the inclosing membrane.

Q. 7. What further of their work?

A. That they are of special importance to the value of the animal, and are the parts most subject to impairment from injury or disease.

Q. 8. What muscles co-operate in the foot action?

A. The two principal muscles that flex or bend the foot are

the perforatus and perforans, and one principal muscle, the front extensor, straightens or thrusts the foot forward. (See Figs. 4 and 5.)

Q. 9. What is the significance of their positions and insertions?

A. Knowing the action of the bones to be straightforward and back, we know that the muscles must act on the same line.

Q. 10. What duty do the navicular and small sesamoids perform?

A. They act as pulleys (and supports annexed to the joints) in facilitating the gliding movements of the muscles which pass over them.

Q. 11. What do we understand by the "soft tissues" of the foot?

A. They comprise various organs of cartilage, fibrous or elastic tissues for the development of other tissues, and for easing concussion on the hard organs.

Q. 12. What are the principal apparatuses thus referred to?

A. The lateral cartilages, the coronary and plantar cushions.

Q. 13. What further do we know concerning them?

A. The cartilages are pads at the sides of the foot, the coronary cushion secretes the horny wall, and the plantar cushion acts as a support to the back tendons.

Q. 14. What are the "sensitive tissues"?

A. The laminal or leafy tissue and the velvety tissue, which are continuous with the membrane covering the entire foot.

Q. 15. What is the function of the laminæ?

A. They form the connection between the internal foot and the encasing hoof, by dovetailing into the horny leaves on the wall, and thus support the action of the two parts.

Q. 16. What of the velvety tissue?

A. This is the covering of the sole of the coffin-bone, the

sensitive sole of the foot, and secretes the outer horny sole and frog.

Q. 17. What relation does the hoof sustain to the foot?

A. It serves as the outer covering or case, and protects the internal parts from external violence.

Q. 18. What is scientific horseshoing?

A. It is a noble artificial skill of man working in conjunction with nature, to keep the foot in its natural formation. The shoe is to protect the foot from external injuries.

Q. 19. How many acts are there to be performed before the foot is properly shod.

A. There are three acts required: First, to remove all the surplus growth, and properly shape the foot to its natural form and size. Second, to select a bar of iron or steel, make and fit a shoe of suitable weight for which the foot and leg requires, and the work the horse has to perform and fit properly to the foot. Third, to nail the shoe to the foot.

Each of these operations must work in entire harmony with the rest, otherwise one would undo the others. Thus, the shoe must be properly adjusted and accurately driven on the foot, or the utility of the preceding acts would be destroyed or crippled.

CHAPTER IV.

PRACTICAL HORSESHOEING

METHODS OF SCIENCE, ART, AND COMMON SENSE.

Necessity of Shoeing.—Since the employment of the horse in many pursuits renders it necessary that an artificial protection be employed to preserve his feet from injurious wear, it becomes a consideration of the first importance to know the proper method of doing this without seriously interfering with or destroying the functions of the foot, and so as in the least, to constrain its natural gestures while employing its fullest powers.

The effects of applying an iron defense to the horse's foot and securing it to the hoof with nails, are no doubt a source of injury to that organ, and even with the best of care a few of them are unavoidable; but they are increased in number and heightened in intensity, when the shoe is badly constructed and attached, whereas a right understanding of the subject will teach that those evils which are unavoidable may at least be greatly mitigated.

There are some points on the question of shoeing notoriously at issue between writers and shoers, theorists, and practitioners, so that hardly any agreement can be found to exist even on essential principles, and this diversity of opinion will probably continue until the known human artifices shall have been superseded by unknown or natural agencies.

All agree, however, that some artificial shield to the horse's foot is necessary, for employed as he is, his hoofs are unable to withstand the severe demands imposed upon them: the wear more than exceeds the growth.

Prof. Wm. Russell, in His Study.

Again, all unite in the belief that nothing more simple, inexpensive and efficient than a well-devised iron or steel shoe can at present be produced to meet the exigencies of the case, nor can the safe and ready method of attaching it by nails be displaced by any other means that we are acquainted with.

Having to deal with the facts as we find them, therefore, let us turn to a consideration of the best means which lie in our power of reducing, as much as possible, the evils so frequently attendant upon the practice of shoeing as commonly pursued.

Past and Present.—Bad and indifferent shoeing are productive of but one result—serious injury to the animals shod—and rendering them more or less unfit for active service. It is the exercise of a higher knowledge and its scientific application that constitutes the true "art, trade and mystery" of farriery, as exemplified in the best practice of to-day; in which science, as well as art and common sense, are operating to supplant the irrational, time-honored customs (which were once a portion of the blacksmith's creed), and are now gradually raising the science of horshoeing above the baneful influences of ignorance and traditional routine, to that position which its practical importance as a great national economic question justly entitles it.

When it is thus conceded that some of the operations and practices of the art have been materially altered and improved upon, it is none the less true that the ordinary system of horseshoeing, as it obtains in average hands, has not kept pace with the advancement noted. In too many instances it is observable that the art of the farrier is at variance with the workings of nature, and what satisfies the one outrages the demands of the other. The result is strikingly conspicuous in the number of lame, maimed, diseased or disabled horses, involving a direct loss of valuable property, as well as much needless suffering in the noblest of our dumb animals. And to misapplied shoeing, a very large proportion of these evils is, beyond all doubt, directly or indirectly traceable.

Important to Horsemen.—The shoeing of horses is a work practically belonging to the smith, but as gentlemen and others who are owners of horses ought to know and be able to distinguish, at least in some degree, when it is ill or well done, it would seem an unnecessary precaution to recommend a matter of such personal interest to their attention. It is really surprising to learn, however, how indifferent or neglectful of the well-being of their horses' feet and legs so many owners and drivers are. The foot is undoubtedly the most important part of the animal, so far as his ultimate usefulness is concerned. And the affair of shoeing is so important in its consequences, both for the preservation of the foot, the safety of the legs, and the ease and comfort of their motion that horsemen and proprietors can not be too attentive to practical recommendations on the subject. For it must be borne in mind that among horseshoers there is as great diversity of opinion in regard to the performance of their work as there possibly can be in any other trade or calling, and theoretical speculations upon this subject have done but little for the farrier or the horse. I am convinced that many of these differences would disappear, together with most of the ailments and afflictions to which horses are liable under existing conditions, if a better knowledge of the natural formation of the foot and of the relative value and office of its various parts, pervaded the great body of owners and trainers as a whole, than now exists. These troubles are caused, speaking generally, by the horse being out of balance on his feet, and, in justice to the much abused horseshoer, be it noted, they are quite as often due to erroneous ideas and "pet theories" of would-be horsemen being foisted into the workshop, as from any lack of ability or ingenuity on the part of the farrier.

In veterinary surgery, too, as an effective remedial or curative agent, for so many of the injuries and diseases affecting the health and soundness of the horse, scientific shoeing should occupy a foremost place; yet it is a matter of deep regret that among this class of practitioners are many men who have neglected to properly study this most important branch of their profession, or, having acquired only an imperfect conception of it through books, are unable to direct it with necessary discretion to any salutary effect; or, as has so frequently come within the trend of my experience, altogether pervert it, to the continued detriment of the patient and of the business interests involved as well. The moral of this is obvious. No humbug use of iron, nor theoretical experiments with it on the one side, nor blind groping in the dark on the other, will ever solve the "problems of farriery," simple and easy as they really are, but made difficult contentions in the hands of quacks and ignorant practitioners.

Essential knowledge.—To rescue the practice from such hands is the work of that higher knowledge to which I have already referred, and it is the application of such general facts of veterinary anatomy as explain the construction and functions of the foot, to the practical business of shoeing that will most largely contribute to this end. How, otherwise, can the smith be expected to understand the normal size, shape and structure of the foot upon which he operates, or how know the correct principles of shoeing and balancing a horse on his feet?

When a horse is at the shoeing forge "it is a condition, not a theory," that confronts the smith, and there is no longer room for doubt, and unless he knows, with positive certainty, just how to preserve or obtain the proper balances and bearings of the foot he is utterly incapacitated to take charge of it. Science and art are combined in skillful shoeing. A knowledge of the structure and normal functions of every part of the foot, as well as of the legs from the knee and hock down, though not necessarily in their ultimate scientific minutiæ, are as necessary to make a perfect shoer as is the mechanical skill to make a perfect shoe.

Condensed Anatomy.—Fully appreciating the importance of these suggestions and knowing that an accumulation of detail often deters the average reader and thus defeats the design of the writer, a concise review of the general anatomy of the horse's foot will be introduced here, containing only the briefest hint of the essential organs of locomotion, which may serve as a convenient reference chart to the general features of the subject under discussion.

Speaking first of the external structure of the foot alone, the parts with which the farrier has to deal, are the wall, sole, bars and frog, all well enough known by name, but less familiar in their relations with other parts and the mode of their co-operation.

The hoof is composed of horny, hair-like fibers, closely matted together and forms the natural protection of the sensitive foot.

The wall is that part of the hoof visible when the foot rests naturally on the ground, and is the main factor in bearing the horse's weight.

The bars are a continuation of the wall forming the angles at the heel, and assist in the lateral expansion and oppose contraction of the heels and quarters.

The sole is contained within the lower margin of the wall, and is a concaved plate of flexible horn covering the ground surface of the foot.

The frog forms the back part of the sole between the bars, and is the natural buffer of the foot for the prevention of injury and jar to the limb.

The wall grows indefinitely, but the sole and frog naturally throw off flakes or scales when they have grown to a certain thickness and are essential in their entirety for the maintenance of the foot in health and its protection from injury. The hoof incloses the coffin-bone, which is the terminal bone of the leg.

To this bone are attached the principal tendons that bend and thrust the foot forward, and to it also grow the tough but tender, leafy tissues which dovetail into horny ridges on the wall; these attachments being technically called the sensitive and insensitive laminæ. These leafy tissues working together, carry the stress of weight with an elastic movement, their variation, under pressure and without, being found to be about one quarter of an inch. The result is a wonderful elastic spring between the end of the leg and the external hoof, and this with the springy action of the coronary and frog cushions and lateral cartilages, acting together with the expansion of the arched bars—all being compressible under pressure—is the wise provision of nature to ward off and minimize the concussion on a horse's foot in motion.

The Center of Gravity.—Having reached this point, let us observe the going as well as the external and internal structure of a horse's foot. The horse then who draws presses first on the toe, then successively on the sides to ease the toe, then upon the heel, from which it immediately rises again. Trotting and running horses press the toe relatively lighter, landing first upon the heel, but in either case the effort of the weight of the horses fixes the real point of support neither upon the heel or toe, but on the middle or ball of the foot—between both, where is located the center of gravity, which is easy to demonstrate anatomically: thus, the cannon-bone presses on the head of the upper pastern, this on the lower pastern, this again on the navicular and coffin-bones, the center from where it is projected upon the ground bearings of the hoof without. In a sound and healthy organization, the succession of rapid movements of the living animal, adducts or shifts the center of gravity toward and through the median line or center of the heads of the coffin-, pastern-, and fetlock joints, in a smooth, even, and equally-balanced movement, and the function of locomotion is performed with perfect and efficient activity. But let any change or irregularity, however slight or obscure, occur among the elements of the case, whether in the relations of co-operating parts, or of form, dimension and location of foot bearings, whereby certain parts of a limb are forced to accept the portion of the weight which belongs to others; in short, whatever tends to defeat the purpose of nature in organizing the locomotory apparatus by interfering with or misdirecting its normal movement will ultimately result in that loss of harmony and lack of balance betrayed by disabled functions and testified by lameness.

Emphasizing the Facts.—In thus digressing it is only to establish certain primary facts relating to the main subject, in the hope of drawing attention to the necessity of every horseman and farrier clearly comprehending this branch of it before entering upon its sequel—the preparation of the foot for the shoe—in order to prove that without it as a foundation upon which to rest the whole *modus operandi*, and as a final resource to fall back upon in all cases where accurate judgment is required, there can be no permanently favorable results secured from any treatment instituted, howsoever skillful or experienced the operator may otherwise be. The value of appreciating this and of knowing the natural formation of the foot, is, practically to know when the foot is losing that natural form, so that it may be shaped and shod to assist nature in restoring it. How, then, shall we shoe a horse to preserve intact the normal conditions of the feet and legs, so as to afford them the necessary protection in the performance of their varied functions under the most exacting conditions which civilization can impose, enabling all to act together in perfect harmony and with absolute efficiency?

Variation of Feet.—From the natural form of the hoof we perceive that it descends obliquely outward, whereby it becomes considerably broader at its basis than at the coronet; it also declines in height toward the heel, and this change of contour, together with the changes of growth, affects its size and the degree of obliquity in its various parts. Too much importance can not possibly be attached by the workman to this variation, for it is of the first importance to discriminate accurately and determine positively the normal and abnormal positions of the limb. It frequently becomes exceedingly difficult to do this, owing to the close similarity between the natural and unnatural positions existing in horses of different breeds, and to do it satisfactorily will often require the exercise of the closest scrutiny and draw upon all the resources of experience, sound judgment, and anatomical knowledge. Horses' feet are alike in their anatomical combination, but they differ in conformation, condition, and size, and what will suffice to level and balance one horse will have no satisfactory effect on others.

The Angle of Incidence.—But in a majority of cases the solution of this first problem relating to the correct fall of the angle of incidence may be easily obtained by carefully observing the outlines of the pasterns, and closely noting the motion of the whole extremity and especially of the joints. Sometimes the overgrowth in length of toe or heel is too distinctly evident to admit of error, but in every instance the shoer must not fail to make the foot the subject of a thorough and intelligent examination, for upon his decision as to its natural position and the succeeding step, namely, leveling the ground surface of the hoof so that its angle will conform exactly to the inclination of the pasterns, is where the art of farriery comes in.

What Rule to go by.—It would be misleading to lay down any arbitrary degree of obliquity, as it naturally varies more or less in almost every individual horse, short pastern horses standing at a greater angle than those with long pasterns, and hind feet more than the fore; hence, the natural bias of the superimposed structures is the only safe guide to follow.

How to get on in the Work.—As the slightest departure from exactitude here renders whatever amount of care that may be devoted to the completion of the work worse than useless, and as every one knows that accurate leveling can not be done by the unaided eye, mechanical means must be resorted to for the purpose, and a scientific leveler and compass should therefor form part of every farrier's outfit.

Farriers' Tools.—All the world over, the simplicity and fewness of farriers' tools, have from the beginning, marked the slow progress of his invaluable art. The buttress, the knife, the clinch cutter, the hammer and the pinchers have comprised his "kit" of tools, and these as a general thing of rude or inferior construction; latterly, however, they are of better design and material, and more effective in use. But now, to be up with the spirit of the times, the shoeing smith needs more scientific tools for expert workmanship in leveling and adjusting the angles of the foot, to secure that precision and perfection imperatively demanded, and to supply this long felt want I am performing a duty which needs no other words of explanation in referring my readers to the " Russell Foot Adjuster," a description of which is inserted here with directions and illustrations for its practical use, as a preliminary guide to the subject proper, and which will follow after in due order of place and connection.

RUSSELL'S SCIENTIFIC FOOT ADJUSTER.

HOW TO USE IT IN ACCURATELY LEVELING AND BALANCING THE FOOT WHEN PREPARING IT FOR THE SHOE.

This device is very simple and effective, consisting of a flat metallic rim or bed-plate, similar in form to an ordinary horseshoe, to which is pivoted at the center of toe a movable quadrant (the quarter of a circle), the arc of which is graduated or divided into 90 degrees, from the horizontal plane to the right angle of the segment above, and which is operated by means of a lever, working the sweep of the quadrant forward and back.

A stationary indicator is also fixed perpendicularly to the toe of bed-plate, and this registers the angles of the foot upon the surface of the quadrant when the lever is brought forward against the wall of the hoof. The lever is also marked to a scale of inches and fractional parts, so that the height or depth of wall is obtained at the same time with its degree of obliquity.

The Adjuster Applied.—This arrangement is best shown by the accompanying illustrations of the adjuster in position for use.

Fig. 16. II, II, upper surface of the bed plate of the adjuster (with quadrant projecting in front).

Fig. 17. Side view of foot with adjuster applied to toe. A, A, rim of bed plate pressed firmly against bottom of hoof. B, B, lever for moving the quadrant and measuring height of wall. C, stationary indicator registering the angular face of the wall. D, arc of the quadrant inscribed with degrees as shown.

Fig. 18. Front of foot with adjuster abreast of the quarter.

Fig. 19. Adjuster registering the angle of quarter as seen from the back of foot.

Fig. 20. Leveling-plate to be used in connection with foot adjuster.

Other Mechanical Aids.—Fig. 21. Compass for spanning and ascertaining the exact height of the wall at different points, necessary in leveling and equalizing same.

In addition to these instruments every farrier should be provided with a metal rule having a scale of about 6 inches, and also a short narrow tape line (18 to 24 inches long); the special uses of which will be made apparent in the explanations to follow.

Method of Procedure.—Fig. 22 shows the uplifted foot in proper position for handling and examining it while applying the adjuster and testing the angles at different parts, as well as afterward, when viewing its levels and proving its balances.

With the foot in this suspended position, we begin the operation of scientifically leveling and balancing it, by starting a line through center of frog-cleft and carrying it forward over the point to center of toe at base of hoof, dividing the foot from front to back in two equal halves. See Fig. 23, line A, B, B.

Mark the point at base of toe (with chalk), then, with a tape line, measure the circuit of the hoof round the top border at coronet (just below the hair), and starting again at frog-cleft, as the center of operations, measure half way round the coronet from both inner and outer sides, and mark point of meeting at top of wall in front, then draw line from point at base to point at top, and you will have the center or median plane of foot and leg as shown by line H, H, in Fig. 18.

Now, with the foot still in hand, take up the adjuster and press the bed-plate firmly against the bottom of the foot and turn the lever down until it rests upon the front toe of wall, as shown in Fig. 17, and observe whether or no the angle of the toe corresponds with the normal slope of the pastern, also if the wall lines up with the straight edge of the lever, evenly and truly from base to coronet. The first consideration is that the obliquity or angle of the toe should be the same as that of the ankle above, and the second is that any abnormal growth or variation in length, convexity, or concavity, should be reduced to a normal or healthy form, according to the principles subsequently laid down for that purpose; and by this process of adjustment every shoer ought to succeed in obtaining a clew to the solution of the first problem in farriery, namely, how to secure and preserve a perfect level and balance in the foot.

Next, measure off about 1½ or 2 inches on each side of front toe at base of hoof and mark same, then draw a line from each of these points to connect with the top of line in middle, to indicate the bearings of the inner and outer sides of toe, as shown in Fig. 18, lines E, E.

After properly noting the foregoing, we may, from thence, the more easily reach our conclusions touching the other parts of the hoof to which the same proceeding applies, that is, in the use of the adjuster on both inner and outer quarters, carefully observing the angle of each and the line of the wall that one side may be made uniform with the other side in height and degree of obliquity.

Next, let the foot down to stand naturally on the leveling plate, Fig. 20, and view it from all sides, to properly gauge and determine its best natural position; then, with the compass, Fig. 21, divide the space between the line E and the heel of hoof into two equal parts, and mark the points at base and at coronet and draw a line to connect same as shown by letter F, Fig. 17. This is to be done on both sides of quarters, and then, in the same way on both sides of the heel as shown by letters A, B, Fig. 19.

These lines are next to be accurately measured with compass from coronet to base of hoof, or to face of leveling plate on which it rests, and the two opposite lines at inner and outer sides of toe, quarters and heels, made to compare and agree by marking any inequality existing and paring the hoof level round the circuit of the wall as directed in a succeeding page and as shown in Fig. 23.

This is always to be done with reference to the normal slope of the pasterns and to having the front line of hoof incline on the same angle with them, which can be easily verified at any stage of the work by the use of the adjuster, with or without the assistance of the leveling plate.

When this is done with one foot, the same method of procedure with each of the other feet will enable the smith to bring them into precisely the same good form; his work will also be done on true scientific principles beyond the criticism of his most exacting patron, and must prove a boon to horseflesh generally.

It will, of course, be observed, that the quarters are straighter or more upright than the toe (compare Figs. 17 and 18), and that the degree of obliquity varies in almost every horse, ranging from 45 to 56 on front toe of fore feet, and perhaps a little more for the hind feet.

But the main points to be impressed here are, that the natural slope of the pasterns is the only safe guide to be followed in all cases, and that the two fore feet of the same animal should always be alike, and the two hind feet alike, whatever difference may exist between them otherwise. In this way the horse will be enabled to tread upon feet of the same relative form in the same relative way, an advantage to their working in perfect harmony over irregular growths and dressings that is simply beyond our power to estimate.

The center line through the leg and middle of heel and toe, as shown in each of these figures, represents the exact axis of all normal leg and foot movements. The weight is precipitated in a direct line downward through the center of the bones and joints until it reaches the fetlock, where it is thrown forward on the angle of incidence formed by the pasterns and coffin-bone, represented in Fig. 17 by letters G, G. In a well-balanced horse, each foot and each part of a foot, combine to perform an equal and uniform function, and to carry an even or equal portion of weight distributed in the natural way. But any unevenness or irregularity of the base of the hoof, which is the final point of application, will displace the physical balance, and a single alteration in the proper balancing of the body will result in a complication of foot disorders which may baffle the best skill to remedy, and leave our burden-bearing servants to succumb to their inevitable fate. Hence the benefits to be derived from the use of these instruments will be apparent to all practical shoers. Instruments of similar intent and purpose are used by mechanics in every trade, even when not dealing with vital, living structures, as is the case in this pursuit, where any deviation from absolute accuracy causes suffering and unrelieved distress.

Different kinds of Feet.—I have previously indicated that a horse's hoofs may, by variation of growth or usage, be either perfect or imperfect, and these last may also be rugged, long, crooked or flat, and the frogs may be broad or the heels narrow, and I have pointed out the necessity of paying due regard to each of these conditions in determining the natural form and size of the particular kind of foot being dealt with, also to the employment of all the farrier's care and address in bringing it to its best form, as there are many apparently trifling circumstances which have much to do with the conditions of orderly soundness and efficient activity which are too often overlooked.

The Natural Model.—If we examine the natural healthy feet of many horses, we will find that their essential shape is the same. Some may have grown more luxuriantly than others, it is true, whereby the crust will be deeper, or the bottom part may be worn and battered, giving the hoof an uneven, ragged appearance; but when this superfluous or broken horn has been removed, it will be found that the bottom of the foot is nearly circular, the sole concave, the frog broad, the bars distinct, the commissures deep and the heels expanded. Surely no one will dispute that this form, which the Creator has given, is the most perfect and far better adapted to all purposes than any that can be given by the most ingenious farrier

Rational Shoeing.—When, therefore, we undertake to get a horse's foot into condition, this rule may be invariably depended upon, that any mode of shoeing and treating the foot which has a tendency to alter the form or design of nature is highly absurd and destructive, while that practice which best tends to the conservation of its natural uses is alone founded upon sound and rational principles.

Fig. 23 shows a natural, healthy hoof properly prepared for the shoe, and clearly indicates the only parts which should be reduced when a foot is being made ready.

Fig. 24 shows the upper surface of the same hoof with longitudinal and tranverse lines, indicating the proper balance of a level foot and the normal center of gravity at intersecting point.

Fundamental Principles.—It may be accepted as a guiding principle that in a natural healthy foot, the outside rim of the horny wall and that small portion of the sole immediately attached to it on which the shoe is to rest, are the only portions of the foot to be interfered with in preparing the foot for the shoe, and, whenever possible, the necessary trimming ought to be effected by means of the rasp. Conditional exceptions to this general rule are, of course, to be fully noted in my observations hereafter, on shoeing different kinds of horses, and in the treatment of diseases. Natural physical conditions are alone treated of in this section.

The feet must be placed upon the same plane and in proportion to the skill displayed in this alignment, will danger of injury be avoided, as the smallest deviation from a perfectly level bearing entails disastrous consequences, not only on the foot but on the entire limb.

Securing the Levels.—In the foot itself, when the weight is borne unevenly, the lowest part receives an undue share; the pressure retards the growth and free play of the parts, and the foot in consequence, becomes, weakened distorted and deformed. In the limb, deflected as it is by an uneven basis, from the ground surface to its union with the trunk, the incidence of the weight is imposed unequally, and bones and tendons mutually suffer from the strain.

The wall, then, must be perfectly level, that is, no more is to be taken from one side than from the other, and this is determined by exact measurements with compass at opposite points all around the hoof, indicated by the lines in Fig. 23, from coronet to ground surface, and having same agree. Details are fully given in connection with the use of the foot adjuster, for which see Fig. 17.

Maintaining the Balance.—Also the foot must be balanced, or in other words, from a line drawn through the longer axis of the frog the measurements to opposite points should be the same on both sides of the hoof; this means simply that a longitudinal line through the center of the frog, must at all points, be the center of the foot or divide it in exact halves, as in this way only will the force of the foot-fall be carried through the center of the column of bones and be equally and naturally distributed upon the supporting apparatus of bones and tendons and the weight-bearing portions of the hoof. The active principle of this indispensable arrangement is best illustrated in Figs. 25 and 26, and is explained with the use of instruments in Fig. 17.

Preparing the Hoof.—In thus leveling and balancing the foot, my practice is to remove only such portions of the sole as nature is about to cast off, that is, those portions which are exfoliating and destitute of the natural moisture and flexibility that exist in a healthy growth, and then to reduce the wall to a level with the untouched, healthy or sound sole. I aim to have every part of the wall, from the angle of the heels to the toe, receive a good, broad, equal bearing on the shoe, unless there is some special reason for doing otherwise. With some feet, having a strong healthy growth, this means a great deal of cutting (especially if shoes have been worn, and worn a long time); then, again, there are feet which require very little reduction, hence, the work must be done with constant and intelligent reference to the inclination of the pasterns as already prescribed. Sometimes the hoof will grow all to toe, and again the growth at the heel will be more marked, or the foot may be run over by having one side too high or the toe worn off excessively. To rectify this, and to better its adjustment a good plan is to look at the old shoe to see where it has worn most and be partly guided by that. The point is to remove so much of the wall as would be a surplus growth, or so much only as will bring it back to its natural form and adjustment. And this after all must depend upon the judgment, expertness, and ingenuity of the farrier, who should, however, never lose sight of the fact that if the heels are allowed to grow too high, an excessive strain is thrown upon the bones, while if the toes are too long the tendons suffer in like manner. The sharp lower rim of the wall should be rounded-off just a little to prevent splinters, and of course all stubs or nails should be removed.

Opening up the Heels.—The junction of the wall with the bars affords a firm natural bearing for the heel of the shoe, and is to be rasped level with the wall and so low as to be exactly even with the frog, but the so-called process of "opening up the heels" by removing the bars, is a most disastrous practice, to be strictly avoided. The bars are the lateral braces and binders of the foot, and the arch which they form on either side admirably fits them to admit and limit, to a proper extent, the expansion of the foot, as well as to powerfully oppose any disposition there may be in the hoof to contract, by assisting the heels in retaining their natural form.

Indefensible Practices.—There may be differences of opinion among authorities as to minor details in shoeing, but there is one practice not open to argument, and which all alike severely condemn, and that is the utterly senseless and atrocious custom so characteristic of the common every-day horseshoer, of thinning out the sole and trimming or mutilating the frog. No man has ever been able to assign a reason for acting contrary to the first principles of his own work by destroying that which he is aiming to preserve, and yet this has been and is the most frequent procedure of so-called farriers in their treatment of the frog and sole. They persist, with an obstinacy which sets common sense at defiance, in paring and hollowing out the sole even to the quick, and to forming an exact "fine frog," regardless of consequences, though these are of the most serious nature and affect the vital integrity of the living animal.

Thinning out the Sole.—From the connection, thickness and flexibility of the horny sole, as well as from its arch-like external contour, it is wholly destined by nature to serve as a cushion to the sensitive sole (velvety tissue) which rests upon it. By hollowing away the sole in paring, it dries and shrinks by exposure; the horse loses his natural defense against violent shocks of a pavement, or any kind of external violence, and thus the sensitive sole becomes easily inflamed by being bruised or wounded (disease called villitis).

Trimming the Frog.—The horny frog is also designed for contact with the ground for the prevention of jar and injury to the limb, and the presence of this thick, elastic, compressible mass of horn in a healthy unmutilated condition, permitted to reach the ground (while the animal is moving, at least), is absolutely essential to the well-being of the foot, the more especially if high speed is desired. The frog is nature's cushion and hoof expander (in connection with the bars), and to alter this state is fatal to its usefulness, for such act causes it to shrink, dry and harden, when, both as a cushion and expander it is a dead flat failure. The frog is also the main support to the plantar cushion, which in turn supports the back tendons, so that without its natural pressure the tendons soon become jaded, inflamed and swollen, and it is thus a main factor of safety in traveling or riding.

Neither the frog or sole ever become too large or thick by natural growth or usage, for they scale or cast off flakes as they pass beyond the life maintaining stage of the producing tissues, and a certain degree of exposure is required for their vitality and resiliency. In cases of existing disease, where resort to the drawing-knife may be required to relieve or assist the affected parts, I plainly treat of such in the subsequent pages; but in normal conditions the sole and frog should, on no pretext whatever, be disturbed by the shoer.

Weight of the Shoe.—Two things must be strenuously insisted on for the shoe; one is, that the shoe be as light as possible, and the other is, that it be made or moulded on its foot-bearing surface to an exact counterpart of the hoof to which it is applied. Bearing in mind that the original and legitimate design of the shoe is for the preservation and defense of the hoof from undue wear, we should not misconcieve this purpose by attaching to our horses' feet any uncalled-for weight. Light shoes proportioned to the weight of the animal and the nature of his work, are infinitely preferable to heavy ones, for these latter are a burden at best and a constant tax on the energies of a horse, as is meaningly implied by the familiar saying "that an ounce at the toe means a pound at the withers." It is not surprising to those conversant with the facts that the majority of our horses are at the decadence of their powers when they should be at their prime, and a prolific source of such disability is the habitual necessity of pounding along on hard roads, with over-weighted, iron-clad feet, ensuing from the conventional mode of shoeing.

Calculating that a horse going a fair trot lifts his feet all round sixty times a minute, and this with shoes weighing two pounds each, the reader will be able to realize how enormous the amount is that can be unnecessarily raised to the wear and tear of the living members.

As an example, suppose a horse shod with shoes weighing two pounds each and traveling at such a jog as requires him to lift his feet all around once in a second or sixty times a minute, keeps up his speed for five hours, how much work does he perform—that is, how much does he lift?

Lifting one foot sixty times a minute; for four feet, $60 \times 4 = 240$. Lifting two pounds each time, in one minute he will lift 480 pounds, which, multiplied by 60, will make in one hour 28,800 pounds, and in five hours, 144,000 pounds, or 72 tons. This calculation is based upon the scientific experiments of Mons. Bouley, of France.

The injury of artificial or excessive weight carried at the extremities of a horse's limbs is always increased as the rate of speed increases. But even for our heaviest draft horses it is not necessary to increase the concussion and battering, inseparable from their bulk, by an aggravation of several pounds of metal on each foot when an equal or greater advantage is to be found in shoes weighing only half as much: and one may well be excused for wondering why horse owners do not deal with this issue as one of self interest.

Form of the Shoe.—The shoe should have a perfectly level, wall-bearing surface; but to mellow and soften any pressure on the sole which has a certain amount of descent under the exertions of progression, the plane of the shoe should be concaved or beveled off inwardly, as shown in Fig. 27.

The web of the shoe should be fashioned substantially, but not unduly wide. Narrow-webbed shoes are eminently the best, as they do not obstruct the growth of the sole, nor interfere with its natural strength and flexibility.

Setting the Shoe.—It is a common thing for writers to admonish that "the shoe must be fitted to the foot, and not the foot to the shoe," and it would seem an unnecessary caution were it not a fact that the average farrier only partially prepares the foot at first, leaving the remainder of the work to be done after he has fitted the shoe—to his eye. Any inequalities or deficiencies then in the shoe are either burned into the hoof or it is rasped off and made, somehow or other, to conform to the size and shape of the shoe. I need hardly add that this practice is wrong, and that the outcome of it is pernicious in the extreme.

Hot and Cold Fitting.—Burning a badly or even well-adjusted shoe, to a badly or well-prepared foot, is injurious, and is to be deprecated under the most favorable circumstances, but the fusing of a red-hot shoe to the foot surface, as is generally practiced, can not be too severely condemned. Burning the sole will, in time, overheat, blister, and destroy the laminated and membraneous structures of the foot, causing lameness or intense pain, and often suppuration and lesion of the living tissues. The horn secreting tissues of the hoof under these circumstances are impaired or suspended, and when closely examined show an absence of the cohesive matter which unites the healthy fibers, which thus disintegrate and become hard, dry and brittle. The advocates of hot-fitting though, present many specious arguments for the furtherance of the practice. It is alleged that shoes can not be fitted so rapidly nor so closely by any other means, and this is generally true, for, by burning the shoes on, an accommodation is forced between the hoof and the shoe, and accuracy is thus secured, but at the expense of the right growth and operation of the foot, and any one who is a practical shoer, with any knowledge of anatomy, knows, without being told, that "mild and careful" work in hot-fitting is rare among workmen, while its indiscriminate and excessive use is a matter of every-day occurrence. Horn, being a non-conductor of heat, is slowing affected by it, and it is claimed that three minutes burning of the lower face of the sole is necessary to produce any indication of increase of temperature on its upper surface. This is a fallacy, as I have tested and proven many times, by operating upon and dissecting green specimens with soles of varied thicknesses, when by the application of hot shoes for the specified time, I found that the soles of ordinary depth were penetrated by the heat and the sensitive sole scorched and the laminal tissues burned and charred. In the living subject these effects would have been disastrous, and they convinced me (if that were necessary) that the foot of a horse is in no sense to be compared to an inanimate block of wood which may be carved or charred at man's unholy will, or to suit his capricious whims.

And because it is a vital organ filled with life and feeling, the necessity which there is of thought, care and skill being exercised in our treatment of it, is pointed out to us by the most indubitable evidences of nature. The economy of time and labor attained in the process of hot-fitting will, I am sure, never counterbalance its evil effects. While it is probably true that more shoes can be fitted in a given time by hot-fitting than by cold, that is no argument in favor of its expediency, for it follows as a logical sequence to be applied here, that it is the consistent business of the shoer always, to give form to the surface of the foot as well as to the shoe, and that the final test of skill and intelligence is in the best adaptation of one to the other, so that the least possible hurt shall be done to the foot.

Fig. 28 illustrates the correct way of fitting a shoe, with proper length at toe and heel, with foot leveled and balanced, and front of wall in line with the natural inclination of the ankle from toe to fetlock, all as clearly defined in the section on the use of the adjuster. (See page 77.)

Whenever the face of front toe does not line out full and straight from coronet to ground surface by reason of deficient growth, excessive wear, or paring down, the shoe should be made to cover out in front to the line of the natural tread, and thus supply the deficiency of the hoof. Also, where a quick going over of the toe is desired, let the shoe supply the same by being rolled or beveled on the ground surface instead of shortening up the toe of the hoof, as is so frequently done.

Adaptation of the Shoe.—From this manner of setting, it may be observed that dangerous compressions will be avoided and the shoe rendered more secure by having it conform to the ground tread of the foot, and by having the nails placed in the quarters, three on each side (directly opposite) being sufficient. In effect, the more easy the shoes set upon the feet the more active the horse will be. So large, long, thick shoes make him heavy, unwieldy, and hobbling. A long, wide shoe is precarious, for the longer the lever the greater will be the drag upon the clinches of the nails, and thus horses will be more apt to trip and strike them off. The body of the shoe being unyielding, the flexibility of the hoof yields to the shoe heel, and the thicker the shoe is and the more it covers the sole, all the more subject is that of the horse to meet it, thus weakening the fetlocks and heels by compressing them as if in a constant vise, because they have always the same inflexible point of support.

Hence, we learn that the shoe must be made uniform with the spread of the hoof, and perfectly plain or flat in its actual bearings, in order to adapt it to a close, even seat all around; not too thick or wide (varying, however, to suit the necessities of the case, for a medium-sized horse being about $\frac{3}{8}$ inch thick by $\frac{3}{4}$ inch wide), nor projecting beyond the natural circuit of the ground tread. After securing a perfect adaptation of the shoe to the foot, the two levels to fit each facing, do not spoil the job by going back to the anvil, as many do, and give it another final hammering, thus altering the foot surface of the shoe and causing a misfit at the last.

Fullering and Punching.—Nail holes should be punched through the shoe straight, or inclining slightly outward, directly opposite one another (except in cases where otherwise directed), that all danger of cramping the foot may be avoided when the nails are driven. The fullering and punching should not be too fine, that is, too near the outside of the shoe, but suitable for the size of the nails, so that they may enter and fill the same, as then they will stand sure and endure longer. If punched coarser, a stronger and better hold may be taken in the wall, and the nails need not be driven up so high as to prick or endanger the sensitive structure.

Concerning the Nails.—Never use inferior nails, for they invariably break off or bend upon slight occasions, and the shoe will work loose from the foot, or be quickly lost. A good nail should have a strong, stiff neck and shoulder, flat, thin shank, and sharp point, without hollowness or flaw. A low, short, thick hold for the nail is better both for the ease of the foot and the security of the shoe. Two of the most common evils in shoeing are using too many and too large nails, and then driving them up too high in the wall. The fewest and smallest nails that will insure the shoe remaining on for a reasonable length of time, is a rule that should never be departed from. For if a perfectly level bearing has been obtained, as ought to be the case if my directions are followed, only a few small nails will be required to hold the shoe securely in place.

Fig. 29 shows a full-size, transverse section of a hoof, with shoe fitted and nails properly driven, to pass obliquely out through the strong, thick part of the wall, away from the cavity occupied by the sensitive structures of the foot.

Driving the Nails.—As much care is required in the final adjustment of the shoe to set it right and fit the foot equally in all places, the two middle or quarter-nails should be driven first, with a few soft strokes of a light hammer, till they are somewhat entered; then see that the shoe fits the outer lines of the hoof evenly and justly, on one side the same as on the other, and that the tread is square and straight. Otherwise, either one or both of the operations—of leveling the foot and fitting or adapting the shoe—may be set at naught by a failure to nail the shoe on in its proper place. When this is done, let the rest of the nails be driven so that their points stand out in line; then cut them off and clinch them, turning the clinches down with the angle of the hoof and hiding them a little by filing or rasping the wall slightly underneath the clinches before laying them down.

The Finished Work.—The shoer's work is now supposed to be completed, and he must know when to stop. He must not, therefore, give any "finishing touches" to the hoof by rasping off the outer crust of the wall, in order to make it seem round about the shoe. An ever-beneficent nature has provided for the entire wall from the coronet to the base a fine film of natural horny varnish—the periople—which is necessary for its protection and perfect growth. By robbing it of this proper horny coating, the farrier inflicts an injury on the foot beyond the reach of art to imitate or repair. Hoof dressings and other oily preparations can not replace the loss of this natural healthy, glossy layer, and their use to polish the hoof is detrimental to the growth or development of the horny tissues.

Sizes of Commercial Nails, with Recommendations for their Various Uses.

No. 2. For plating running horses and colts.
3. For "training shoes" on running horses.
4. For the track horse.
4½. For the roadster.
5. For the roadster.
6. For general business and hack horses.
7. For omnibus and stage horses.
8. For light draught horses.
9. For heavy draught horses.
10. ⎧ For the heavier breeds of draught horses, such as the
11. ⎨ Norman, wearing extra heavy shoes (from 6 to 8
12. ⎩ pounds), for which extra long nails are required.

94 SCIENTIFIC HORSESHOEING.

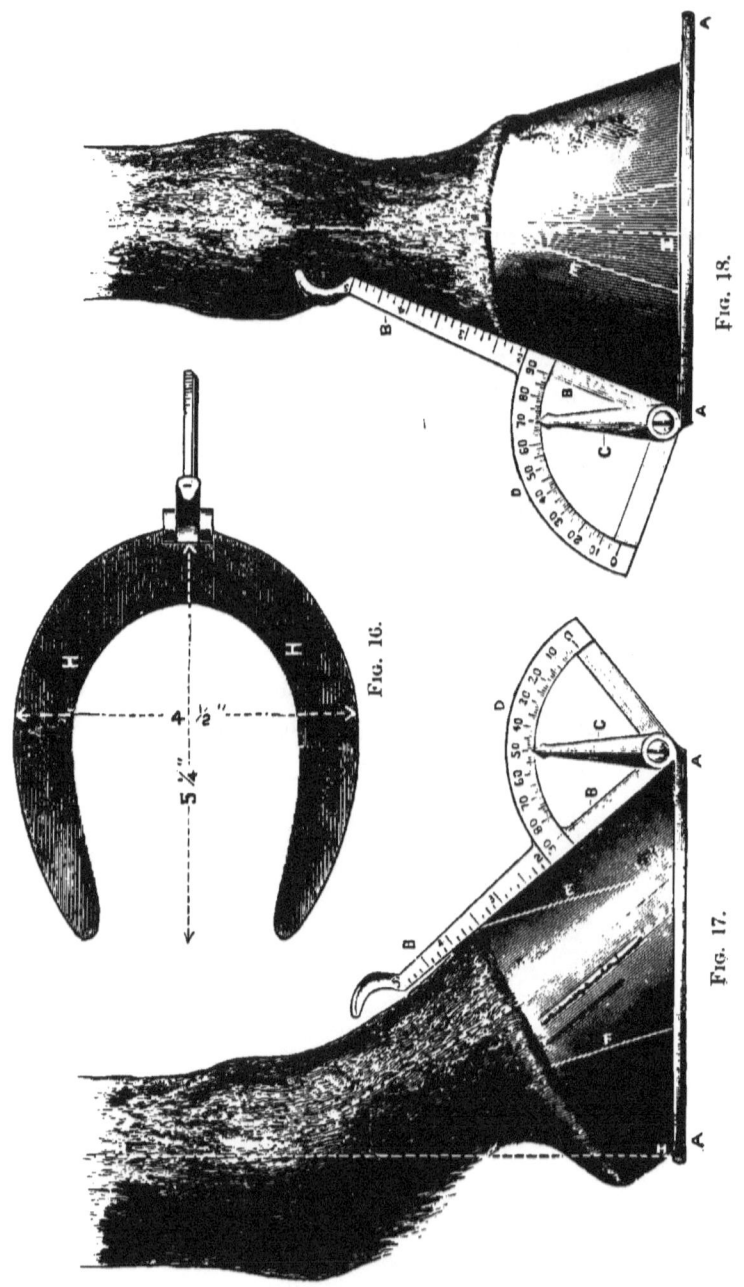

Fig. 18.
Fig. 16.
Fig. 17.

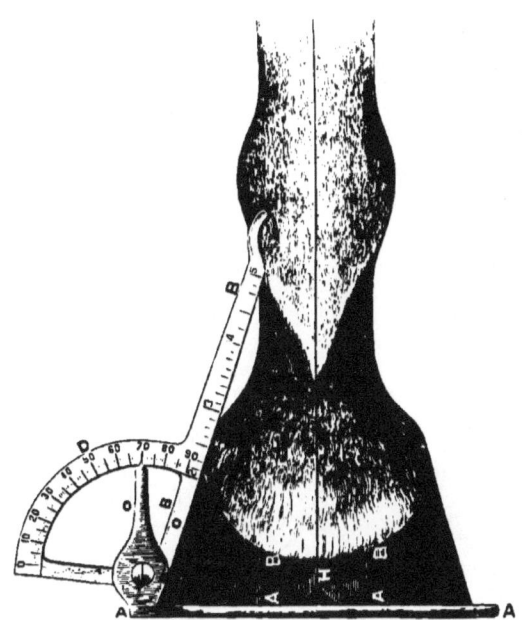

Fig. 19.

Fig. 20.

Fig. 21.

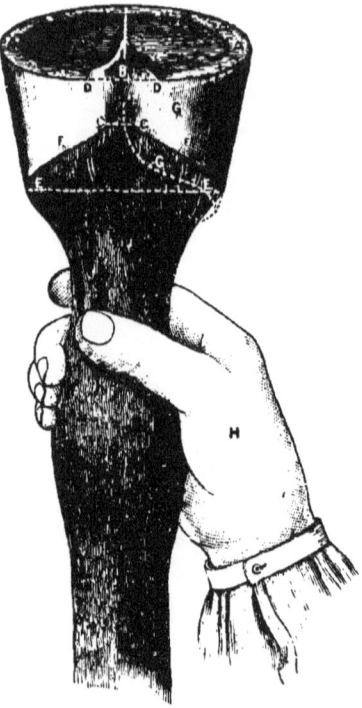

FIG. 22. POSITION OF FOOT, UPLIFTED, IN THE MOST CONVENIENT WAY FOR HOLDING SAME IN OBTAINING LEVELS, ASCERTAINING ITS GRADATIONS AND DULY PROPORTIONING IT BEFORE SHOEING.

A, A, Wall-bearing surface leveled and prepared for the shoe.

B, Cleft of frog, marking line through center of heels to middle of toe.

C, D, C, D, Heels leveled and equalized from coronet to ground surface.

E, E, The wall leveled and lined up equally from coronet to base opposite the quarters.

F, F, Coronet level from upper border to base at each side of heel.

G, G, Dotted line showing how one side of the heel may be twisted out of its proper position by an unequal bearing of the foot, produced by uneven wall (high or low on either side), and improper shoeing.

Any overgrowth of hoof will displace the natural balance of the horse and cause him to dispose his feet in or out, or carry his legs forward or back in the direction of the greatest bearing point, while with feet leveled and balanced, as they should be, he will **stand correctly and** move with ease and comfort all the time.

PRACTICAL HORSESHOEING.   97

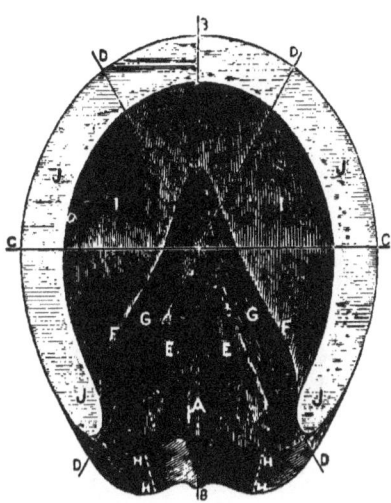

FIG. 23. SHOWING UNDER SURFACE OF A PERFECT FRONT HOOF PROPERLY PREPARED FOR THE SHOE, WITH GUIDE LINES FOR LEVELING AND BALANCING THE FOOT.

A, Center of frog cleft in line with the insertions of front and back tendons, and parallel to their straight line of movement. **B, B,** Line through longitudinal center of foot, dividing it into exact halves and indicating middle of heels and front toe. **C, C,** Line transversely across center of foot, midway through inside and outside quarters. The point of intersection of these lines indicates the normal center of gravity. **D, D, D, D,** Intersecting lines marking the width of inside and outside toes and heels. **E, E,** Branches or forks of the frog on either side of the median cleft. **F, F,** Bars on either side of the frog. **G, G,** Commissures or grooves between the bars and frog. **H, H, H, H,** Line marking height of heels from coronet to base. **I, I,** Concave surface of sole. **J, J, J, J,** Wall-bearing surface leveled and prepared for the shoe.

These lines indicate the main points where the wall of the hoof is to be measured from the coronet to the lower rim or base, in order to obtain equal and exact levels around the entire circuit. The height of any two opposite points on either side of line B, B, must correspond, that is, the sides of toe and heels and quarters must be alike to insure proper levels, and the width from the converging center, near point of frog, to any radiating point on opposite sides must be equal to secure a perfectly-balanced foot.

7

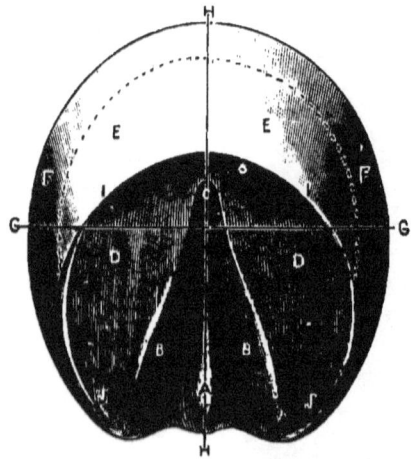

Fig. 24. UPPER SURFACE OF A PERFECT HOOF, CORRESPONDING WITH THE UNDER SURFACE SHOWN IN THE PRECEDING FIGURE.

A, Internal ridge or spur of the frog-stay dividing the fissures.

B, B, Internal fissures, or depressions between the bars and frog, in which the plantar cushion finds lodgment.

C, Internal point of fissures corresponding with external summit of the horny frog.

D, D, Internal surface of the horny sole.

E, E, External upper face of wall.

F. F, Dotted line indicating thickness of wall.

G, G, Transverse line across center of hoof midway through quarters.

H, H, Longitudinal line through center of hoof marking middle of toe and heel. The intersection of these lines locates the normal center of gravity.

I, I, Upper margin of the coronary band called the periople ring and continuing to the skin.

J, J, Laminar leaves of horny tissue coming out from the internal face of the wall and extending over the bars.

PRACTICAL HORSESHOEING. 99

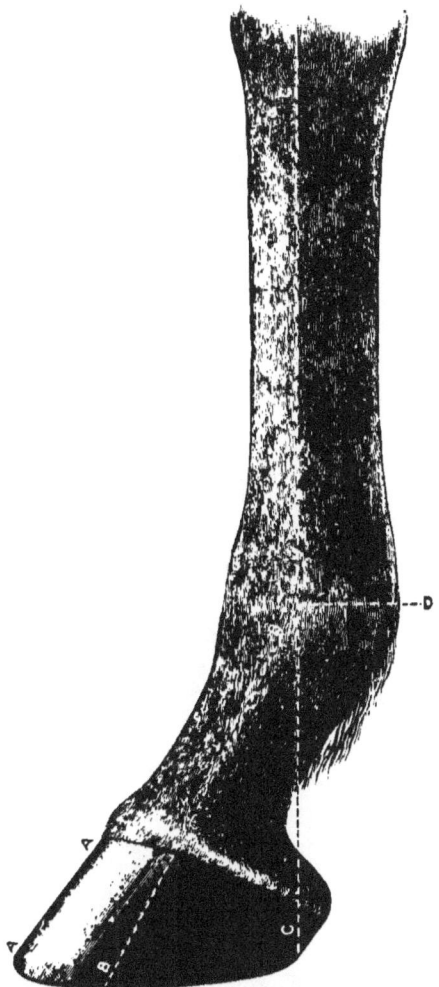

FIG. 25. SIDE VIEW OF A PERFECT FORE FOOT AND LEG, STANDING NATURALLY, AFTER IT IS LEVELED AND BALANCED ACCORDING TO DIRECTIONS GIVEN.

A, A, Front or toe of hoof, lined up with inclination of pastern, at an angle of about 50 degrees. B, B, Angle of incidence, through axis of the terminal bones, and center of foot joints, locating the normal center of equipoise at the base. C, C, Line of vertical descent, through axis of leg upon which the stress of weight and momentum pass to fetlock and pastern. D, Center or pivot of fetlock joint where the stress is imparted or deflected through the phalanges of the foot, and thrown out on the bearing surfaces of the hoof.

100   SCIENTIFIC HORSESHOEING.

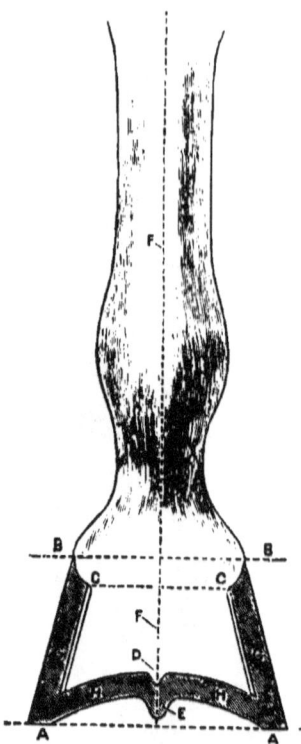

FIG. 26. TRANSVERSE SECTION THROUGH QUARTERS SHOWING THE NATURAL BACK POSITION OF FRONT FOOT STANDING AFTER BEING PREPARED FOR THE SHOE AS INSTRUCTED.

A, A, Base or spread of the hoof accurately leveled and balanced.

B, B, Upper border of hoof showing levels at coronet.

C, C, Cutigeral groove or cavity in which the coronary cushion rests.

D, Interior fissure in which the plantar cushion is imbedded.

E, External projection of summit of horny frog near center of sole.

F, F, Vertical line cast through axis of the bony column locating the normal center of gravity in a balanced foot.

G, G, Wall of hoof across the quarters, lined up on both sides, equally from coronet to base.

H, H, Arch of horny sole crowning the ground surface.

PRACTICAL HORSESHOEING. 101

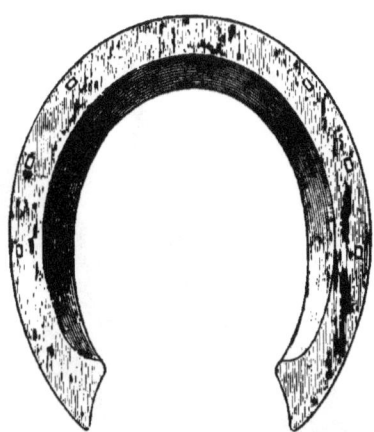

FIG. 27. FRONT FOOT SHOE FOR GENERAL ROAD OR BUSINESS PURPOSES.

This shoe may be regarded as a standard pattern for general use, and should be about ⅜ in. thick x ¾ in. wide, to weigh 12 ounces, varying when necessary to suit the horse to which it is applied. The above view shows a good flat wall-bearing surface and the inner rim concaved or beveled to avoid pressure on flat, soft, or weak-soled feet. For ordinary driving six nails are sufficient, three on each side placed opposite each other in the quarters as indicated. The shoe should fit the toe and heel and follow the circle of the wall neatly, and the ends of the branches are to rest strongly on the bars at each side of the heels. The ground-bearing surface of this shoe should ordinarily be perfectly flat.

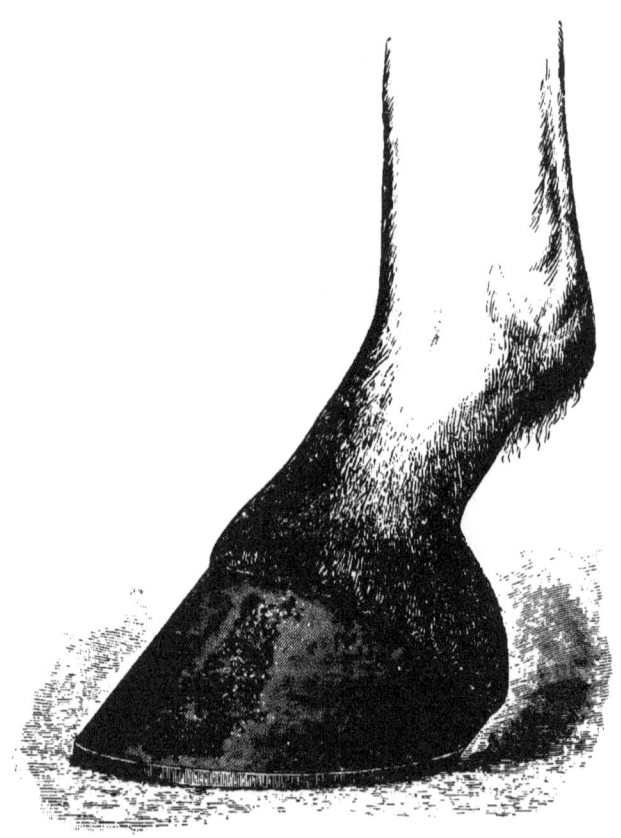

Fig. 28. NATURAL POSITION OF A PERFECT FORE FOOT ON THE GROUND, LEVELED, BALANCED AND RIGHTLY FITTED WITH SHOE IN ACCORDANCE WITH THE RULES LAID DOWN.

This figure shows to advantage the proportions of a symmetrial foot and pasterns of right size, length, and slope to give the desired strength, vigor, and suppleness. It will be observed that the angle of the hoof at toe and heel are continuous with the natural bias of the pastern, and that thus the poise of the leg and foot is unconstrained and perfectly adapted to sustain the weight and perform the functions of locomotion with ease, comfort and security. The shoe is adjusted to the natural-ground tread of the foot following the circuit of toe, heel and sides, being affixed with three nails directly opposite one another on each side. In this way the foot lands evenly, the strain is equally distributed between the bones and tendons, the expansion is uniform all around, and all danger of foot or leg soreness is entirely avoided.

PRACTICAL HORSESHOEING.   103

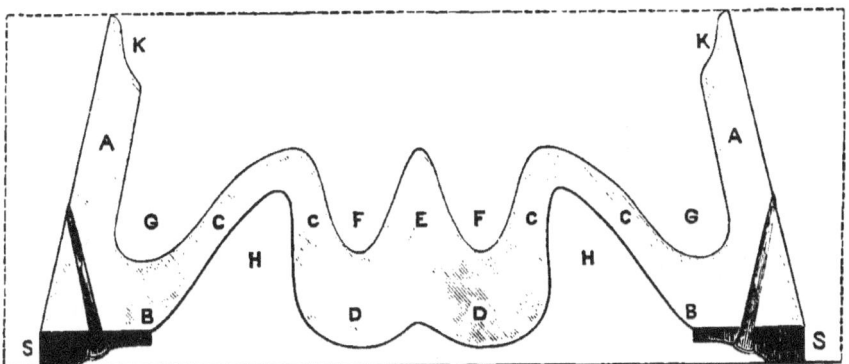

FIG. 29. FULL SIZE, TRANSVERSE SECTION, THROUGH HOOF NEAR THE HEEL, SHOWING ACTUAL THICKNESS OF THE VARIOUS PARTS IN A HOOF OF MEDIUM SIZE.

A, A, Thickness of wall at quarters.

B, B, External junction of bars and sole at base of wall.

C, C, C, C, Continuation of bars, overarching and joining themselves to the frog and sole.

D, D, External bulbs of the frog forks divided by the cleft.

E, Internal frog-stay or spur projecting into the thick part of the plantar cushion.

F, F, Internal fissures divided by the frog-stay, designed to receive the plantar cushion.

G, G, Internal cavities which form the seat of the wings of the coffin-bone.

H, H, External gaps, called commissures, separating the bars and frog.

K, K, Cutigeral groove, or cavity, in which the coronary cushion rests.

S, S, Shoe properly applied on the level bearing provided by the under rim of wall, with the nails driven at right inclination to take a strong, short hold and come out of the wall with the least injury to its fibers and without hurtfully compressing the sensitive structures of the foot.

The marginal line surrounding the hoof shows its relative angles and levels with the rectangular border.

Practical Balance of the Foot and Leg.—The principal points demanded in the training and development of a perfect and sound horse are, for a driving horse speed and endurance, and for a draught horse, strength and endurance. How can the utmost speed or greatest strength with endurance be best attained? These are the ends aimed at by the skillful and experienced farrier, and after the practical experience of a lifetime extending beyond the allotted years of man, I am ready from that practical experience, and from my observation of the practical experience of others, to give to the world what measure of practical knowledge has come to me in the way of the development of speed, or strength, with endurance, of the highest class in the horse.

In the first place, it is undeniable that the whole value of a horse depends primarily and always upon the soundness of the feet and legs; and in the second place, upon the skill, competency, and good, practical judgment of the farrier. The most important thing the farrier should know is that the more equality of pressure obtained at all points of the feet and legs, at each footfall, the greater will be the speed, or the more effective the strength, with endurance, attained—and this stands to reason. There are three very essential points which he should bear in mind to attain to these desiderata. First, the farrier should know how to obtain accurately the natural angle of the foot—that is to say, he should know when to cut and where to stop cutting. Such a man is master of his trade. For any damage to a horse from a neglect or ignorance in this particular can only be repaired by time, which means loss of money to the owner, if not lasting injury or death even to the horse. The proper preparation of the horse's foot for the shoe is therefore of paramount importance in farriery. The horse's hoof corresponds to the human finger nail, and a perfect knowledge of the hoof can only be obtained by dissection; and it is much more humane to acquire that knowledge by operating upon the dead subject than upon the living animal, as has frequently been done. Any one can attest to the pain and annoyance of having the finger nail cut to the quick, and yet our suffering is as naught to that of the horse who has undergone the same operation.

Before proceeding to dress the hoof, observations should be taken from in front of as well as the rear of the horse, to ascertain whether the foot is directly underneath the leg—that is, if the center line of the foot is in the same vertical with the leg; then from either side take notice of the vertical line, and whether the upper and lower pasterns are on a line with the front wall of the foot, when the horse stands on a level floor; that is, to see whether the leg tilts in or out. In either case the hoof is not level on the ground surface. Equalize by sight as acute as possible the wall, and determine how much should be removed by the rasp and at what point or points, in order to obtain the desired equal bearing on a level surface; then proceed to remove the superfluous horn. In dressing or paring the feet, so as to obtain equal heights for the front feet and also for the hind feet, the eye can not be trusted. Guesswork must now cease; mathematical accuracy is demanded. This can only be obtained by resorting to the use of mathematical instruments, and for this purpose the six-inch compass, foot and heel adjusters, have been invented and adopted (pp. 94 and 95). The method of procedure described on pages 77, 78, 79, 80, 81, shows the use of the instruments. The front feet being of the same length from the top of the coronet to the ground tread, and shoes of exactly equal weight being used, the stride of the front feet will be of the same length at each footfall when up to speed. The correct rule for the angles of the front feet to be observed is, when the former stand at an angle of 48 degrees, the latter should be at 50 degrees, for the reason that the hind legs constitute the propelling powers of the horse. This has been my never-failing rule

Before going into detailed description of the different conformations of feet met with in our daily work, we will assume that every animal had perfect feet, or we will take a colt never shod, and go with him through life; and we will also assume that it is impossible to adjust a shoe to the horse's foot without some injury to that part of his anatomy. Now the duty of the farrier is to reduce that injury to a minimum, so that the shoeing will not shorten the career of the horse or reduce his value.

The parts of the foot to be carefully observed are the wall, sole, frog, and the angle of obliquity of the wall at the toe, which varies in different animals. The breed, labor, and also the roads on which he works, play an important part, and each case must be treated in a different manner. The horse that works on the farm will travel sound and show no inconvenience with shoes that would lame him on artificial paved streets and roads, and again the shoes used in our cities would not answer for the agriculturist; the latter are too long, and are liable to be pulled off in the soft ground. Be that as it may, the same careful preparation of the foot for the shoe should always be demanded. Too strict adherence to these rules can not be observed, to insure sound feet and legs.

The angle of the wall varies in different animals; what that angle should be in each instance must be determined by a lateral survey of the foot and leg, so as to have the strain or weight equally divided. If the toe is too long, the flexor tendons and suspensory ligaments are overtaxed. If the toe is too short and the heels are too high, there will be damage done to the bones and ligaments of the joints. As a consequence the animal will be deprived of that elastic, bounding, graceful footstep, which is so beautiful in the colt, and results from a well-balanced foot. In removing the horn, as the wall and sole are rasped off together, a line of demarcation will present itself about three-eighths to one-half an inch from the outer edge of the wall. This line shows where the sole abuts; it is united to the wall, and is of value as a guarding point, showing how much of the crust can be removed with safety. The dividing line will show the outer wall thicker at the toe than at the quarters or heels; shorten or reduce it by careful manipulation of the rasp against the edge of the crust to an equal thickness all around with the *plantar* surface of the foot in view; then turn, and with the hoof placed on the knee, smooth the lower edge of the wall, to obtain the desired results. If the foot is balanced, the weight is equally distributed on the laminated tissue.

Each portion of the anatomical structure bears its share of labor and performs the functions nature intended in a rational manner. The external portion of the hoof is a modified continuation of the outer or scarp skin, with similar functions to prevent evaporation of moisture and protect the sensitive structure, beneath which, if too much of nature's protecting envelope be removed, a sensitive surface is the result. The outer wall is more liable to become hard, dry and brittle, and lose that elastic spring, where the shoe, never intended for it by nature, is attached to the foot. If the foot, as a rule, is kept properly balanced, we seldom meet with lame horses.

The frog is composed of spongy horn placed in the center of the foot between the bars, beneath the column of bone, and when in a healthy condition is very elastic. Its office is to break concussion, and under no circumstances, except for a surgical operation, should it be touched with a knife. Too strict adherence to this rule can not be enforced. Not even the rags should be removed; if left alone they will do no injury and come off at the proper time.

The bars are a continuation of the wall, bent at a very acute angle, at the heels. They form stays to the quarters and should be cut with judgment—that is to say, that portion which projects below the sole, especially on heavy draft horses working on city pavements. These are more liable to be afflicted with what is termed broken bars, similar to quarter cracks; but the latter are in the external portions of the hoof, although they may penetrate deeply into the soft tissue, often producing lameness. This sole, like the frog, exfoliates, and when left to nature the old horn is cast off at intervals as the new is strong enough to take its place. But when, after the foot has been shod, the squamous tissue is protected from wear and held in place by the protecting shoe, that dead portion should be removed; but do not use the knife too freely. The sole should be left as strong as possible in perfect feet.

It goes without saying that the after usefulness of a horse depends upon the good judgment and practical experience of the farrier shoeing him. It is not a question of how cheap, but how good? As the old adage holds: Any thing half done is not done; "any thing well done is twice done."

As to shoeing speed horses, no man can intelligently shoe one without seeing him in harness; and, while standing in front, he should watch him as he approaches and passes, and notice how he picks up his feet and puts them down on the ground. If the horse's motion is level and smooth, his front and hind strides will be of the same length; if he is hitching and hopping behind, these strides are unequal. A skillful, practical horseshoer can overcome this by close observation. Again, the farrier may have properly balanced the feet; but the driver can undo all the good done by unbalancing the body in checking up the head too high. The fault may not be in the shoeing, but with the driver.

To balance the foot and leg is, therefore, the first and all-important step, before shoeing. And the work will not be complete or well done until they are made to stand directly underneath the body, as before enjoined. To neglect this is the greatest mistake, from which certainly may result any of the diseases which impair the foot and leg, and ultimately, if not at once, ruin the horse.

The next and equally important point is to make and fit the shoe to suit the diseased condition of the foot and leg, so when the shoe is nailed to the foot the horse will stand with his feet and legs naturally under the body. When this is done, two-thirds of the victory is gained. I have never seen any disease of the foot and leg where there was a permanent cure effected, unless the foot and leg were made to stand naturally under the body.

My sole object in getting out the fourth edition of my treatise on Scientific Horseshoeing is to give my former as well as other patrons the benefit of the new illustrations, showing the different diseases to which the feet and legs are subjected. As I maintain always, seventy-five per cent of the foot and leg diseases are caused from unbalanced feet.

CHAPTER V.

SHOEING YOUNG HORSES.

TO BALANCE AND REGULATE ACTION AND GAIT.

Conditions of Action.—Not to go too deep into the literature of the subject, it seems that the walk, trot, and gallop have always been the natural gaits common to horses, influenced by their environments and the nature of the ground over which they traveled. On the other hand, the ingenuity of man has evolved various breeds and given them different phases of action, in order that certain demands not naturally existing, but arising in a later day civilization, might be fitted. This shows that the quality or characteristic of action is, in a measure, artificial, because as soon as the natural necessity for any specified gait ceases to exist, the gait ceases with it, unless training by man is substituted for the original demand. At the present day, therefore, we notice that all breeds of horses are distinguished by some special method of action, which is an essential factor in determining the intrinsical and fancy value of any of their representatives. The trotter that can not trot, or the hackney that can not lift his knees and hocks, is generally an unsalable commodity. It would serve no special purpose to go more fully into the details of this section. What I am most anxious to show is that the natural conditions of the ground over which horses must travel should regulate their gaits, and that for any given method of progression the proper style of shoes must be adapted and applied with a nice intelligence so that the exercise of their legs and feet may be fully sustained without violent waste of effort. In animated beings, soundness of parts and liberty of movement constitute the perfection of existence; hence it becomes a paramount duty that the training and gaiting of horses be primarily conducted within this scope, a prerequisite of which is the observance of certain rational details appertaining to the affairs of shoeing which all horsemen should understand.

Care bestowed in Colthood.—While attention is being continually drawn to the foot of the horse after it is shod, few references are made to the hoof of the shoeless colt. The latter is, by some peculiar oversight, left to take care of itself, as if it required no preparation whatever in the early stages of its existence. Consequently the limbs and action of many young colts are impaired from neglect of proper supervision of the most important of all his aids to locomotion—his hoofs. I have visited many breeding establishments of racing stock, where the last consideration of the proprietors appeared to be the importance of supplying conditions under which the feet of their youngsters could have every chance of proper development. Many times there may be seen promising two- or three-year olds with ragged, uneven feet, growing into all shapes but the right, when the most simple early attention would avert disease or deformity. If the bearing surface of the young animal's foot is uneven, it most surely results in weakness of the limb or visible deformity when he arrives at maturity. Defective hoofs are of as a serious nature in the immature colt as in the full-grown or aged horse, and as much to be counteracted as in the horse regularly shod by the expert shoeing smith, and neglect may bring regret at a later day; for, in the case of the former, permanent injury is the result of inattention. He may grow in or out at the toes, either calf kneed, bent kneed, or knock kneed, just as the bearing surface of the hoof maintains its relations to the joints, ligaments and tendons of the limb of which it is the base.

First Trial of Shoes.—The horse's hoof is after all a good deal of what we make it, and if our horses from colthood up, had their feet more carefully attended to, the period of their active usefulness would be greatly extended, and in every way they would be found better suited for the work required of them. I am in a position to know some of the main causes that are responsible for imperfections of gait and action in horses, and one of the foremost among them is the first shoes that are put upon a youngster. To shoe a colt for the first time and shoe him scientifically, put a very light shoe on him, and every shoe the same weight front and hind, then you have your horse balanced perfectly, as nature made him, and if pure gaited he can always be shod so. Afterward if he betrays a lack of balance, faulty action, or an uneven gait, a driver of keen observation can certainly discover the imperfections and apply the proper correctives. To force a change in his way of going must be at the expense of the joints and tendons. For if the articulation is such that the limb is forced to go in a wrong direction, any irregular or increased weighting of the foot to force it to go in a different direction will undoubtedly result in serious trouble. A broken gait and unbalanced movement comes from some evident cause. Remove that cause and the ill effects quickly disappear, and the animal becomes comfortable in his action, with the result of an increased desire, as also increased capacity to speed faster, and in such a smooth, rythmical way that it becomes a real pleasure to the noble animal.

Modifications of Action.—In the course of my long experience as a shoer, I have necessarily had a great deal to do by adaptation of shoes to the balancing and trueing of irregular and mixed gaited horses, representing every type and condition of foot soundness and soreness. I have thus come in contact with many horses where the cause of such disordered action seemed obscure, or where the true seat of trouble had its origin or location elsewhere, while apparently leaving its mark or making its sign at the extremities of the limbs. It is proper to suggest, therefore, that, when beginning examinations at these points and failing to identify the trouble, you should not suspend investigations without subjecting other regions of the limbs and trunk to a close scrutiny, until the real cause of the ailment is discovered and you have satisfactorily remedied it before permanent injury ensues from neglect or inadvertence. It may be that the horse is not well-balanced in physical build. If the shoulders are very straight the feet will not be properly flexed, nor will they if the pasterns are short and upright. He may have long legs and a short reach underneath, or he may have long, sloping or weak pasterns and be unnaturally close coupled in the back, or exceptionally open-angled from hip to hock. Also he may be long in his sweeps behind or he may carry his head too high or too low for a proper balance on his limbs, and any one of these so-called structural defects—by insufficiency or misdirection of purpose—may give rise to a derangement in the movement of extention or flexion, to take effect in action or gait, or may lead to injury of the feet or limbs, as I will amplify in the section on "Faults of Conformation."

Care of Horses' Mouths.—Illustrations in point of probable or remote causes assisting to disturb the action and break the gait of horses—which shoeing will avail nothing whatever toward remedying—may be found in the horse's mouth.

This is one of the most sensitive organs of the equine economy. All young horses coming three or four years old should have their mouths and teeth carefully examined when any symptoms of tenderness or irritation are shown, as it is at this age that some of the deciduous molars are replaced by the permanent teeth. In some cases this gives rise to much pain and annoyance to horses, affecting their temper and sensibility. Again, in some horses, the structure of the teeth is of a comparatively soft nature, and wears upon the grinding substances in a ragged and uneven manner, which severely cuts and lacerates the tongue and cheeks, or, by a driver repeatedly lugging on one rein or the other, hard, sharp, spur-like points are formed or irregularly grown on the borders of the teeth, which become an exciting cause of injury to the gums and membranes of the mouth, impairing the natural processes of mastication and contributing at the same time to a bad way of going; also, the animal may suffer from toothache, due to a displaced crown of a temporary molar, or from ulceration, which will cause it to champ fretfully upon the bit and lurch to one side in such a sudden manner that he "looses his feet," by becoming bad in his action and tangled in his gait. If a horse pulls his head and neck out of line with the median plane of his body the hind limb on that side is correspondingly misdirected, and its foot is forced to land between the front ones instead of in line with them, this cross-firing naturally impairs the steadiness of his gait and injuries are liable to occur from it. If a humane treatment of the teeth is pursued by people who own horses they will obviate these changes of locomotion, and at the same time be amply repaid by the improved appearances of their animals through proper mastication of their food and in their general order of movement.

Handling Young Horses.—In gaiting young horses, much lies in the understanding how to equip and handle them. A driver or trainer can make or unmake the "thoroughbred close up," as he is wise to see that which is good, proves it worth, and holds fast to much that is tried, until it grows from the stage of experiment to law of permanent action. A horse may have plenty of spirit and yet be free from the undesirable habits of shying, breaking his gait and losing his balance, if the reins are made to deliver their right message. You might take a good horse, properly shod, and handle him like some cranky drivers do, and you could never judge just how a horse would best handle himself. The horse that is least governed is the best governed, when you want to get at the point of how light or how heavy his shoes should be to get the best speed and style of action. Trotters are changed to pacers and pacers are changed to trotters simply by an adaptation of shoes to the animal's way of going, and instances are on record of horses trotting in one race and pacing in another, the change being effected simply by shoeing. It is true that this can not always be effected for some families pace naturally, and again it is nearly impossible to make a pure square line trotter into a pacer, but some have naturally an interchangeable gait, and if the possibilities of scientific shoeing were more thoroughly understood, we would see less crooked-legged, knee-padded, tendon-booted horses led out to display their forced speed, and its utilities would make their own demonstration in every department of horse enterprise.

Determining the Gait.—You can not have strained tendons, swelled joints, and irregular-gaited horses if the feet are trued and balanced and the shoe properly adjusted to carry out the balance. Do this, and their action will be true and their gait equably sustained all the time.

In developing a horse's gait and speed, shoeing is a matter of the utmost importance, and one which requires the greatest study and care. It is, in fact, half the battle. Careful, patient experimentation, extending over many days, or even weeks, may be necessary to ascertain these points. Not until they have been ascertained and safely met is the colt ready for a "trial of speed," or for the adjustment of any settled gait. For a green colt, no matter how pure-gaited he may be, is almost certain to cut his shins or his knees by striking them with his feet when he begins to travel at a high rate of speed. The skillful horseman will carefully study all these varying points. The shoeing will largely depend upon the individual necessities of the animal and other similar conditions.

Regulating the Gait.—With a view to correcting and balancing with proper shoes and weights any faults he may have, carefully note every point in the action of a young horse while giving him a little preliminary driving. If the action is disproportionate, or the propelling power of the hind limbs excessive and their stride longer or more rapid than that of the front ones, their movements can be regulated and equalized in this way. The feet must first be leveled and balanced in the manner provided for when shoeing the perfect foot. (Fig. 23.) Very light shoes are then to be put on all round. For the front feet, use the pattern of scoop-toe shoe seen in Fig. 121, as this will quicken their revolution. Then, by using the shoe (Fig. 139) for the hind feet, having the ends of the branches calked lengthwise and turned outward beyond the heel $\frac{1}{2}$ inch or more, the flexion and extension of these limbs will be retarded to a degree that will accommodate them to the difference in movement of the front limbs.

In all such instances, however, the weight of the shoes must be adapted to suit the style of action, some horses requiring more and some less weight, to fulfill the purpose in view. In cases where light shoes fail, or where the horse has a low, swift gait behind and does not use his hocks sufficiently, it is necessary to shoe heavier behind than in front—the hind shoes to weigh, say, from 4 to 5 ounces more—because the greater weight on the hind feet will cause him to use his hocks and muscles more in picking up his feet, and this will naturally tend to slow the action behind and thus allow time sufficient for the front feet to get out of the way.

If the action is naturally well-balanced, the shoes should, of course, be of the same weight all round.

Balancing the Action.—It is sometimes a matter of great difficulty to balance and square the action of horses, especially trotters. The requirements are so many and varied that various expedients must be resorted to in securing the benefits of shoeing.

Some horses are long, low striders, and others high, short steppers. Some require heavy and some light shoes, and every style of open, bar, flat, concave, rolling, and weighted shoes, with different lengths of toes and heels, are necessary, amongst the rest, for times and occasions, to regulate and balance the action of different horses; and much of the success that should attend the acquirement of a pure gait, or the correction of a faulty one, depends upon the discretion exercised in the selection of the right kind of shoe.

When the action of a horse is short, high, and quick, or "choppy," in front, it will generally be found that the toe of the foot is too short and the heels too high, or that the pasterns and shoulders are upright. This can be remedied in effect by lowering the heels as much as possible, which will bring the foot more to the ground. In case the front part of the hoof has been rasped or pared too short, the shoe should be extended over and beyond the toe, and thus acquire a proper extent of ground surface. The weight of the shoe must be determined by the driver or owner as to what is best adapted for the horse to carry with ease and safety.

When the action in front is long and low and stiff-kneed, put the foot in shape as for the perfect foot (Fig. 23), and use the scoop-toe rolling-motion shoe shown in Figs. 121 and 134, which will shorten the stride by lessening the extent of the ground tread, and at the same time effect an increase of knee action. A still more efficient aid in these respects will be found in the use of the plain rolling-motion shoe (Fig.125), for in proportion to the increase of the roll in the shoe, so will be the increase of the action in the knee. The roll heightens and hastens the action, imparting, as it were, a "down-hill" impulse to the ste

A common cause of bad action in speed horses is tenderness

or soreness in the feet, resulting from improper shoeing. To shape and properly adjust a shoe to meet the varying requirements of a horse's foot is an art that is not as thoroughly understood as it should be (as I have elsewhere shown), and there are still many primitive methods associated with the professional practice. No man is fit to shoe a horse unless he can balance and level a foot scientifically so as to preserve or restore the natural bearings of the joints and hoof, which is, after all, the main thing necessary, and the quantity of skill displayed in this respect constitutes the real difference between the skilled and unskilled workman. An ill-fitting shoe is as inconvenient and painful to a horse as a tight boot is to his owner, and the comparison more than justifies itself when it is borne in mind that the horse's shoe becomes a fixture not to be discarded at will, whence follow impaired action, distorted hoofs, corn bruises, inflammations, etc. A foot thus shod may be tortured by the cramping of nails around the toe or be "underpunched" and driven upon the sensitive parts; or by scooping out the sole and then shoeing with too light, thin plates, causing what is known as "foot scald." Other penalties are inflicted by burning, causing the hoof to become hard and dry; and in destroying the right angle of the foot by having high heels and short toes, or *vice versa*. A horse with a low gliding action behind can only move efficiently with light-weight shoes, as the labor in such cases devolves mostly on the muscles of the thigh—the hock not opening wide, and much weight on the foot soon becomes fatiguing. The shoes for the hind feet should therefore be light as can be safely worn, and be well concaved on the ground surface, without heel-calks, as shown by Fig. 149.

The Useful Gait.—It only remains to be added in this connection, that it will pay horsemen to cultivate that most useful gait for any horse—however restricted it may appear—namely, a good walk. The steady, good, four-miles-an-hour walk is the gait that "gets there" with the most regularity and with the least amount of wear and tear of team and vehicle every time. The team that walks steadily and well, without being required to mar the walk by trotting over part of the road, generally reaches its destination before the one that divides the distance into periods of brisk trots and very slow walks. To improve the walk of a team, it should be taught to work persistently at that pace, without alternating the performance by any other style of going, for the time being, for that would spoil the salutary effects of the lesson.

CHAPTER VI.

SPECIAL AND GENERAL SHOEING.

DEALING WITH DIFFERENT KINDS OF FEET.

That there is a wide margin of difference in respect to the conformation and proportions which characterize the feet of different kinds of horses, or horses reserved for particular uses, is too constant and well established a fact to require formal assertion here, and that it is.the practical difficulties of adjusting suitable shoes to meet these varied requirements that most of the failures of farriers is due, can not for a moment be denied. There is always a choice of modes and instrumentalities available to the farrier, a question of preference as to this or that alternative in shoeing, and it often involves a considerable amount of practical ingenuity and good judgment to decide on a procedure that will insure good final results.

This, indeed, constitutes the most difficult part of the art of shoeing, for it is plainly evident that all feet, differing as they do in conditions and uses, can not be alike operated upon, nor can one kind of shoe be supposed to answer the purposes of all. The safety, speed and endurance of a horse greatly depend upon the adaptation of his shoeing to the nature ef the work he has to perform, and at all times a careful application of it to the state of his foot.

In general terms this represents a comparison applicable to the science of horseshoeing in its best state, that, in its degree, it demands as much expertness, knowledge, and attention to details, as is required in the construction of a delicate musical instrument that it may keep in tune and harmonious action.

The mode of dealing with each foot, therefore, should be influenced both by its kind of condition and the kind of service for which the horse is designed. A want of attention in this respect or a disregard of the consequences entailed by such neglect, is largely responsible for the disasters that wait on misapplied shoeing; not only marring the utility of shoeing to all intents and purposes, but rendering it a menace instead of a protection.

Without being an alarmist, and not presuming to claim a monopoly of advantages in criticizing the objectionable features most noticeable in the common run of horseshoers' work, I again refer to my observations in Chapter IV on the importance of settling and balancing the foot on the normal center of equilibrium, which it must be understood inclines, and is fixed or altered according to the natural or unnatural growth of the hoof; then, in the right adaptation of the shoe to maintain and carry out this balance. Reiterating these primary facts, all the more from the frequency of the instances where they are wholly disregarded (there being one good intelligent shoer, it is safe to say, where there are ten others ruining horses right along), and to the further fact that they are at the very beginning of all inquiries relating to the proper shoeing of horses of any and every kind, as well as to the cause and treatment of many foot ailments. Hereafter my references and comparisons in dealing with the other portions of my subject may be considered as constantly applying to, or as being based on, the general matters of shoeing advanced in the chapter just mentioned.

The Running or Galloping Horse.—The running horse occupies a legitimate position at the head of field racing. Aspirants for distinction in this class must have physical merit to make prominent those qualities which alone prove most accept-

Fig. 30. RACING PLATE FOR RUNNING OR GALLOPING HORSES.

able on the track—vitality, strength, speed, and endurance. The running horse concentrates the full power of a perfect animal organism in his terrific bursts of speed, and is rewarded according to his deserts. Considering the immense length of stride, or the distance covered with each forward movement or jump in the act of galloping, when each front and hind pair of bipeds are extended to their utmost in rapid succession to receive, sustain and transfer the weight of the body, as well as the burden of the rider, it will be readily appreciated that the result of these efforts (sometimes prolonged in hard contests) must prove a severe test of the structural makeup of any horse, and that in the eliminating process where exceptional speed marks the "survival of the fittest," a large proportion of all running and racing horses soon cease to be available for speed or any other profitable purpose. From the violence of their exertions they are liable to sprains of tendons and ligaments, and a sprained leg must always remain a weak leg.

The great sprain producing or "breaking down" pace is the gallop, but (as this injury more nearly concerns the limbs above the fetlock) as a rule, running horses have much better feet than trotters. This is due to the softer tracks over which they course, and to the consistent use of light thin shoes, so that the frog impinges the ground with such a firm tread as to overcome any interposition to the expansive capacity of the foot while in action, we must, for the most part, ascribe that better condition observable in the feet of running horses.

To preserve them in this way, despite their hard manner of going, it necessarily requires judicious care and the barring out of most of the objectionable features to be found in shoeing. When properly applied according to their natural requirements, the training shoes of running horses are quite light, placed on with only a few small nails, not to unnecessarily crowd, split, or weaken the wall; then, before racing these training shoes are removed, the feet accurately leveled and balanced like the form in Fig. 23, and racing plates substituted. The latter are a light, narrow rim, about $\frac{3}{16}$ in. thick x $\frac{3}{8}$ in. wide, weighing, say, $1\frac{1}{2}$ to $2\frac{1}{2}$ ounces, though this must be proportioned to suit the conditions of going, gait, balance, etc. These plates should be well concaved on the ground surface, with a fine edge all round, to catch the first impulse of the spring at the toe without slipping, and be adjusted to the precise line of the hoof, just covering the wall-bearing to insure perfect action without compressing or touching any other part. The nails should have thin, narrow blades and sharp points and be driven around the sides and heels even to the extreme ends of the branches of the shoe, as shown in Fig. 30; to point out through the thick lower margin of the wall, and thus secure a solid, permanent hold, as shown in Fig. 29.

In this way, the task (worthy of the most intelligent farrier) to combine the right and useful utilities of the work will be insured, to the desirable end that "violence during locomotion," which constitutes the serious and irreparable accident termed "breaking down," will, at least, be restrained in so far as shoeing can effect it.

The Trotting Horse.—The trotting horse must be considered in the light of a pattern road horse—generally useful in form, gait and docility, to meet any demand—combining the ambition of a gentleman's driver and the reliability of a lady's phaeton horse. The influence of the trotting-bred animal is favorably seen in its effects upon the general character of our roadster stock, which it has greatly improved for all practical purposes and enhanced in all desirable respects. In other lines his public performances on the turf have given the trotting horse a prominence unequaled as his excellence, and he is everywhere fancied as the favorite among speed horses. In this respect the distinctive trotter is an example of modern evolution; as will be seen by a reference to the following table, which gives a list of the standard, record-taking performers, in and subsequent to the year 1806, from which date the development of the trotting classes are credited.

CHAMPIONS OF THE FAST-CLASS REGULATION MILE-TRACKS.

YEAR.	NAME.	REC'D.	YEAR.	NAME.	REC'D.
1806	Yankee..	2 59	1874	Goldsmith Maid	2.14
1810	Boston Horse	2 48½	1875	Lula	2.15¼
1829	Topgallant, 3 miles	8 11	1876	Smuggler	2.15¼
1834	Edwin Forrest	2 31	1878	Rarus	2 13¼
1839	Drover	2 28	1878	Hopeful	2 14¾
1844	Lady Suffolk	2 26	1879	St. Julien	2 12¾
1844	Unknown..	2.23	1880	St. Julien } same date	2 11¾
1849	Pelham, converted pacer	2 28	1880	Maude S. } same date	2 11¾
1849	Highland Maid	2.27	1881	Maud S..	2.10¾
1849	Flora Temple	2 24½	1881	Maud S.	2 10¼
1855	Pocahontas, pacing to wagon	2 17½	1884	Jay Eye See	2.10
1859	Flora Temple	2 19¾	1884	Maud S.	2 09¾
1867	Dexter	2 19	1885	Maud S..	2.08¾
1867	Dexter	2.17¼	1889	Guy..	2.10¾
1868	Lady Thomas	2 18¼	1891	Sunol..	2.08¼
1869	American Girl, 31 oz. shoes..	2 19¼	1892	Nancy Hanks..	2 04
1871	Goldsmith Maid	2.17	1894	Alix (against time)..	2.03¾
1872	Lucy	2 18¼	1895	......	.....

(It is freely predicted that a speed of two minutes is not only possible, but probable, in the immediate future.)

This gradual development of the trotting horse to his present state of excellence, and the still greater excellence to which farther development in the future will certainly elevate him, can not fail to improve all kinds of light harness horses in general use. The trotter will train on and breed on. People who are not horsemen, in the strict acceptance of the word, but who,

SPECIAL AND GENERAL SHOEING. 119

nevertheless, enjoy a ride behind a good horse, will become more and more impressed with the fact that it costs no more to keep a good horse than a poor one, and that in horses, as in everything else, the best is the cheapest. The demand for good horses will therefore increase, and as the general horsekeeping public become more and more learned in the knowledge of what a good horse really is, they will take nothing else.

In the evolution of the trotting horse the most vital and imperative points commanding the attention of horsemen and farriers have been the acquirement of constantly improved methods and skill applying to the intelligent supervision of his feet and legs, the most important parts of the animals structure, upon the soundness of which its capacity for speed and power of endurance greatly depend. I have already referred (in the chapter on "Shoeing Young Horses") to the many perplexities to be encountered in the progress of shoeing trotting horses, owing to the variety and velocity of movement, and because each single front leg is required to alternate at certain successive moments in bearing all of the weight and impetus of moving, instead of sharing it with its counterpart, as in the act of standing or running, in all of which there is always an increase of the difficulties of shoeing.

The weight and style of shoe, are, therefore, to be regarded with the utmost nicety of judgment, and such matters must be thoroughly understood in adapting the shoe to its proper intent. It is necessary for the shoe to be well adjusted to a close, strong bearing upon the wall, and that it be sufficiently wide to sustain the usage required without bending or twisting, nor yet to touch or bear against the sole. The shoe should therefor be beveled off inside of the wall-bearing and fit the hoof to the best advantage uniformly around all parts, with a firm seat toward the heels, and in all other respects let it be made and fitted like the shoe for the perfect foot, Figs. 27 and 28. By having the ends of shoes beveled off on the same angle as the heels of the hoof, the force of landing will pass through the ball of the foot on the right axis of the leg, without injury to the back tendons. Three nails on each side of shoe opposite each other will allow the foot to expand equally on both quarters and thus avoid the danger of foot and leg soreness. It should be borne in mind that pressure from the shoe must be kept off around the front part of the foot to prevent toe soreness, as the hoof grows more at the toe than at the quarters.

Some horses may require scoop-toe shoes, or shoes concaved on the ground surface, others, small heel calks; but these points, together with weight of shoes, etc., must be adjusted to suit the stride and gait of the horse. When starting trotting horses in their spring work after a long winter's rest, it is advisable in some cases to have their front shoes weigh four or five ounces more than the shoes worn in the fall races, as these heavier shoes will assist them in getting up more quickly to their stride. Reset the shoes every ten or fifteen days, so that the foot may be kept level and balanced, and at all times fit the shoes snug around the hoof to avoid striking them off by an overreach.

Another point worthy of note in this connection is, that by watching the action of a trotting horse and attentively listening to the sound of each footfall, the rhythm of their movement may be observed and any irregularity detected. Thus, if the action is balanced the succession of steps will fall in regular 1-2-3-4 time, but if any irregular interval occurs—either slower or faster —there is a difference in the length of stride. Where there is a long interval, the stride of the slow-moving limb is longer than its fellows, and where there is a short interval, the stride of the quick-moving limb is shorter than the others. These irregularities may be due to some inequality of the foot—a high heel or short toe will cause an unbalanced gait or an unequal stride. A foot shorter on the ground surface—that is, with short toes—is shorter in stride and quicker in its fall than the others. If the front feet are upon the same angle, same height.

of wall from coronet to base, same length of ground tread from heel to toe, and carry the same weight and style of shoes, their action and stride should be the same, and this rule applies also to the hind feet.

To supply any insufficiency in ground tread of hoof, the shoe should be made to project over the toe enough to line up with the correct angle of hoof and pastern, all as explained and shown in Chap. IV, with Figs. 16 to 29.

The Pacing Horse.—Having shown in the preceding chapter that the necessity for action of a certain kind has in some cases been the cause of breed evolution, and in others breed evolution has necessitated the development of action of an entirely different character, I come now to speak of one of these artificial gaits as displayed by the pacing-bred animal. The pacing horse shows his ability to successfully compete with other distinctive "speed horses" in their own sphere, but he will not compare side by side in popular favor with the trotter as a road horse. The action is a succession of changes from one side biped to the other, resulting in the active swaying and balancing of the body with a sidelong shifting movement, developing in the best types, great reach of stride at speed in an easy frictionless manner, with much force and power of action.

For horses of this kind use as light and thin shoes as will suffice for the protection of the hoofs from concussion in swift movements, but no more. They should be concaved on the ground surface to make landing secure without spreading or sliding, and for the same purpose the hind shoes may have low-heel calks, Figs. 140 or 149. In all other points observe the order of procedure in leveling the foot, adjusting and nailing the shoes, according to conditions noted in connection with perfect foot, Chap. IV., Figs. 23 and 27.

The Racking Horse.—Another acquired gait is called the

FIG. 31. ENGLISH SEATED SHOE FOR HACKING OR SADDLE HORSES AND FOR GENERAL DRIVING PURPOSES ON HORSES HAVING GOOD STONG ARCHED FEET.

rack, which is especially adapted for saddle horses, being a rapid, attractive style, graceful and pleasant for a rider—though, as horsemen know—exacting on the stamina of a horse. The gait is performed by the action of each lateral biped in rotation. The revolution of the front feet exhibit a high knee action, full of mettle, with a hard, almost perpendicular descent; in consequence of which there is an aptitude in horses of this class to overreach and thus strike off the front shoes by the forward thrust of the hind feet.

The objects to be looked to in shoeing the racking horse are to provide a secure footing and avoid unnecessary concussion or the mischance of picking up stones. The shoes for the front feet should therefore be of a light concaved pattern, such as the English seated shoe shown in Fig. 31, or in case of overreach use the scoop-toe rolling motion shoe, Fig. 121, as this will quicken the action of the front limbs; and for still quicker movement over the toe, use a plain roller-motion shoe, such as Fig. 125. For the hind feet the addition of heel calks to shoes, as shown in Fig. 140, will give a more effective footing by sinking deeper into the ground. In all cases, however, the feet should be kept strong in all parts and the shoes fitted accurately to a firm position on the wall, as for the perfect foot, Fig. 28.

The General Purpose Horse.—This class of horses may be held to include numerous miscellaneous representatives of all classes in all sorts and conditions of life: from the sleek, well-groomed, and handsomely appointed, light-stepping roadster of the successful professional or business man, to the "general utility" animals of the coach, omnibus, and livery lines, as well as the workaday horses of the common carriers and the sedate looking, steady going, well known family carriage horse.

Thus classified, or grouped, there is enough diversity in size, style, and general character of performance to apparently tax the ingenuity of the shoeing smith; yet there is nothing formidable in this array after all, and all may be treated with great ease and simplicity, though with that regard and attention which each may seem to demand. The same process of shoeing as appertains to my formula for the perfect foot, and the same shoe as shown in that connection (Fig. 27) applies here, and may be followed with general success throughout, as this shoe will prove most serviceable for all horses going at a "jog trot," especially for summer wear on the front feet. I would not recommend the promiscuous use of calks on shoes, for where such cramps seem of use to the support of a horse by the impression they make in the surface, it will be seen from my method of shoeing race horses, where the frog comes to the ground, notwithstanding the course they run over is often slippery and they are up to their speed, yet they seldom fall, and this style of even, plain shoeing, would seem to be well calculated to answer for the same purposes generally. Still, when toe and heel calks are required, it is well to state that the toe calks should be of good length, set slightly back from the front rim of the shoe, as this will assist the easy going over at that point without deviation or hindrance to the action.

The Draft Horse.—Dropping from the higher types to the draft horses we still find that conditions of environment have given to the different breeds of this class their own characteristic ways of going. The true gait of the draft horse is the walk, though the candidate for the best honors must show that he can go faster than a walk when necessary, but still maintain his legs in such a position as to enable him to exert the maximum of his strength as occasion may require. A typical instance may be selected from the Clydesdale family, whose long continued use in the heavy soil of Scotland has caused him to lift his feet squarely up, flex his ankle joints deeply, turning the sole of his feet squarely up, and then, with a long swinging stride, implant them on the earth again, indicative of his perfect ability to carry or draw the burden to be thrown upon him. The hocks of draft horses should not be carried too wide apart, for that detracts from their power (resulting from muscular fatigue) in the exertions consequent on heavy hauling. That the feet of such horses should be strong and healthy, with firm hardness of hoofs, will be readily inferred from a consideration of their important, special uses as supports, from whence proceeds, as the base of action, whatever there is of bodily strength or physical power to work or strive "with might and main" within the sphere assigned them. Yet how frequently do we see horses of this class with weak, tender feet, marked by mishaps from careless exposure to irregular, hard, loose bodies upon which their heavy tread may chance to fall, or lame from the lodgment of flints and pebbles between the sole and shoe, to which the customary method of shoeing greatly contributes by paring down the sole and frog, and weakening the heel by opening up the space between the angles of the bar and wall, and then setting the toe and heels too high from the ground, otherwise removing them too great a distance from the point of support, which tends all the more to an excess of pressure upon the coffin-joint, as well as to the fatigue of the nerves and tendon upon which it rests, by the distention they undergo at every step the horse takes. It is not to be supposed that teamsters, traffic-men or farmers give their horses' feet the particular attention given to the higher class of racing and pleasure horses, but they can most assuredly give them common-sense care, and this will often spare unnecessary punishment to, or save the life of, a useful and valuable animal.

"Experience keeps a dear school," but a wise man will learn to profit by the mistakes of others, and this particular advantage everyone may reap from the foregoing references to the present subject of inquiry, namely, to keep your horses' feet strong as nature made them, level and balance them as I have sufficiently pointed out and amply explained under the head of "Practical Horseshoing." Pare away as little of the sole, frog, and bars, as possible, to accomplish this end in the proper way, then adjust as plain and light a shoe as accurately to the hoof as may be done, and, lastly, fasten it on with no larger nor more nails than are judged sufficient to make it secure in position for a reasonable length of time; and I will guarantee on the strength of long years of experience and close observation, that the fruitful source from which arise the many dangerous compressions, inflammations, etc., already mentioned, will be obviated, and you will have learned, without the aid of other tutor, the great scientific lesson of rational horseshoeing.

But though this method may not be so generally adopted by all in its utmost extent, for the reasons previously announced, that from the different formation of horses' hoofs, which in some will always demand a particular method of shoeing, yet it undoubtedly applies to the majority of horses generally met with, and the exceptions remain to be further noted.

The shoes for draft horses should be only moderately heavy, not too thick, and as narrow in their covering as the case admits, so as not to endanger the elasticity of the sole.

Figs. 32 and 33 indicate the patterns usually adopted for front and hind feet respectively, showing four nails on each side exactly opposite one another, to do the best service with the least injury. Toe and heel calks are in general vogue for shoes of this kind, and they should always be of equal height and low

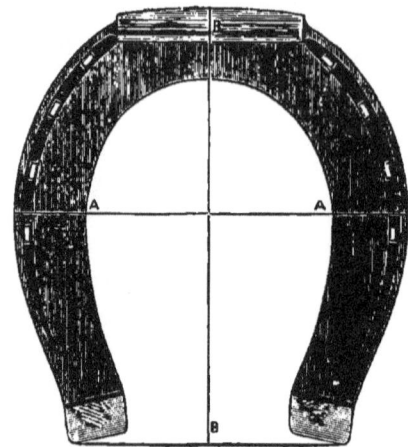

FIG. 32. FRONT FOOT SHOE FOR DRAFT HORSE.

A, A, B, B, Figs. 32 and 33, Lines showing the equal adjustment of shoe to the normal center of foot from heel to toe and across quarters, thus placing the weight upon the right portions of the foot and the shoe under the right weight bearers.

as possible—the lower the better for the ease and safety of the horse. The expediency of calks may sometimes be questioned especially on the front feet, howsoever convenient or successful they may be in respect to the hold they secure, for they aggravate the inequalities of bearing and deprive the feet of liberty of accommodation, and work injuries to the freedom of the locomotory apparatus as previously mentioned.

Resort to toe clips, and burning them into the hoof to assist in the retention of the shoe, is often productive of injury to and soreness in the foot—as I shall illustrate further along—but when applied they should be carefully turned up with reference to these effects, and also in line with the angle of the hoof, using a knife to notch the hoof where they are to be buried.

By the method of shoeing proposed in connection with Fig. 27, and since referred to according to the perfection or imperfection of

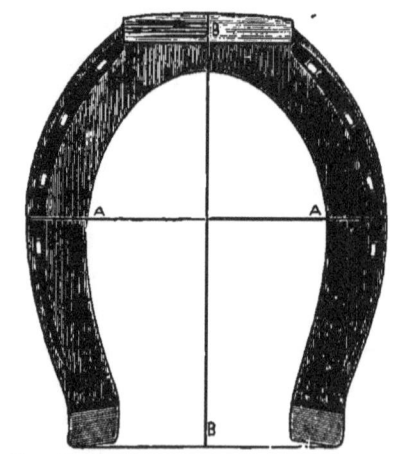

FIG. 33. HIND FOOT SHOE FOR DRAFT HORSE.

the hoofs under consideration, it will be seen that the advantages arising from the plain and simple processes recommended are, that the free action of the extremities in going with ease is preserved, by not setting on any more iron than is necessary; and that in not removing the frog, the foot rests more evenly from toe to heel, thus multiplying its points of support and giving it a stronger and more adherent landing, without lessening the surface of ground tread nor yet increasing its friction or fatiguing the stride.

It is observable that a horse goes easy or escapes soon being jaded if the frog receives a certain amount of pressure, as it is the supporting cushion to the back tendons, also defending the sensitive sole against many inconvenient bruises, so that if it is kept at a distance from the ground by high heels or by paring it away, an inordinate distension of the tendons will happen, causing relaxations, swellings and soreness, which are occasioned more by paring the sole and frog than by hard driving or the distance traveled. Experience has shown that the frog, being of a soft, flexible substance, by its natural elasticity, yields to the weight of the horse the instant his foot touches the ground, and immediately recovers itself again, thus giving a natural expansion to the foot with every step taken. When contracted feet have to be expanded, the most simple, safe, and at the same time, effective means of attaining that end is to be found in this action of the frog. An overgrowth of hoof, that is, high heels and long toes, displaces the normal balance of the foot and bearings of the joints, and causes contraction, weakness and a curl under at one or both sides of the heels, forcing the foot bones upward—twisting the coronet—producing malformation of the wall and an atrophied condition of the internal parts from defect of nourishment and loss of strength caused by pressure of the hoof; all of which defections may be entirely averted if the foot is properly dressed as directed. Or before becoming permanently established, they may be overcome if the foot is leveled and balanced so as to restore frog pressure, when the latter speedily recovers its lost characteristics and, again, in a healthy condition, gradually and naturally accomplishes one of the very purposes for which it was put there.

However, there may be cases whereby sudden frog pressure might occasion soreness for the time being, when it is still hard and dry, or when a horse has worn shoes for a long time, having thick, high heels; but by leveling the frog on a line with the hoof when preparing the foot to its proper bearing angle as directed this disorder is soon remedied.

Proportions of the Hoof.—It is apparent from the anatomy of the foot that there is a fixed limit beyond which the growth of the hoof should not proceed, though this growth is, in itself, constant or indefinite, enlarging the base of the hoof as it proceeds. In a natural, unshod state, attrition or wear by the strain of the animal's mere weight is sufficient to keep the hoof in such size and condition that the balancing of the body is properly distributed upon the digital regions, thus obviating the impairment and lameness which result from improper shoeing, as well as the premature breaking down of horses through the overgrowth and unbalancing of their hoofs.

No definite rate can be assigned to the growth of the hoof, as some develop more rapidly than others and in different parts, though it is claimed by some writers that it requires a year to renew a complete wall. The toes of the fore feet and the heels of the hind feet are relatively the thickest and strongest parts of the wall, and consequently the growths there are more marked than at the quarters. In a naturally well-proportioned horse the ground tread of the fore feet is longer from heel to toe by from $\frac{3}{4}$ in. to 1 in. than across the quarters, and in the hind feet from $1\frac{1}{4}$ in. to $1\frac{1}{2}$ in.

These is no use in mincing matters for the more one knows about shoeing, the more he knows that the common mode of doing the work is so frequently destructive, that we seldom meet with a horse whose feet have not in some degree lost their natural form, and this deviation from their original shape is generally proportioned to the length of time he has worn shoes. We may learn from this that the horse in a state of bondage is a subject fit for our gravest consideration and worthy of every care and attention that we can bestow. Certainly it is true that this applies with particular directness to the matter of shoeing, where extra precaution should be adopted and intelligent observation maintained, in order to guard against unnecessary punishment, and secure the best results.

Resetting the Shoes.—It not infrequently happens that horses go lame from an overgrowth of hoof by allowing the shoes to remain on too long. A false economy about shoeing bills on the part of the owner—by persisting in the continuance of shoes on his horse after they have been outgrown by the hoof—is wrong and unreasonable, as the infliction of an unnecessary punishment. Under ordinary circumstances and conditions of hoof growth the general purpose and draft horse should have his feet adjusted and shoes reset every four weeks, and on the track or speed horse, every two weeks to preserve the necessary harmony of action and balance in the foot.

Owing to the fact that the hind feet differ from the front ones in shape, operation, and mode of growth, a different method of shoeing should be applied to them. The action of the hind limbs, as previously outlined, carries the sweep of the feet nearer the ground, and the lighter force of weight in these parts gives less fixity to the tread; hence, it follows, that calks are less objectionable on the hind shoes, as they tend to keep a horse from sliding on a descent, and secure the footing by a deeper clutch on the ground. Calks, however, should be rather flat and the shoes generally narrower in the web than the front ones (though stiff enough to insure substantial form) as a better grip is thus secured in the act of springing, and no loss of power sustained in the extension of the stride. The shoes also should be attached well back of quarters and heels, as these are the stronger parts of the wall; but in all cases, both front and back shoes should follow the exact marginal line of the wall from toe to heels, and if any deficiency exists in the length or width of hoof, the shoe is the thing to supply it with; then if the foot is leveled and angled aright, the shoe is to maintain the level by being of uniform thickness, and wherever the foot requires to be raised or lowered let the shoe be thickened or thinned to suit the emergencies of the case.

Comments on the Gait of Speed Horses.—Some interesting comparisons are suggested by the records of the phenomenal "time beaters" tabulated on page 118.

Selecting, for an example, the recorded performance of Nancy Hanks in 1892, when she trotted a mile on a regulation track in the remarkably quick time of 2 minutes and 4 seconds, a simple calculation will serve to indicate the rate of speed required for its execution.

The line measure of our standard mile being 1,760 yards or 5,280 feet, it is seen that in dividing the distance traveled by the time expended (reduced to seconds), we have 5,280 feet by 124 seconds=$42\frac{18}{31}$ feet—or the rate per second traveled by Nancy Hanks in the foregoing race.

By another process the gait of horses or the length of their stride will be similarly conveyed. Assuming the stride of the horse to measure 16 feet, it will require 330 such strides to complete the circuit of a mile. If the stride is a rod long (or $16\frac{1}{2}$ feet), there will be 320 to the mile; and if **17 feet** in length, the number of strides to the mile will be $310\frac{10}{17}$.

CHAPTER VII.

LAMENESS AND DISEASES OF THE FOOT.

PATHOLOGICAL SHOEING.

We can scarcely overestimate the value of sound legs and feet in the horse, and having their condition and efficiency for a subject, it also naturally follows that the pathology of these organs becomes a special topic for inquiry, for their situation and uses naturally expose them to a greater liability to injury and disease than any other portion of the animal organization.

The advantages to be derived from a safe and scientific mode of shoeing in the treatment of many of the varied troubles to which the feet and legs of horses are constantly subject, are attracting more attention among horsemen than formerly, even as the results to be obtained from such treatment are their own best proof of the merits of the agency employed, which need but to be seen and understood to be indorsed by all. It is the verdict of experience that a rational, approved method of shoeing will not only protect the horse's foot from injurious wear, and thus prevent the certain damage otherwise ensuing, but acting on the doctrine that "like cures like," it will transmute the evils that men do into good, through its instrumentality as a corrective for the manifold crimes committed in its name. This, in truth, is the legitimate mission of farriery—"preventing, curing, or mitigating diseases." Veterinary surgery—indispensable though it be as a healing art—is not competent to deal successfully with even the most frequent and familiar of the troubles that beset or waylay the horse at almost every footstep, though there are only too many cases in which horses are retired to the hospital, or unnecessarily subjected to the torture of "fire and blister," while all the fault lies at the bottom of the hoof, in an overgrowth of the wall.

It is of such diseases as have their origin in, or otherwise affect the feet, and which may be relieved or cured by rational methods of shoeing, that I purpose treating under this head.

The different character of the diseases as manifested by disorganized structures or deformities of the foot and hoof, are illustrated by typical specimens carefully drawn and selected from many similar examples which I have in my possession—the collection of years spent in such research—which form a complete exhibition of the morbid effects resulting from neglect, abuse, and improper management of the horse's foot.

Many foot troubles, when allowed to exist by neglect, or when improperly treated, are oftentimes obstinate and difficult of cure, or are productive of permanent injury or total disability; others yield readily to a seasonable application of proper remedies, and may thus be completely overcome and the foot restored to perfect strength and vigor.

Most generally the nature of the symptoms, as shown on the joints, tendons or coronet, are directly traceable to an improperly shod or unbalanced foot, and the eye trained to recognize such tokens will be quick to note that there are no existing conditions in the limb that will make it possible for them to find birth in it, and as ready to know that all there is to be done is to have a competent farrier straighten the foot, and shoe it accordingly, to restore the natural conditions and functions of the locomotory apparatus.

Causation of Diseases.—It is estimated that 75 per cent of all the diseases that horse-flesh is heir to, are due to the so-called "necessary evils" of shoeing, and it is found that most of this long category arises from a disregard of the primary principles of establishing a level footing for the horse to go upon. Hence I find myself incessantly repeating again and again that the first and last object of attention —the source and center of success in farriery—is to bring the feet to a perfectly level bearing, so that they will point straight and true in line with the limbs, and the action of locomotion will be performed with easy continuous regularity like the movement of a pendulum. By keeping this principle steadily in view, I feel assured that I have done more for the improvement of the strength and perfection of the horse's foot than could have been done by learning all the mysteries of the veterinary school. Without it, all the soaking tubs, bandages, liniments, etc., are so much time and money wasted.

Though the first condition of incipient trouble has thus been pointed out and evidently proved, the matter does not end here, for an uneven and unbalanced hoof—high heels or long toes or inequalities in height of wall, which displace the natural angle of the foot—is, after all, not difficult to detect when knowing how and where to look for them, and may easily be regulated by any one who will attentively consider the principles of adjustment as defined in connection with the use of the instruments, Chapter IV.

If the heels are allowed to grow too high the greater part of the weight is thrown forward upon the toe and bony structures of the limb, and the bones of the foot are forced forward against the wall in front. Inflammation of the foot and soreness in the joints and bones soon follow. If the toes, on the contrary, are allowed to grow too long, then the excess of weight is thrown upon the back part of the foot and the flexor tendons become sore, strained or ruptured. If one heel or quarter is permitted to grow higher than the other, the high side will receive the first jar in landing, which bruises the heel on that side and causes inflammation and corns. The hoofs, therefore, must be pared or dressed in such a way that the weight of the animal will be equally distributed upon the ball of the foot between the bones and flexor tendons, in accordance with the instructions given for leveling and balancing the feet, as described in Chap. IV.

The use of toe and heel calks will also produce soreness or lameness in fast horses by their uncertain or unequal contact with rough, stony pavements, causing a side rocking or tilting motion in the limb, racking the joints of the foot which are not capable of much lateral motion.

Another cause that is generally overlooked is the attachment of shoes with an unequal number of nails on either side of its branches. For example, if four nails are used on the outside and only three on the inside branch of the shoe, the inner side, with the least number of nails being less permanently fixed, yields to the outside more firmly seated on the unyielding shoe, and thus by growth and tension the inner side (with less nails), is gradually forced in or under the leg, while the outer side (with more nails), is correspondingly carried outward and away from its normal center and thus the hoof becomes deformed and its movements deranged. Then, by a reversal of the above arrangement, that is to drive four nails on the inner side of the shoe and only three on the outer, the process will in two or three shoeings, return the foot to its natural form and straight position by the same means and in the same manner through which it had lost them. This demonstrates the necessity of shoeing according to the principles already defined—having the nails alike on both sides and set opposite each other, as directed with Fig. 27.

Locating the Lameness.—No horseman or farrier need be told the effects of splints, sidebones, curbs, spavins or ringbones, or how they make themselves known by the condition of the organs to which they extend. Hence I shall not now attempt to define their symptoms, as they will be succinctly dealt with hereafter, but confine the present inquiry to a search for more obscure conditions which may attack the foot, while having their location elsewhere, or otherwise appear in remote regions when the foot itself is at fault.

The nicest observation is sometimes demanded to identify and locate the causes which produce certain derangements of the locomotory apparatus, where a horse is said to "go sore," or exhibits signs of tenderness. Simple or severe lameness, where the condition of disabled functions is plainly manifested by the animal refusing to use an injured leg, or to bear any or an equal portion of its weight upon a disabled foot, may easily be detected; but mere tenderness or soreness is more difficult to locate. Serious results may at times follow from the obscurity enveloping the early stages of many foot ailments, for in the absence of early treatment, which a correct diagnosis would have given, they may easily develop into more complicated maladies or become transformed into chronic, incurable cases. Hence the importance of early symptoms, how they betray themselves, and what region or structure is affected.

A little observation on the part of the driver will readily detect any irregularity or change in the movement of his horse, but just where lies the fault is not so easily determined. If the horse is trotted slowly down hill and shows more evident signs of lameness than when going on the level, it is an indication of high or bruised heels; again, if more distress is shown in going up the grade, long toes are the probable cause. Soreness of the shoulder muscles is also betrayed in a dragging movement of the toes when going up hill.

In case these preliminaries are not conclusive, lose no time in turning the horse over to some competent farrier. The next proceeding is naturally the removal of the horse's shoes to examine the soles and hoofs all around, for nail pricks or punctured wounds and external injuries or bruises of any kind. Having closely observed these parts and settled their connection with any symptoms of lameness, proceed to examine for internal soreness by using my foot testers (Fig. 195), to compress the lower margin of the wall all around, from toe to heel as high as the nail hole. If there is any soreness in this region the horse will flinch or shrink from the pressure, but if nothing is manifested in this way continue the same process up around the coronet by gripping it between the base of the hoof in the jaws of the tester, same as before. Then if the cause of the trouble or its seat still remains in doubt, pursue the investigation to other regions of the limb or trunk as recommended for "modification of action," page 106.

Laminitis, or Founder.—Under this double head is expressed one of the most insidious of all foot ailments. The former gives "a local habitation and a name" to the disease as applied to the laminar tissues, while the other recognizes it more in effect as indicating the "sinking" or falling of the foot structures or the failure of their functional activity as implied by the word "foundered," by which name the malady is most familiarly known. Its particular character is an inflammation of the sensitive laminæ, and its general symptoms are so well manifested by the impairment of the bodily vigor and power of locomotion, or weakness and stiffness in the limbs, accompanied with signs of acute pain which the suffering animal attempts to relieve by disposing his weight on the sound members, that its presence is not easily mistaken. It may be confined to a limited region, or it may involve the entire tissue of one or all four feet, though the front feet are the ones most affected. Various causes are assigned as productive of this disease, such as drinking too freely of cold water while overheated, rapid changes from heat to cold by exposure to cold wind, rain, or washing the feet and legs in cold water when the animal has been violently exercised or is exhausted by work, over-exertion and at times over-feeding of certain grain, especially corn; bad shoeing is also—here as elsewhere—a prevalent factor by paring out and weakening the foot, or by applying high heeled shoes, etc.

Primary or Passive Stage.—The early stages of this disorder may consist only of a simple congestion of the sole tissues, but as it develops rapidly, if suffered to run its course, the morbid process will involve other regions in its destructive changes, and severe lameness—extremely difficult of cure—or entire physical disability will result. The most prompt and efficacious treatment should therefore be resorted to at the first symptoms of an oncoming attack, as the conditions are then favorable for speedy relief, and the disease may be checked or cured in one or two days' time.

When the evidences of soreness or weakness appear, or the horse stumbles and shifts his gait by declining to use his feet in the natural way, have the farrier remove his shoes and pare the sole of the foot thin, that the resistance of the horn may not obstruct the after measures, then lightly replace the shoes by tacking them on with two nails on each side. Cover the body, neck and legs warmly with several blankets (strapping them on closely all around) and place the feet in tubs of warm water—heated to a good temperature—which should be kept so by replacing the water as it cools with a warm supply, as in this way the return flow of blood will be increased. Warm drinks are also recommended to stimulate internal circulation, the congestion will be overcome or re-absorbed, and by continuing this treatment for twenty-four hours, the symptoms will subside and the normal functions be practically restored without disorganization.

Acute stage Villitis.—When this form of congestion spreads or progresses into a more acute stage it is attended with more evidences of soreness and lameness, evidenced by greater unwillingness of the animal's movements as well as by the various positions which it carefully assumes in attempting to alleviate the distress of weight on the inflamed member. This secondary or extended stage is known as villitis, because it is principally confined to the villous tissue of the sensitive sole; but the point of greatest sensation, is naturally, in the region of the toe, where the sole and laminal tissues blend into each other; which increases the vessels of that part, hence the sensitive laminæ may also become congested or inflamed. The treatment for these acute cases is the same as for the more passive cases above prescribed, and usually the symptoms will pass away or recovery be accomplished within a comparatively short space of time.

Imperfect recoveries, however, naturally impair the secretive powers of the sensitive sole, and thus renders it liable to after effects, which may be obviated if properly managed.

Chronic or Violent Stage.—True laminitis is the sequel of the progressive development or culmination of the acute stage, when the inflammation becomes general throughout the laminæ and the tendency to injurious changes of the structures become more marked. When this stage of the disease is reached, the symptoms are greatly increased and the distress of the animal correspondingly intensified. The inability to support weight often causes it to lie down, and constitutional disturbance by loss of appetite and feverish restlessness are attendant characteristics of this phase of the disease.

The vital connection which these laminæ sustain to the entire animal economy and their situation between the horny hoof and the bony structures of the foot, necessarily renders any compression or inflammation of them one of peculiar injury and suffering to the horse. When thus affected they are no longer able to perform the function of weight bearers, their power of withstanding the work imposed on them is lessened, and the pressure upon them gradually weakens and destroys their attachment to the hoof, letting the bones descend upon the sole, resulting in that condition of helplessness and disability known as "founder." This indicates that when laminitis becomes firmly established or deep rooted, various complications are inevitable. Other organs are invaded, the parts affected become useless and the animal either becomes an incurable cripple or is soon relieved by death.

This illustration gives a correct impression of the ravages of laminitis, when its processes continue to the chronic stage, whereby the joints, tendons and other structures of the foot are alike involved and their functions impaired. The disease has destroyed the laminal connections, a forced separation of the parts has turned or dished the hoof, and depressed the coffin-bone upon the sole, which has thus become weak, thin, and bulged or dropped downward. The space between the bone and hoof being filled with a fungous deposit resembling honey-comb.

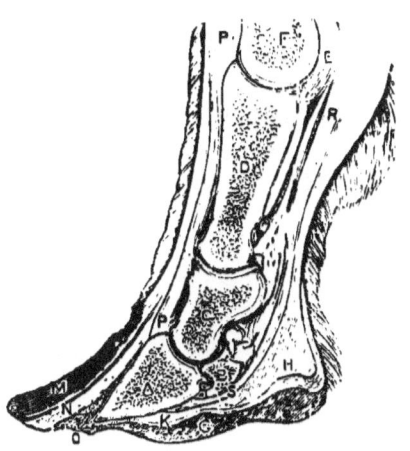

FIG. 34. MEDIAN SECTION OF A "FOUNDERED" FOOT, SHOWING THE SEVERE EFFECTS OF CHRONIC LAMINITIS.

A, Coffin- or pedal-bone. B, Navicular bone. C, Lower pastern. D, Upper pastern bone. E, Sesamoid. F, Lower end of cannon bone. G, Horny sole. H, Plantar cushion. K, Velvety tissue or sensitive sole. M, Wall, dished or turned up toe. N, Laminal tissue—the seat of laminitis. O, Fungous growth. P, Extensor tendon. R, Flexor perforatus. S, Flexor perforans.

In dressing a foot of the kind shown in Fig. 34, it is first necessary to foreshorten the toe as much as can be safely done without injury, by rasping around the front and sides and taking out the "dish," and restoring the hoof to its natural shape as far as possible. In feet of this kind, the sole is thin and weak, hence care must be taken that it is not cut or pared in any way around the point of the frog. When leveling the wall for the shoe, commence at the heels and lower both sides as much

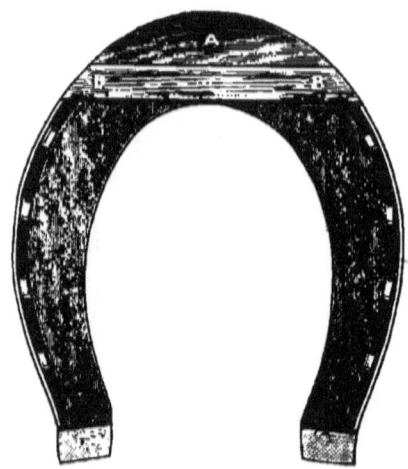

Fig. 35. FRONT FOOT SHOE FOR DROPPED SOLES AND FOR FLAT, WEAK SOLED FEET.

A, Bevel on toe from calk to outer rim.
B, Long toe calk set back from front.

as can be safely done, and this operation must be carried forward toward the quarters. In some cases where the sole is badly dropped, it will be found impossible to get more than two and one half to three inches level bearing for the shoe. When the foot is thus prepared apply the style of shoe shown in Fig. 35.

By having the toe set well back on the shoe, the center of gravity will fall more directly under the bearing of the foot and leg bones, and thus the strain will be partly taken off the weakened laminæ. If the foot be too wide at the heels and quarters, clips should be drawn up on both sides of the shoe, opposite the wings of the coffin-bone, that the hoof may be retained from further expansion. Clips are not to be used in front; bevel the front part of the shoe at the toe on the ground surface in order to prevent the horse from stumbling or tripping. Reset the shoes every three weeks, by lowering the heels again, and, in four or five shoeings, the sole will return to its natural concave form. Do not file or rasp the new growth.

The shoe being nailed solidly at the heels, it will be readily seen that the front part being released, and an open space intervening between the foot and the shoe, the foot will press down to meet the shoe at every step which the horse takes forward, and just in proportion as the foot springs down, the sole will be returned to its natural cup-like form.

DROPPED SOLE CAUSED BY BAD SHOEING.

Three views from a single specimen.

The illustrations on this and the following page are typical examples of the condition of a foundered foot, or dropped sole resulting from bad shoeing.

Springing the shoes off the heels, thereby breaking down the quarters will cause such effects, especially in large draft horses that have low, broad heels, and Figs. 36 and 37 show an instance of this kind. It is plain that such style of shoeing must prove disastrous in the extreme, whereas if the shoe had been fitted so that the heels would have corresponded with the dotted lines F, F, F, F, Fig. 37, the trouble would have been avoided. The excessive width of this foot as compared with its length from toe to heel indicates that the quarters have been broken down, the heels worn low and

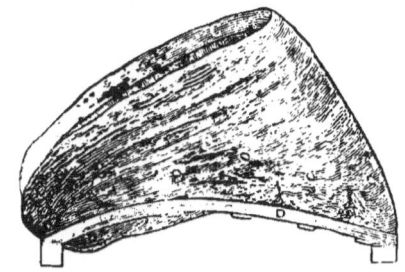

FIG. 36. SIDE VIEW OF HOOF SHOWING THE EFFECTS OF SPRINGING THE SHOE OFF THE HEEL.

A, Lower margin of horny frog. B, Side or quarter of wall. C, Cavity for the coronary cushion. D, Shoe on the hoof.

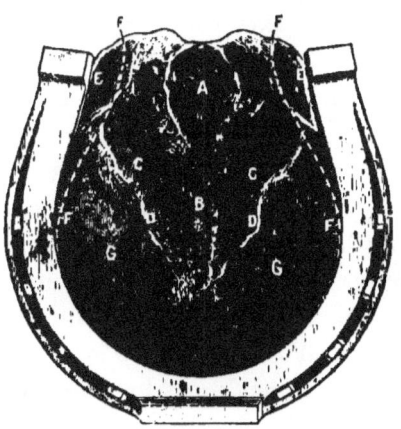

FIG. 37. BOTTOM VIEW OF SAME HOOF.

A, Cleft of frog. B, Horny frog. C, Commissures. D, Bars. F, F, F, F, Dotted lines showing where the shoes ought to have been fitted to cover the quarters and heels. E, E, Bulge of heels pressed through shoe by too wide fitting. G, G, Lower face of horny sole.

Fig. 38. SIDE VIEW OF COFFIN-BONE OUT OF THE FOOT, FIGS. 36 AND 37.

become bruised and curled under or bulged below the shoe, and low heels will produce a "wheel" foot, such as shown in Fig. 36. Fig. 38 shows the coffin-bone from same foot much distorted from its original form by the effects of faulty shoeing, as well as of disease resulting from the same.

Peditis is the term applied to this serious complication of laminitis, where not only the laminæ but the periosteum and the coffin-bone are also subject to the inflammatory process which sometimes involves the coffin-joint.

Depression of the coffin-bone is oftentimes accompanied with suppuration, where the separation of the reticulum from the bone takes place, and gangrene and superficial caries are common results.

The destructive effects of this disease upon the internal structure of the foot are well displayed in this drawing. The bone has become much distorted from its original form, from the pressure of the part constantly under weight when the sole has become dropped; the upper surface has "dished," as it were, or fallen in, until only one half its original height, while an immense number of small spines or thorn-like spurs have grown all over it, and the lower part of the bone has convexed in an extreme degree, bulging down until it had lost all semblance of its original shape.

In a preceding chapter instructions have been laid down for the management and shoeing of the feet of draft horses, and if they are carefully followed the most satisfactory results will be obtained.

In paring and dressing such a foot as shown here, the operation must be the reverse of that described in Fig. 34, that is the height or depth of toe being excessive in this case, it must be reduced as much as possible, and the heels left intact. The shoe bearings then, thus obtained, being around the front part of the shoe, use shoe Fig. 35, but nail around the toe instead of at the heels. Or it may be necessary to resort to a bar shoe for restoring the foot, but this will depend on the judgment of the farrier.

Seedy Toe.—Among the complicated effects of chronic laminitis is a peculiar dessication of the hoof commonly known as "Seedy Toe." This condition is well represented by the appearance of Fig. 39, in which is also seen the evidences of neglect in dressing and leveling the foot.

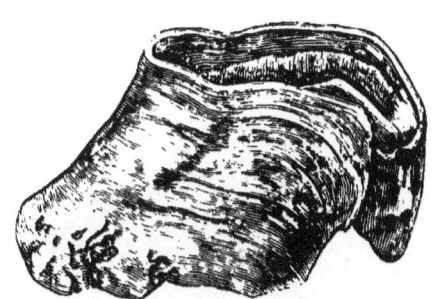

FIG. 39. SPECIMEN OF SEEDY TOE.

In this specimen the wall is twice its natural thickness on the side in view, it will be noticed that it is also scarred and seamed with rough ridges—due to irregular secretion of horn—while the heel is abnormally high, the sole being fully 1¼ inches too thick, and the toe turns up from an overgrowth at least two inches too long. Laminitis does not always involve the whole of the leafy tissue—even in the present instance—the morbid process appears to have destroyed only certain regions, where the leaves take on a regular honey-combed appearance, while other portions present a comparatively sound and healthy structure. But in most cases it develops rapidly, and if unchecked, continues to spread until the entire region is involved, with structural changes of the most serious character.

For a foot affected in this manner, pare the hoof level and as low as possible, rasp the wall thin from coronet to ground surface, and get the hoof back near as may be to its natural shape. If there is any tenderness in the sole it must be protected by using a plain, flat, broad-webbed shoe, well concaved on the sole-bearing surface, the nail holes to be punched where the foot is least affected, and the shoes reset every two or three weeks. It is difficult to describe any particular style of shoe to meet the emergencies of such cases, and the farrier must judge what is best. Cold water bandages around the coronet will assist in keeping the horn moist and allaying fever and pain.

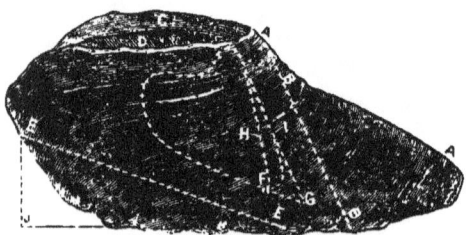

FIG. 40. ANOTHER EXAMPLE OF SEEDY TOE.

A, A, Angle of hoof as it stands, 34 degrees. **B, B,** Line to which surplus growth of front wall should be removed. **C,** Cavity for coronary cushion. **D,** Horny laminæ. **E, E,** Line to which surplus growth should be removed at base. **E, J,** Indicating how much heels will be lowered by reducing the base of hoof. **F,** Point to which coffin-bone was wasted. **G,** Normal extent of coffin-bone. **H,** Line indicating front angle of coffin-bone to be 75 degrees (should be 50). **I, G,** Line to which coffin-bone will conform when hoof is reduced as directed.

Fig. 40 illustrates the further ravages of chronic laminitis, in which its destructive effects (coupled with the mismanagement of the foot) are perhaps more plainly discernible. In this instance the heels have been allowed to grow to such an extent as to raise them far above their normal position. The normal angle of the heel from the ground surface to the coronet is the same as the angle of the front part of the foot from toe to coronet. In proportion, however, as the toe lengthens, just so much will the angle of the ground surface of the foot be carried forward, as seen in the above diagram, which shows the growth at the back of the quarters to be of unusual height, raising the heels up out of their natural angle, and, as the heels are raised up, just so much the heels of the coffin-bone are elevated, and the point of the bone is pressed forward against the front part of the foot, preventing the action of the secretive powers, bringing on inflammation, burning and scalding, and destroying the life of the foot, causing what is called seedy toe. In shoeing a foot of this description, great care must be taken that none of the sole be removed around the point of the frog. Remove the surplus growth from quarters to heel as shown by line, E, E. By removing surplus growth the heels will be lowered as shown from E to J, and the pressure will be relieved on point of coffin-bone. Remove the surplus growth in front to the line B, B, after which the foot will be placed upon its natural angle of 46 degrees. Compare this foot with Fig. 41. As the sole will

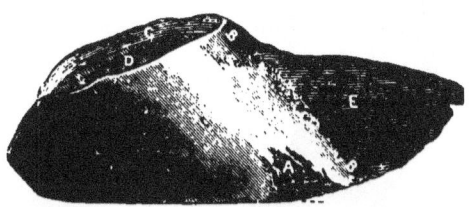

FIG. 41. THE SAME HOOF WITH ONE SIDE PROPERLY PARED AND STRAIGHTENED, AS INDICATED BY DOTTED LINES IN FIG. 40.

A, Effects of disease on horny laminæ. B, B, Correct angle of toe after removal of surplus growth as shown—46 degrees. C, Cavity for coronary cushion. D, Horny laminæ. E, Surplus growth to be removed on the opposite side. F, Elevation of toe of hoof above shoe, to obviate pressure.

be quite tender and sore at the point of the frog, the shoe must be well concaved around the front. Use shoe shown in Fig. 35. Rivet leather at the heels, letting it extend all over the shoe. Take fat pickled pork out of the brine, and cutting in slices, cover the bottom of the foot well, and then nail on the shoe slightly. Afterward stand the horse in a soaking tub of warm water for three or four hours. This will melt the pork, and thus assist in speedily removing the soreness. Bear in mind to keep the pressure off around the point and sides of toe, and thus give great freedom to the diseased parts. Keep the soaking swabs around the coronet wet with warm water. Reset the shoes every two or three weeks in order to check or keep down the undergrowth of heels and quarters.

I have often taken feet when the coffin-bone had worn through the sole at its point, and by the above treatment have restored them to their normal condition, and they have ever afterward remained sound.

The effects of chronic cases of founder or laminitis upon the foot are seen in Fig. 42; and not only the foot, but every tendon, joint and bone from the knee to the foot is seriously effected. These evils can be reasonably attributed to the want of skillful knowledge of horseshoeing and of the management of the hoof.

In paring a foot of this kind, follow the instructions laid down for paring the flat foot; always bearing in mind the necessity of getting and keeping the foot in its natural position. Use shoe described in Fig. 35.

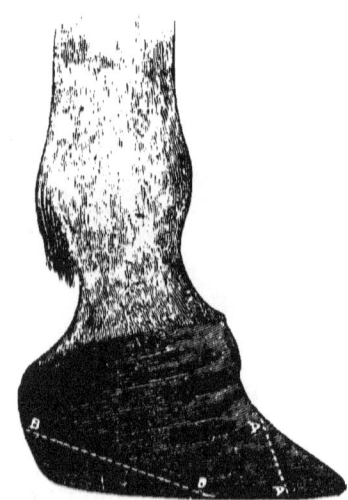

FIG. 42. DISHED FOOT AND DROPPED SOLE.

A, A, Line to which surplus growth at toe is to be removed. B, B, Ground line to which surplus growth is to be reduced from heel to quarter.

When describing the lateral cartilages in the chapter on "The Foot of the Horse," a brief reference was made to certain derangements of their natural structure by process of inflammation, through which they lose their soft elastic qualities and are changed into bone. Fig. 43 represents a typical case of the disease mentioned, which is often met with in practice, especially in heavy draft horses, though speed and saddle horses and also well-bred carriage horses, are not exempt from

LAMENESS AND DISEASES, ETC.

FIG. 43. COFFIN-BONE WITH SUPPLEMENTAL ATTACHMENT OF SIDE BONE OR OSSIFIED LATERAL CARTILAGE.

A, Body of coffin-bone. B, Lower margin of its wing. C, Side bone or ossified cartilage surmounting the wing.

its attacks, and in some instances it is hereditary.

There are numbers of conditions which may be the exciting cause of this bony formation; various diseases of the foot may occasionally involve the connective tissues, such as ulcered heels and laminitis; but contraction, violent concussion or injuries, and over distension by weight, bad shoeing and unlevel feet are the prevailing causes of ossific development. The present example is to be classed with others resulting from bad shoeing, and is the outcome of the next morbid specimen, here introduced as a dismal relic of perverted appliances.

In this case, the distorted condition of the hoof—the twisted heel and corrugated coronet—the diseased appearance

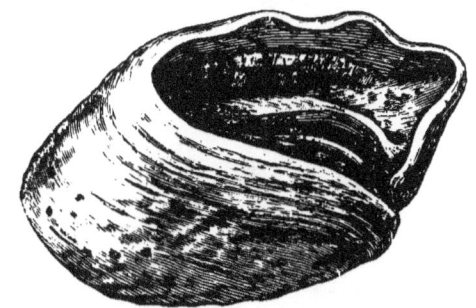

FIG. 44. VIEW OF THE HOOF (OF RIGHT FRONT FOOT) IN WHICH THE BONE (FIG. 40) WAS IMBEDDED AS INDICATED, BY THE DISTORTION OF THE OUTSIDE HEEL.

of the laminæ, and the disorganized character of the whole structure generally, are the consistent product of one common actor, namely, an uneven ground-bearing of the foot. To still further illustrate and explain the subject, I insert here two opposing views of the bones of the front foot and leg in order to establish a comparison between the normal and abnormal position of which they are the representations.

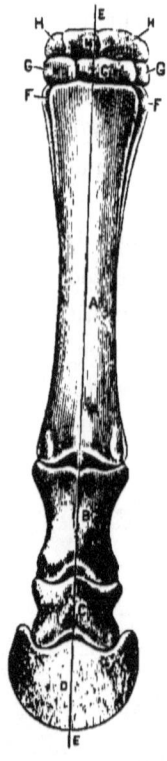
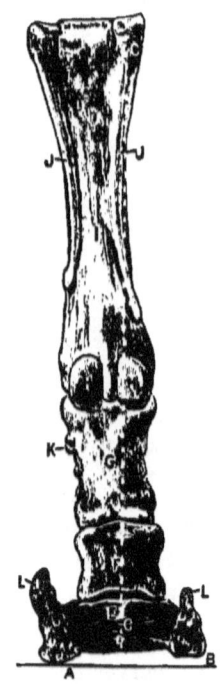

FIG. 45. NORMAL POSITION, FRONT VIEW.

E, E, Vertical line through axis of joints. A, Cannon-bone. B, Upper pastern. C, Lower pastern. D, Coffin-bone. F, F, Inner and outer splints. G, G, G, Lower row of knee bones. H, H, Upper row.

The knees and hocks are formed of several small bones placed in two rows, articulating with the larger bones above and below, as shown and described in skeleton, Fig. 2.

FIG. 46. ABNORMAL POSITION, BACK VIEW.

A, B, Level to which the foot should conform. C, Vertical line locating center of axis and indicating the displacement caused by unlevel base of foot throwing the weight on the outside heel. D, Coffin-bone. E, Navicular. F, Lower pastern. G, Upper pastern. H, H, Sesamoids. I, Cannon-bone. J, J, Splints (the highest one diseased). K, Morbid enlargement of upper pastern. L, L, Side bones or ossified cartilages.

The parallel of these views is self evident, and but little is to said in addition to my former observations on leveling and balancing the foot. When the bones and joints are in their natural relations, as shown in Fig. 45, the precision and accuracy of their functional activity is assured. The weight is carried through the normal centers of the limbs, the foot rests naturally, with every part of the apparatus sustaining its proper share of the burden, and when springing from the ground it is in direct line with the median plane of the body, and its movement forward and back is as regular as the swing of a pendulum. But when the ground-bearing of the hoof is uneven, as shown in Fig. 46, the incidence of the muscles is misdirected, the bones and their articulations are displaced from the extremity of the limb to its union with the trunk, and derangement of the entire structure is the inevitable result. To simplify the matter by a further description of Fig. 46, it is seen that the base of the foot is not level with the line below, and that this deflects the bony column out of the perpendicular. Assuming the width of the hoof to be four inches, and the distance from the base to the knee to be twenty inches, any unevenness, starting at one side or the other of the base, increases in the ratio of five to one; thus, a displacement of one-fourth of an inch at the bottom of the foot, will amount to a displacement of one and one-quarter inches at the knee. Improper paring of the hoof is of too frequent occurrence, and this illustration is only one of the many serious results following from a disregard of the first principles of shoeing. Impaired nutrition, diminished and obstructed secretion, abnormal growths and structural changes are always associated with it. It is impossible for a horse to spring from the ground or land on it in a line with the movements of his body unless his feet are straight in that direction and level in their bearings, and from a neglect in these regards or want of precaution to secure them, arise many maladies of joints, bones, tendons, cartilages, laminæ, and other structures of the feet and legs.

Fig. 47. OUTSIDE APPEARANCE OF SIDE BONES WHEN DEVELOPED.

A, Enlargement of cartilage transformed into bone. **B,** Its effect shown by bulge of wall at heel. **C, C,** Abnormal height of heels. **D,** Extension of side bone over pastern. **E,** Prolongation of side bone over the quarter.

The structural change of cartilage into bone arises from a deposit of lime salts, and may be of rapid or slow growth. The usual symptoms are manifested by the presence of fever-heat around the affected part, attended by more or less soreness, stiffness or lameness, and as the change advances it will be apparent by enlargement and by a sense of hardness to the touch. This illustration indicates the general appearance of a foot in this condition. When thus invaded the tendency is to increase, and no permanent cure can be effected as the cartilage tissue can not be restored; but in the early stages of the disorder the calcification may be arrested and the thickening re-absorbed by the application of a sweat blister. There are many variations of side bones, but the front feet are most liable to suffer from them. If both cartilages on the same foot are attacked at the same time, it is noticeable that they are less liable to cause lameness than if but one side is affected.

My drawings are samples of the development of side bones on one side of the foot as a consequence of one heel of the hoof being higher or longer—from coronet to base—than the other which is provocative of such malformation.

Where shoeing can be altogether dispensed with it will be better for the natural relief of side bones than otherwise, but where shoes are necessary they must be made to suit the conditions of the foot and the nature of the work to be performed.

In all cases, however, when dressing the foot, follow the directions given for the perfect foot, Fig. 23. This will equalize the bearings throughout, then, if the conditions are favorable for natural frog pressure, use flat, thin heeled shoes. If only one side bone exists, use the three-quarter shoe, Fig. 59, but if both sides are alike involved, it is better to insert a simple tip around the toe—the object being to place both shoe and nails to the best advantage, that all avoidable pressure may be removed from the diseased region. Reset the shoes at frequent enough intervals to keep the foot true to its natural balance.

Fig. 48. The laminal leaves of the horse's foot are, as already mentioned, peculiarly susceptible to the influences of disease, concussion, injurious burning, compression, etc. The present subject is a characteristic example of the evils last named. Spurs of the horny laminæ arise from external compression upon toe of the wall, and appear upon its inner surface in the form of a hard, callosity of varying thickness and length. In the above figure the growth has extended the full length of the leaves, imbedding itself against the coffin-bone, which has wasted away as this extraneous growth proceeded. Fig. 49 is a view of the lower face of same hoof and completes the story of the case. It shows a severely contracted quarter and heel on one side, and a large surplus growth around the front of the other, and all over its surface are the visible signs of hot fitting and bad shoeing. The bars and frog have been pared away and the strength of the

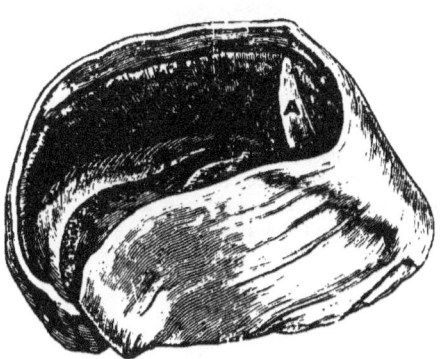

FIG. 48. HOOF OF DRAFT HORSE, INDICATING THE DESTRUCTIVE EFFECTS OF HOT FITTING AND CLIPPING.

A, Spur of horny laminæ, produced by clip on shoe.

152   SCIENTIFIC HORSESHOEING.

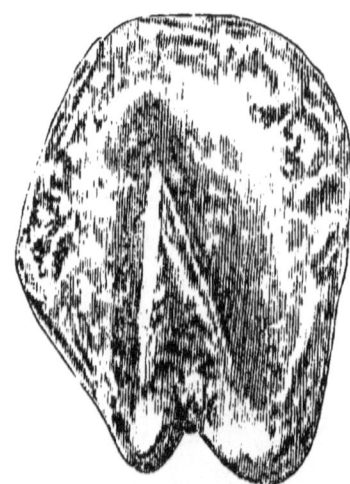

Fig. 49. BOTTOM OF SAME HOOF, AS IN FIG. 48, SHOWING CONTRACTION FROM QUARTER TO HEEL ON ONE SIDE, AND AN OVERGROWTH FROM QUARTER TO TOE ON THE OTHER.

foot destroyed, together with its balance. In a natural foot the frog is the right dividing line from heel to toe, but in this case the narrow or contracted side was forced to accept two-thirds of the whole weight, as indicated by its relative proportions.

From obstruction to its secretions, the sole was deprived of its elastic properties, and the entire hoof was similarly exhausted and reduced to a hard, dry condition throughout.

Compare with Fig. 23 and remove the surplus growth of the full side and supply any lack of ground tread on the contracted side by carrying the web of the shoe wide enough to cover out the deficiency.

Figs. 50 and 51 will serve to still further illustrate the tendency of hot fitting and clipping to work destructively upon inner structures of the foot.

Clipping is not injurious if properly done. Skillful farriers can resort to

Fig. 50. MEDIAN SECTION OF HOOF SHOWING FURTHER EFFECTS OF HOT FITTING AND CLIPPING.

A, Cavity for coronary cushion. B, Leafy tissue of horny laminæ. C, Side of internal fissure. D, Section of bulb of plantar cushion. E, Section of horny sole at margin of coffin-bone. F, Section of horny sole at point of frog. G, Section of horny frog. H, H, Section of spur of horny laminæ. I, Fungous deposit at toe. J, Section of wall at toe. K, K, Height of wall at toe, angle 45 degrees.

this expedient for a lifetime without injury to the foot; but in the hands of ignorant men, a horse shod by this method is subject to certain injury. In general I do not hesitate to say from practical experience that I believe hot fitting and clipping injurious if the feet have lost their proper angle. In the endeavor to accommodate shoes that are too short for the feet for which they are intended, ignorant and unskilled farriers often cut out the front of the foot until they draw blood, then burn in the clip so as to stop the flow of blood, and worse than all, hammer the clip back into the foot.

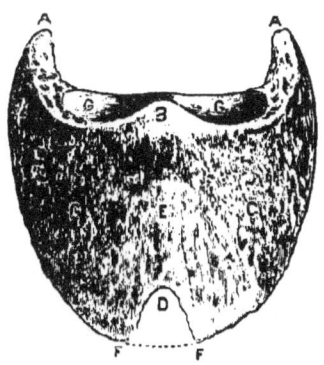

Fig. 51. UPPER FACE OF COFFIN-BONE, SHOWING EFFECTS OF HOT FITTING AND CLIPPING.

A, A, Extensions or wings of heels. B, Eminence on which is inserted the extensor tendon. C, C, Lateral faces. D, Groove worn by spur. E, Depth to which this groove sometimes extends. F, F, Margin to which the bone should conform. G, G, Articular surface of coffin-joint.

The result of such malpractice is to cause the heat to penetrate into the sensitive parts, dry up the secreting nourishment and cause an unnatural compression against the insensitive laminæ at their union with the sensitive laminæ around the lower margin of the toe. Fever sets in, drying up and destroying the parts under compression, and the formation of a decayed, pithy, horny substance is the result.

But in addition to clips, there are many other spur-producing causes, which for want of space can not be defined in the present work. Mere mention, however, may be made of a few that have come under my notice, such as the driving of large, thick-bladed nails into thin shells. This, it is true, may not lay up the horse, but the spur which will result will make him tender footed, and if not at once remedied, the trouble will in time become aggravated. In a word, any improper management of the foot tending to produce an unnatural compression of the insensitive and sensitive laminæ, thereby destroying or preventing the action of the secretive powers, will cause the formation of a spur, large or small, which, if not attended to, will in the end develop to the great injury of the foot and the horse. I have in my possession many specimens of hoofs in which spurs are present, and an examination of them will show conclusively the cause of the spur in each case.

Diagnosis for spur in the toe, and its causes, will show the horse to be restless on his front feet, stretching or pointing first one foot forward, then the other, and this action always indicates trouble of some kind in the front part or toe of the foot. If a decayed, pithy, horny substance, as shown in Figs. 48 and 50, be found, it should be probed and cut out as deeply as safety will admit, being careful not to draw blood. Fill the cavity with my foot salve, prescribed in the latter part of this book. Finally apply a shoe suitable for flat feet, care being taken to keep the pressure off the toe, as elsewhere shown. If for a draught horse, use shoe, Fig. 35. Dress the foot to make it conform as near as possible to Fig. 23, and follow the directions given for that purpose. It will be found impossible to straighten the foot at once, as the new growth proceeds slowly from the coronet. File or rasp the outside crust in front from coronet to ground surface, as that will tend to release the internal structures from pressure. Apply hot-water bandages around the coronet, for the purpose of stimulating a new growth.

Contraction is almost always the result of improper shoeing and mismanagement of the foot, primarily due to overgrowth of the hoof at toe and heels. At times the shoes remain on too

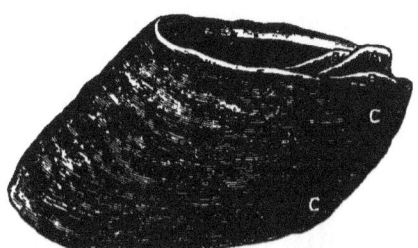

Fig. 52. CONTRACTED HOOF.

A, Spur of frog forced above level of coronary band. B, B, Bars forced above level of coronary band. C, C, Abnormal height of heel from coronet to ground surface.

long and the growth of hoof becomes excessive, or the horse may be allowed to stand in his stall in hot dry weather without sufficient exercise, whereby his feet become dry, hard and feverish, and such conditions are exciting causes of contraction, and horses thus affected are also more apt to stumble and cut themselves than would otherwise be the case. Fig. 52 shows a contracted hoof produced by an abnormally high wall. The appearance of the same hoof on its ground surface is represented in Fig. 53. The base of the hoof had wired together until the bars and spur of frog were raised above the level of the coronary band, against which the coffin-bone was also compressed by being forced upward, impeding or altogether stopping the functional activity of the vascular tissues, and causing a calcareous deposit or bony formation around the coronary cushion, producing stiffness in the foot joints. By the contraction across the quarters, the foot was relatively elongated, the heels narrowing and closing the commissures with an overgrowth of sole, and pinching the frog, as it were in a vise, between the bars, destroying all the expansive powers of the foot. Contraction may be easily

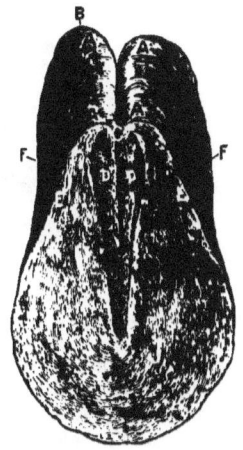

Fig. 53. LOWER FACE OF SAME HOOF.

A, A, A, A, Abnormal height of heels from coronet to base. B, Difference in height of heel at coronet. F, F, Contracted across quarters. C, Contracted cleft. D, D, Contracted bulbs at frog. E, E, Contracted quarter at base.

11

avoided or overcome by proper care of the feet and right methods of shoeing. The main feature is to keep the feet as near as possible to their natural shape, and this can only be done by leveling and balancing them as directed in Chap. IV.

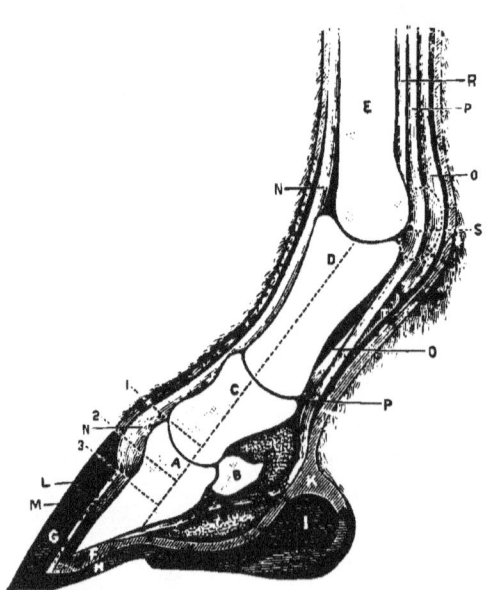

FIG. 54. MEDIAN SECTION OF FOOT, SHOWING DISPLACEMENT CAUSED BY CONTRACTION.

A, Coffin-bone. B, Navicular. C, Lower pastern. D, Upper pastern. E, Lower end of cannon. F, Section of velvety tissue. G, Section of wall. H, Section of horny sole. I, Section of horny frog. K, Fragment of plantar cushion. L, Horny laminæ. M, Sensitive laminæ. N, N, Extensor tendon. O, O, Flexor perforatus. P, P, Flexor perforans. R, Sesamoid ligament. S, Sesamoid bone (dotted line). T, T, Branching of flexor perforatus. 1, Pyramid of coffin-bone displaced. 2, Its normal position. 3, Normal position of coffin-joint.

The complications brought about by contraction include not only the effects visible on the external parts of the hoof, as shown in the preceding Figs. 52 and 53, but its tendency is to work many destructive changes in the apparatuses of the internal foot, as is here partially indicated by Fig. 54, which represents the displacement of the bony structures from such cause. When the hoof contracts and wires under around the base, the sole and frog are forced upward, together with the bones and other organs of the foot, until they are all tightly cramped by the closing in of the horny box. The unnatural pressure around the sole inflames the various tissues, causing a disease of the sensitive sole, called villitis, which may diffuse itself to the laminæ, producing laminitis; and this progressing may involve the coronary cushion in a process of hardening and thickening which may terminate in coronitis—an ossification of this organ (similar to that of the lateral cartilages when side bones are forming), which may be plainly felt when examination is made around the coronet at the quarters. No definite rule can be given for shoeing that would cover all cases of contraction; the farrier must be governed by his understanding of the case confronting him. Good judgment will direct that the hoof must be reduced and pared low as necessary to bring it to a good level bearing, as per Fig. 23, foreshortening the toe within the limits of safety. If the frog is hard and dry, pare it level with the wall and open up the commissures along the sides of frog and remove the horny sole to its union with the wall by thinning it until serum exudes, as this will give freedom to the action of the frog. Also if the heels are curled under (like an in-growing toe nail) open them up as deep as can be safely done, and in thus giving expansion to the bottom of the hoof, it will relax at the top and allow the necessary freedom at the coronet for the structures to assume their normal relations. After dressing the foot, apply the raised split-bar shoe, Fig. 154, as this will assist in expanding the hoof. Rivet a good solid piece of leather at the heels of the shoe to cover the bottom of the foot, then fill the bottom of the foot with a warm application of my foot salve, covering the same with an overlay of cotton or oakum, then nail on the shoe and leather pad and keep pressure off around the front part of the toe. After shoeing let the horse stand with both front feet in tubs of warm water (to fully cover the feet eight or ten inches) for two hours a day until soreness disappears. Reset the shoes every two weeks, pare the growth off the base of the hoof and keep the sole thin so as to allow it to spring under the weight of the body; at the same time have the feet washed around the coronet daily with warm water and castile soap (as described in prescription No. 1), and the horse may be worked right along without hindrance.

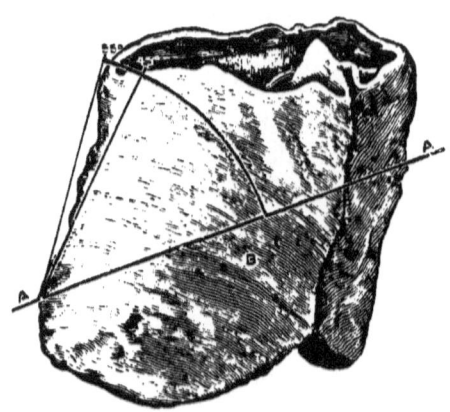

FIG. 55. MULE'S HOOF SHOWING EFFECTS OF OVERGROWTH PRODUCING CONTRACTION.

A, A, Line to which overgrowth should be removed at base. **55°** indicates the present angle of hoof. **45°** indicates the angle to which it will conform when surplus growth, **B**, is removed.

This specimen represents the effects of contraction by having the wall grow too deep, the heels wiring in until they came together, from coronet to ground surface, and the foot was hardly more than half its natural diameter. The heels overlapping each other had crowded the bars, frog and inner spur up above the coronary band. As the crowding of the bars thus necessitated a displacement of the internal structure, the coffin-bone was raised behind, the weight presses it forward against the laminæ. The laminæ in this part being overtasked, soreness and finally lameness ensues.

In many instances the mule is treated for lameness or strains, when the proper remedy was to have had his feet properly dressed and suitably shod. Do not permit the heels to grow to an extreme height, pare them down as much as can be safely done.

In shoeing a foot of this description, open the heels and

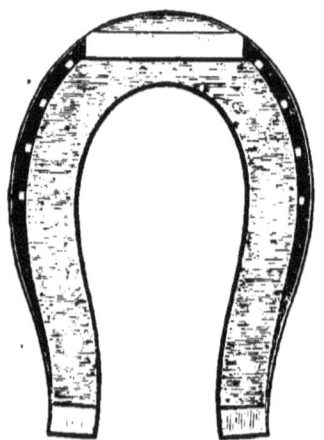

FIG. 56. MULE SHOE.

weaken them at both sides of the commissures, as thin as safety will permit; keep pressure off the toe. In shoeing for drafting purposes, toe and heel calkins will be required. In such cases, have them low, and of the same height, that the foot may be kept as close to the ground as possible, and the animal will travel with more ease and safety. Let the shoes be adjusted in a manner so as to fit the wall; and to avoid the possibility of cramping the foot, use small nails, with the nail holes straight punched and driving so as to take a low, short, thick hold. Reset the shoes every three or four weeks.

The horse's hoof, as described in Chap. III, is so constructed that any exertion may be best carried on by a given elasticity from the center of the toe, as the fulcrum of a reciprocating motion or spring around each side to the heels. Should the natural conditions of the foot be altered, however, by being deprived of sufficient moisture to preserve in it that degree of combined toughness and flexibility, the foot loses its power to yield to pressure and return, and when force sufficient to overcome its resistance is exerted, the hoof, no longer capable of springing to it, suddenly gives way by splitting.

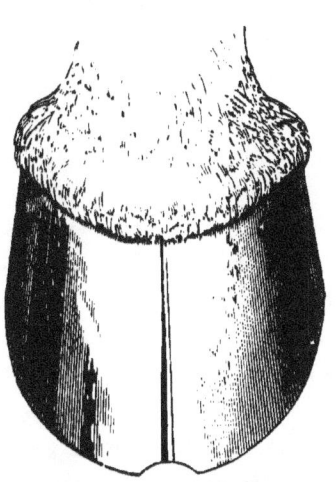

Fig. 57. FRONT VIEW OF THE HOOF PROPERLY DRESSED FOR TOE CRACK.

This breakage occurs wherever the strain is the greatest—at either of the sides from the quarters to the heel, or directly through the middle of the hoof in front.

The condition generally present, then, in the splitting of the horny hoof, is a hard, dry, brittleness, and this may arise in a variety of causes. Hot fitting and clipping, as well as high toes and heels on shoes which prevent the frog from coming in contact with the ground, high heels on foot or shoe, flat feet and long toes on draft horses, and the paring away of the frog, sole. bars and heel, whereby the foot becomes contracted, are prolific sources for bringing the hoof into the above-mentioned state.

Any horse whose feet are thus placed is exposed to fracture either on their anterior or lateral surfaces. With these conditions toe crack is produced by the foot acquiring an uneven ground surface, and being thrown into an unnatural or forced position. If the heel of the foot, through ignorance or neglect, is suffered to grow to an unusual height, the pressure and thrust of the coffin-bone against the front wall will almost surely result in fracturing it in that region. A peculiar accident to which horses are sometimes liable, will also produce the same result. When a horse, being shod with heel calkins, overreaches himself, that is, treads on his hoof with another foot, and bruises the coronet or crust, the crease thus made oftentimes extends itself until the crust is split from the coronet to the ground surface.

Toe cracks most generally attack the feet of heavy draft horses, doubtless owing to the coarse method of applying their shoes, as well as a greater stress being placed upon their toes than upon those of other horses in the exertions of drawing heavy loads.

In treating this disease, the first care must be to thoroughly cleanse the foot, after which the crack must be pared out smoothly on either side, as deep as the horny substance extends, thus widening the crevice so as to prevent all friction between the separated parts of the wall. Pressure must be taken entirely off the toe, and a groove, as in the accompanying figure, should be cut into the bottom of the crust at the toe.

Having done this, if the foot be contracted at the heel, pare it to a level. The toe of the foot is then in turn to be shortened and the heel weakened by paring out the commissures between the bars and frog as much as, in the judgment of the farrier, the foot can safely bear. The pattern of shoe represented by Fig. 35 should be used upon the horses intended for draft purposes, the nails being placed from the front of the quarters back toward the heel. Clips should be used upon each side of the toe of the shoe, so that when placed upon the foot on each side of the fracture, they will prevent the foot from further expansion, by keeping the pressure off from the toe, as shown in Fig. 57. The toe calkin being placed well back from the toe, lightens the stress at the point where the greatest weakness exists, and allows of an easier play to the foot when in motion. When the split occurs in the foot of a general business horse, lower the heel and shorten the toe, as much as safety will permit, and thin the heel of the shoe to obtain strong frog pressure, removing the pressure around the toe of the foot as before directed.

Quarter Cracks.—Quarter cracks are longitudinal fissures in the hoof, occurring near the heels. They are generally occasioned by improper shoeing, or neglect of the foot; or by allowing the horse to stand on hard floors for a length of time, or in the overgrowth of the crust; or when the frog, sole and bars have been pared away, and the heels weakened; also by burning the foot in shoeing, or springing the shoe off at the heel.

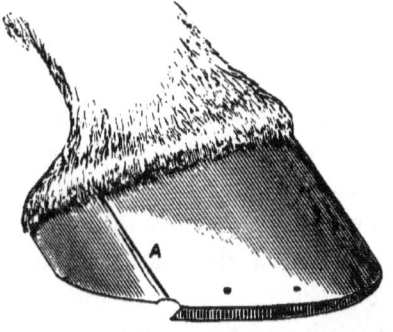

FIG. 58. A SIDE VIEW OF THE FOOT, WITH CRACK OPPOSITE THE WINGS OF THE COFFIN-BONE (A), PROPERLY DRESSED AND THE SHOE ADJUSTED, THE TOE BEING ROLLED OR BEVELED, AND THE HEEL PROPERLY CUT FOR THE BEARINGS AT THE QUARTER.

Fig. 59. A HOOF PROPERLY SHOD FOR THE CURE OF A QUARTER CRACK, THE SHOE BEING WELL BEVELED AT THE TOE, AND CUT OFF IN THE BRANCH, FORWARD OF THE SEAT OF LAMENESS AT **A**.

and throwing the weight of the horse upon the wings of the coffin-bone —the hoof becoming dry and brittle—are some of the causes which produce a disposition in the hoof to contract, which, occurring at a time when it is dry and inflexible, results in its lesion or splitting. In speedy horses, where the heels are allowed to grow too high, the crust loosing its elastic toughness, and becoming hard and thickened, there is liability, by the repeated jar of alighting on his heels in violent action, to burst in the quarters—the break occurring where the stress falls heaviest, back of the heel, or at either or on both sides.

In paring a foot of this kind, reduce the wall (especially at the heels), as much as the safety of the foot will permit. The next object is to remove the contractile disposition in the hoof, by rasping it at the quarters until an appearance of serum, after which open both sides of the crack with a drawing knife, so that friction of the fractured parts may be avoided. Then rasp or cut out the bottom of the crack so that no part of it may bear upon the shoe. After the wall has been lowered, should the frog project below the bottom of the foot, pare it flat. By so doing, the frog will be aided in growing wider, and assist the foot in expanding. When the cracks occur well back at the heels, I sometimes find it necessary to protect the weak parts from the violence of concussion by applying a bar shoe. Commence thinning the shoe at the center of the quarters, and carrying it off both toward the heels and toe, having the shoe light and the bar good and wide, to obtain strong frog pressure. When the cracks occur opposite the wings of the coffin-bone, level the foot and shorten the toe as much as can be conveniently done. If the crack occurs on one side only, use the shoe shown by Figs. 58 and 59, allowing for strong frog pressure. If cracks happen on both sides, shoe with a three-quarter tip. File or rasp the wall on both sides of the crack, from coronet to the ground surface, as thin as safety will permit. If toe and heel calkins are required, apply a four-calkin shoe, well rolled on the ground surface. If the foot be sore and tender, my foot salve may be used with advantage, by warming and saturating with it a pledget of cotton, and applying it to the affected parts, securing same with a bandage. A new growth of horn may also be stimulated by keeping the hoof moist with cold-water bandages around the coronet. Remove the shoes every three weeks, in order to prevent an excessive growth of horn. By following these instructions, this form of disease may be easily cured and the horse regularly worked.

Corns.—There are several forms in which these troublesome growths manifest themselves, though their cause and location are generally the same.

The seat of corns is always in the sole of the foot, or its lower connection with the wall and generally in the posterior portion of the hoof, at or in the angle made by the wall in its return to form the bars.

Fig. 60, on the following page, shows, however, that corns do not always come in the heels. The letters, A, A, show three hard, callous corns bulging up in the inner sole, at point of frog, producing tenderness and lameness around the toe.

The primary cause of all corns in the horse's foot is an uneven ground surface, resulting either from the improper level-

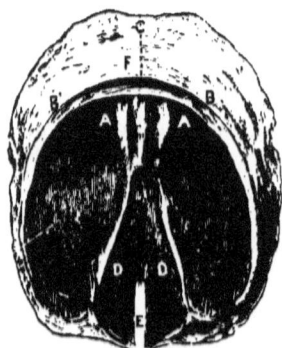

Fig. 60. INSIDE VIEW OF HOOF, SHOWING EFFECTS OF DROPPED SOLE AND HARD CORNS.

A, A, Seat of hard callous corn. B, B, Coronary band. C, Dotted line from coronet to ground surface at toe, showing shallow wall due to wasting away of toe from hot fitting and clipping. D, D, Internal fissures. E, Ridge of internal spur. F, Front face of wall.

ing of the foot by the farrier or its previous neglect. Let the foot always be pared level, and the shoe properly adjusted to the wall, and corns will find no abiding place in feet possessed of these conditions.

To determine where the seat of lameness is, take my foot testers (Fig. 195), and clasp around the union of sole and wall. If the horse does not flinch or yield, grasp the foot at point of frog. If he yields to the pressure, thin the sole at that point. On close examination you will find a hard, callous substance, somewhat resembling the hard corn on the human foot. Pare the sole at this point quite thin, so as to allow it to spring when the horse is bearing his weight on the foot; this will give relief at once. Apply shoe, Fig. 35, to the foot, and punch nail holes in shoe to meet the conditions of the foot. It may be advisable to poultice the bottom until soreness is removed.

Hard corns are protuberances growing upon the inner sole, at its junction with the horny laminæ, and lie beneath, as well as at the side and rear of the foot bone. They consist of a hardened excrescence of the skin, which crowds in upon the sensitive surfaces, and thus become the source of much trouble and pain. The corn may be generated by severe contusions upon the inner sole, but it generally arises from a lateral compression of the horny hoof inward upon the sensitive parts.

The vertical pressure of the horse's weight upon the foot bone is oftentimes so severe, and its winged extremities are pressed down upon the underlying tissues of the sensitive sole so suddenly and forcibly as to bruise them against the horny sole or shoe without. The bruise thus established develops the wet or sappy corn, which consists of an effusion of blood or serum into the pores of the horn, marking its location by leaving a stain upon the outer sole. When the stain appears dark, and is easily removed by paring away, the corn is old and working out, but when the stain appears bright and ruddy, by penetrating further into the horn, the corn is new and needs attention. These corns may be aggravated by additional injury, and terminate in a more serious form, known as the suppurative, in which case the sensitiveness will be greatly increased, causing intense pain, and, as a necessary consequence, acute lameness, or finally resulting in laying the foundation for a quittor.

In preparing the foot for the shoe, if the horn should exhibit signs of moisture or discoloration, caused by the exudation of a sappy or wet corn, open the center of the part indicated, and gradually remove the sole, until the foreign matter is released. The foot must next be dressed down until it acquires a perfectly level basis. For draft horses, let the toe be shortened and the heels lowered; apply a shoe with toe and heel calkins, the toe calkin to be set well back from the front of the shoe, as seen in Fig. 35, and relieve the pressure at the heels. For horses of general business and road purposes, pare the foot as low down as safety will admit, shorten the toe, and cut the shoe off on the side in front of the corn, as seen in Figs. 58 and 59; but if the corn be established on both sides, shoe with a three-quarter tip, in order that the shoe may not come as far back as the affected parts. In some cases it may be advisable to use a four-calkin or bar shoe, as determined by the judgment of the farrier.

Navicular Disease.—The navicular bone, from its position in the center of the foot, and the important protection which it receives from the surrounding surfaces, is seldom visited by disease or disturbed by accident. It is protected at either end by

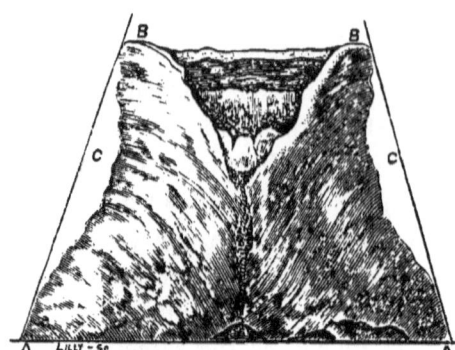

Fig. 61. HOOF, SHOWING THE EXTERNAL CHARACTER OF NAVICULAR DISEASE.

A, A, Base or ground line over the center of the quarters. B, B, Upper edge of the coronet. C, C, Falling in of the hoof opposite the seat of disease. The white line across the hoof indicates the superfluous growth of the hoof, and the extent to which it should be reduced.

the wall and wings and cartilages of the coffin-bone and on its upper face by the lower pastern bone, and beneath, where lies the greatest possibility of accident, it is guarded by the flexor perforans, the plantar cushion and horny frog. (See Fig. 5, and read the anatomy of the parts mentioned.)

In this disease the flexor perforans becomes ulcerated where it slides over the under face of the navicular bone (at times involving the sesamoid sheath in the process), and the severe pain experienced is from its play over the rough, diseased portion of that bone. This disease is sometimes inherited, but once contracted, is incurable; a great deal may be done, however, to ease the animal. Two-thirds of the cases of this malady, I believe, are caused by improperly dressing the foot, cutting the frog away, weakened the bars, and thinning the sole; and then driving over uneven roads, provoking inflammation in the tissues and membranes of the foot, which finally communicates itself to the bones and their attachments with one another.

Fig. 62. DISEASED NAVICULAR BONE, TAKEN FROM THE HOOF (FIG. 61), ONE-HALF SIZE.

A, Diseased portion of bone.

The above (Fig. 61) represents the back view of a hoof showing the effects of navicular disease by the shrinkage of the outer wall upon the living parts of the foot, immediately below

LAMENESS AND DISEASES, ETC.

the coronary band, crowding the cartilages in and stopping in a measure the circulation. The foot become dry, hard and feverish and the wall thick and deep. The white line across the heel shows where the foot should be reduced around the base. When the disease becomes well established, the horse manifests it by continual restlessness, standing on one foot and holding the other backward, with heel elevated and toe touching the ground, or by twisting the toe out and resting the heels of one on the coronet of the other; and by constantly shifting and flexing the fetlock and knee.

Not one-third of the cases of navicular disease which have come under my observation are chronic; and, indeed, many cases which are thus wrongly termed should be considered only navicular joint lameness, which if allowed to run might become chronic, but are curable if taken in time.

In dressing the foot for the shoe, proceed as per Fig. 23, then, after properly leveling and balancing it, open up the commissures and pare out the sole within safe limits. If the frog projects above the heel, pare it flat on the ground tread. In most instances the bar shoe shown in Fig. 63 can be used with satisfactory results. It can be easily made, being of the same thickness in both branches from the heel to the center of the quarters; in front of the quarters it is gradually thinned, and at the toe it is rolled or beveled, as indicated at B.

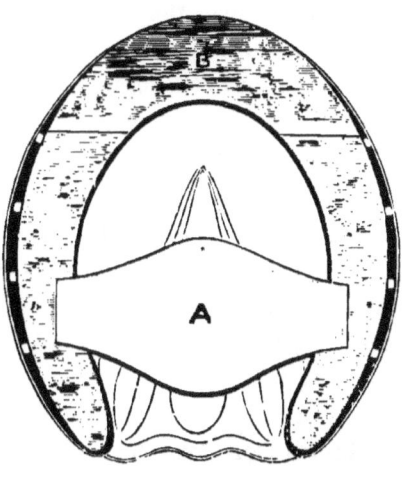

FIG. 63. BAR SHOE FOR NAVICULAR DISEASE.

A, Plate welded on the shoe over the seat of navicular disease. B, Roll or bevel at the toe.

After the shoe is prepared for the foot, a thin plate of steel must be welded on level with the face of the shoe, as represented at A. The plate being placed directly over the seat of the disease, will protect the affected parts from any evil results of severe concussion. The bar thus placed must not bear upon the frog, as frog pressure would have a tendency to aggravate the disease. An open space of considerable depth must be suffered to exist between the plate and the foot, sufficient to permit the removal of dirt, etc., which may secrete itself.

Rivet a firm piece of leather under the heels of the shoe to cover the bottom of the foot, which fill with my foot salve as prescribed. Have heel calks welded on both side branches of the shoe, to be about 1½ inches long, tapering the shoe gradually from heel to toe and of good height at heel point, say ½ inch.

Elevating the heels will lessen the friction on the flexor tendon in its play over the diseased bone, and the action of the foot joint will be firmer. After nailing on the shoe stand the horse in soaking tubs of warm water, two hours a day for a week or ten days, together with warm water bandages around the coronet. By having the shoe rolled on the ground surface in front of the quarters to the toe, the horse will get over the toe with the least possible strain on the affected parts. The shoe should extend as well back at the heel as can be safely worn, and by this manner of shoeing much relief will be afforded. Reset the shoes every two or three weeks to keep down the surplus growth on ground tread.

Raised Coronet.—This disease implies a violent alteration of the coronary band at the heel; consequent upon either side of the heel being uneven on the ground surface. This position of the hoof is fully shown in Fig. 64, on the opposite page.

This complaint arises from mismanagement of the foot, and its continuance is owing to bad shoeing. In slight cases, when a horse is let run at grass without shoes, it will generally be found sufficient to effect a cure. In obstinate cases, however, or when the horse travels or works regularly, recourse must be had to a careful plan for dressing the foot and shoeing it.

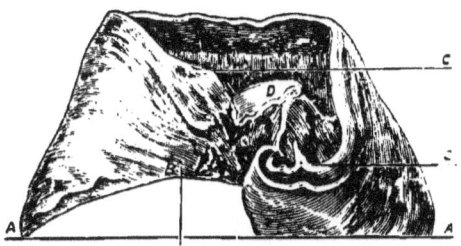

FIG. 64. BACK GROUND SURFACE VIEW OF RAISED CORONET.
(In dressing foot, see Diagram No. 41, p. 145.)

A, A, Line of ground surface. B, Base of raised heel. C, C, Difference in height of the sides of the heel indicated at the coronet. D, Inner spur twisted and deformed.

In such cases, in order to restore the foot to its natural healthy state, the mode of obtaining levels I have pointed out must be attended to, see Fig. 23. The higher part of the heel is then to be reduced, but the strength of the foot on this side must otherwise be carefully preserved, that it may be sufficiently firm to make up as much as possible for the deficiency of the full heel. On the other hand the raised or twisted side must be weakened as much as can be conveniently done, so that it will readily yield to the pressure of the animal's weight; the sole and bars being carefully thinned, gradually lessening the paring as the toe is approached. The shoe which is applied should be cut off on the side where the crust turns up, that that part may not be exposed to any pressure from it.

If the shoe is applied in the manner indicated, the nails being placed in the quarter of the high side, and stopped at the toe of the raised side, the crust on that side, it is observed, will be kept at a considerable distance from the ground.

The flexibility which the horn possesses, therefore, allowing it to yield in a small degree whenever the horse's weight is thrown upon it, gradually restores the foot to its natural condition without the liability of further pain. Whenever the hoof appears to be too dry and hard, or to have lost its pliancy, it may be kept moist by applying several folds of flannel round the coronet constantly wetted with warm water, also by having the horse stand in warm soaking tubs for two or three hours a day.

While Fig. 65 is introduced in order to illustrate the extent to which disease may effect a foot through any mismanagement, it is not proposed to suggest any cure for such an affection; but rather to state that, by careful attention to the preparation and shoeing of a foot, such diseases may be avoided. It is the moral of the old but true adage, that "an ounce of prevention is worth a pound of cure."

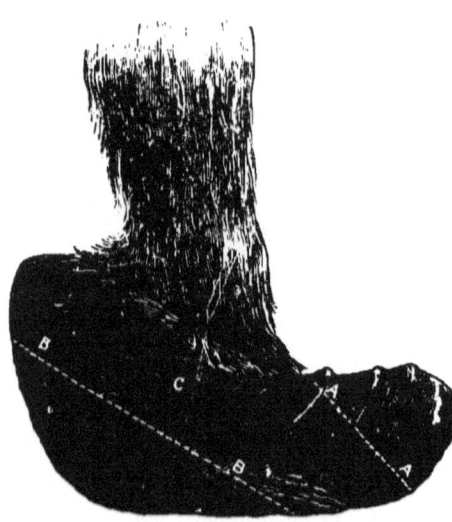

FIG. 65. EXTERNAL APPEARANCE OF HOOF DEFORMED BY PEDITIS, AND OVERGROWN BY NEGLECT.

A, A, Dotted line, to which surplus growth at toe should be removed. B, B, Dotted line, to which surplus growth at heel should be removed. C, Wall of foot.

Fig. 66, on the opposite page, is a section of the preceding figure, through axis of leg from front to rear. The unnatural position of the foot is noticeable; the surplus growth at the heel has raised it out of position, and the decayed coffin-bone is evidently due to peditic degeneration. This is regarded as the very best illustration of this disease in print, and speaks for itself.

Dished-wheel Foot.—Fig. 67, page 172. To shoe a foot of this kind file or rasp the surplus growth on the dished side from B to C, C, and the surplus growth at base from D to D. Open up the curled heel overlapping the cleft of the frog from E to E, as deeply as the horn extends. In fitting the shoe, the weight must be equalized through the axis of the leg and foot when placed on the ground, as shown in Fig. 26.

If toe and heel calkins are required, use shoe, Fig. 73, letting the toe calkin extend over the curled line. The shoe must gradually widen from quarters to heel so as to cover the heel up close to side of frog. Place side heel calkin on as shown in diagram; the projecting toe calk and side heel calkin will serve to widen the ground tread on the dished side.

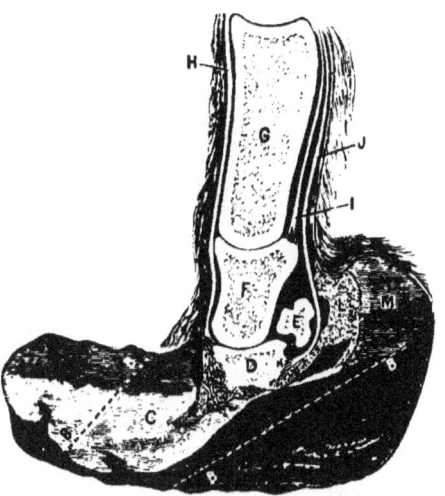

FIG. 66. MEDIAN SECTION OF SAME FOOT AS FIG. 65, SHOWING THE DESTRUCTIVE EFFECTS OF PEDITIS IN THE DISORGANIZATION OF THE LIVING STRUCTURES.

B, B, and B, B, Dotted lines to which surplus growth at toe and heel should be removed. C, Remains of imperfect horn. D, Fragment of dead coffin-bone. E, Navicular bone. F, Lower pastern. G, Upper pastern. H, I, J, Withered tendons. K, Slight insertion of flexor perforans. L, Plantar cushion. M, Bulb of horny frog. N, Base of hoof on opposite side.

The shoe must be beveled from the foot surface on the angle of the foot so as to assist in gaining ground tread. Forge a clip on the quarter of shoe on curled side; the clip will hold the shoe firmly to the side of the foot, and as the foot grows, the shoe will carry the foot to the curled side.

If flat shoes are required, use non-paddling shoe, Fig. 124. The shoe upon curled side should have the nail holes punched outwardly, so as to take a short, thick hold, to avoid cramping the foot. Have the shoes reset every two or three weeks. If

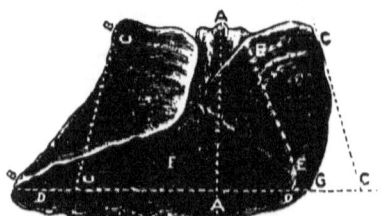

FIG. 67. BACK VIEW OF DISTORTED DISHED QUARTER AND CURLED HEEL.

A, A, Center line through frog. **B, B,** Angle of dished quarter, as the foot stands, 55 degrees. **C to C,** Line denoting portion of dished quarter to be filed or rasped off on one side, and the extension of shoe on the other side to give proper width of ground tread, and make angles on both sides the same—75 degrees. **D, D,** Ground line to which base of hoof is to be reduced. **E, E,** Curled heel overlapping center of cleft of frog, also showing where heel is to be opened with the farrier's knife as deeply as the curled horn extends. **F,** Horny sole deeply concaved. **G, C,** Shows distance inner quarter is curled under center of foot on ground-bearing surface.

the above instructions are carried out, the foot will become straight and natural.

The dished foot shown on page 173 is a result of overgrowth of the hoof. The toe is lengthened and the heel raised in such a way as to throw the foot out of its natural angle. This produces an unnatural pressure at the toe, on the ground surface, and at the coronet, thus preventing the action of the secretive powers; more or less inflammation sets in and as the internal part wastes away the outer wall conforms to the inside. It has been observed that if the foot be allowed to remain in this condition for any length of time, the upper pastern becomes enlarged, which to me is conclusive proof that it has been overtaxed.

Horses accustomed to slow work do not suffer from this as much as road and track horses. When the heel and toe are allowed to grow to an unusual height and length, the angle of the heel with the ground line is carried forward under the leg, thus causing the weight to be thrown out of the axis of the leg and foot; and when the horse is at full speed, the height of his heels prevents the natural expansion of the foot, from heel to quarters, at each foot fall, and he lands his foot upon the ground with a dead jar, like that experienced by a man walking on a wooden leg. This jar will not be transmitted through the axis of the leg, pasterns and foot bone, as would be the case if the foot were on its proper angle, but up into the back tendons, thus causing their overtaxation.

If the hoof is pared in accordance with the indications given (see Fig. 68), it will stand upon its proper angle. All dished feet are thin at the point of the frog, where great care must be taken in dressing the foot to leave sufficient sole, and in shoeing observe the necessity of keeping pressure off from front part of foot.

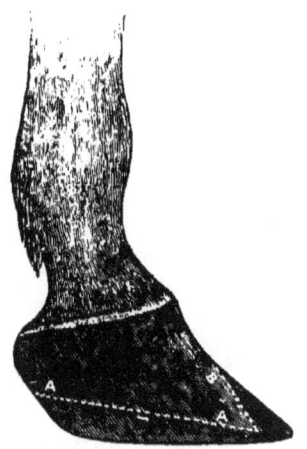

FIG. 68. VIEW OF DISHED FRONT FOOT.

A, A, Dotted line to which surplus growth of wall should be removed. B, Dotted line to which surplus growth of wall at toe should be removed.

Wheeled Foot.—Fig. 69, on the following page, is what is termed a wheeled hind foot, having low heels and high, deep toe, the reverse of the defect in Fig. 68. The unnatural growth is due to mismanagement of the foot. The weight which should pass through the axis of the leg drops back of the heel, bearing upon the back tendons and greatly overtaxing them.

When the foot, in this case, is lifted over the toe, the weight, which bears upon the arch of the coffin-bone, raises the point of it by the overgrowth of the toe, and draws the coffin-bone back from the front part of the foot, thus allowing the front wall to thicken up as seen in the figure.

Common sense declares against permitting a foot to remain in this condition, when it can be placed upon its natural base.

A reference to Fig. 69 shows where the foot ought to be pared in order to bring the toe to the ground, and allow the foot to fall more directly under the leg. This will relieve the

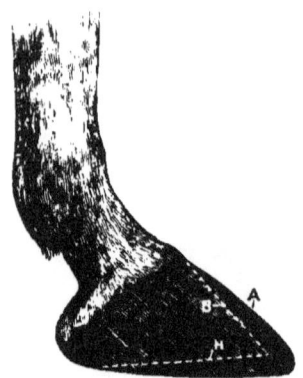

Fig. 69. WHEELED HIND FOOT, SHOWING LONG TOE AND LOW HEEL.

B, H, Lines to which surplus growth should be removed at front of foot and from toe to heel.
A, Unnatural thickness of wall in front.

back tendon from overtaxation and assist nature in bringing the foot upon its natural angles. Pare the base of the hoof as shown to dotted line, H. File or rasp the front wall to dotted line, B. After the foot is dressed, apply shoe (Fig. 115) with heels extended well back of foot, and their height varying with the emergencies. If the shoe is properly adjusted, the best results may be expected.

Defective Ankle Joints or Knuckling.—The catalogue of diseases, defects and deformities in the feet of horses has by this time, the reader will perceive, grown to a considerable length. In tracing them to their small beginnings, we find a striking instance of the serious results springing from the "unconsidered trifles" of shoeing. The weakness peculiar to some horses in their hind ankle joints, next suggests itself. This troublesome affection, in many cases, arises from the overtaxation of the fetlock during colthood, and, again, from hoofs or shoes having high toes and heels, or from hereditary influences. This defect is found to be more prevalent among speedy horses having long pasterns than those of any other kind. Short upright pasterns in conjunction with high heels and short toes; also improper shoeing—allowing the toes to grow too long and low heels—will render speed horses

Fig. 70. DEFECTIVE ANKLE JOINT.

A, A, Line to which base of hoof should be reduced.

LAMENESS AND DISEASES, ETC. 175

liable to this troublesome ailment. Hard pulling will also develop it and no horses are exempt from it where they are in a position to overtax the muscles and ligaments of the pastern and fetlock joints. Certain conformations of the foot or ankle region, together with improper modes of shoeing, as indicated, are always classed with the predisposing causes of this defection. The weakness is generally manifested when the horse is traveling at a slow gait and renders him less sure footed, though not always attended by lameness. When driven on the level the upper pastern occasionally bulges forward, and going down hill the horse knuckles at every step, but the driver will observe that when going up hill the horse never knuckles. I call particular attention to these points, as the style of shoe proposed for the relief of knuckling is on the order of up-hill movement.

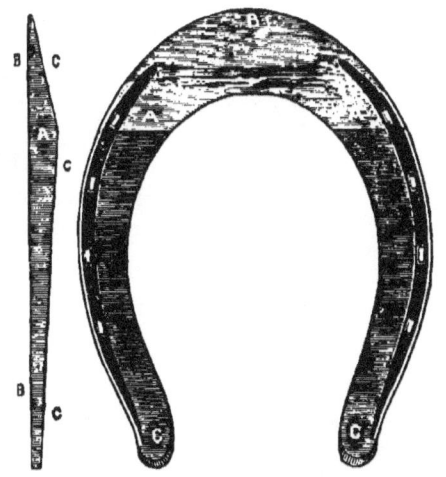

FIG. 71. HIND FOOT SHOE TO PREVENT AND CURE KNUCKLING.

The straight bar indicates the shape of shoe seen from the side. **A**, Point from which shoe should be tapered to toe and heel. **B, B**, Sole-bearing line. **C, C, C**, Ground line.

It will most generally be found that unevenly-grown and unbalanced feet are present in conditions where knuckling exists, and in preparing the foot for the reception of the shoe, the surplus growth should be removed as shown in Fig. 70, and the foot leveled and balanced as per Fig. 23. In this way the toe will be foreshortened, the heels lowered, the ground tread lengthened, strong frog pressure obtained, and the fetlock or weak joints thus be made to rest more easily in a normal position. Fig. 71 is the shoe recommended for the cure of this disease, and may be easily made. A, A, on face indicates a point from the toe about one-third of its length (or two-thirds from the heels), from which the ground surface of the shoe is to be drawn forward to toe at B, and back to heels at C, C, leaving the high point at A, as shown in side bar—usually three-eighths of an inch, to vary with the extent of knuckling. The shoe should be made of steel, quite thin and light, that the horse may have his foot as near the ground as possible, as well as to receive the benefit of strong frog pressure. The effect of a shoe with such a ground-bearing surface will be to place the horse upon an incline, as though ascending a hill, and, when in a standing position, the upper pastern will keep its place in its articulation with the fetlock joint, and when in motion, the foot will be able to slide over without straining the parts affected.

FIG. 72. POSITION OF THE LEG WHEN KNEE SPRUNG.

A, A, Angle of this foot 45 degrees. B, B, Line to which hoof should be reduced to its normal basis.

Knee Sprung.—Many indefinite causes have been assigned by various writers as the originating source of the condition known as "knee sprung;" but, it generally appears as if the ligaments and bandages of the knee had become strained and enlarged, in which also the front and back sinews may become involved by overexertion of those parts, when the bones of the knee-joint being no longer properly retained in their places, become bulged or sprung forward. (Compare Fig. 72 with perfect knee of skeleton, Fig. 2.)

In many cases the formation of the animal, such as undue length of limb from the knee to fetlock, is a natural predisposition to weakness at knee; also, abnormal presentation at time of foaling where knees are doubled under the body, may produce a similar tendency.

Young horses subjected to an excess of hard pulling before they are seasoned or matured, are most liable to injure their knees in this manner. Care should therefore be taken in working them that their limbs are not overtasked while under the age of seven years.

Horses employed in constant "up-hill" work, where the stress upon the knee is continued and severe, or in suffering them to stand in stalls where the slope is considerable and the floor hard, necessitating exertion in the muscles of the leg, and keeping the ligaments constantly in a tense state, will expose them to a deformity in their knees, by their leaning or bowing out in consequence of the ligaments and tendons becoming weakened. When the proper angle of the foot is destroyed, as is most usually produced by improper shoeing, such as having high toes and low heels, causing the lower pastern to bear down upon the navicular bone, which in turn presses back against the flexor perforans, will produce an over distension of the muscles; and similarly, sore or bruised heels will cause a constant leaning forward on the knees to relieve the pressure on other parts, and thus produce this defect; or, should the foot even be properly pared, and the shoe then applied be thick at the toe—the heels of the hoof being low—the effect of always ascending would be the same, and result in the malformation of which we treat; or, if the shoe is too short—indeed, any mode of shoeing that will unbalance the foot, may cause the knees to spring forward.

When the disease becomes chronic, and the ligaments and tendons so much relaxed as to be no longer able to respond to the treatment, a radical cure may be impossible; but, if taken in time, and the foot properly dressed and shod, the disease can be cured.

In dressing the foot for this disease, pare it level and lower it to its proper angle, bearing in mind the directions given in Chapter IV.

The style of shoe which I have found to be best adapted for the relief of sore tendons and knee spring, are the scoop-toe rolling motion, Fig. 126, rolling-motion shoe, Fig. 125, and four-calkin shoe, Fig. 101; having the shoe adapted to extend as far back at the heels as the safety of the foot may seem to require. This extension and elevation of the heels usually affords speedy relief. Either of these patterns, by shortening the ground surface at the toe and strengthening the knee when the horse is moving forward, will relieve the strain and enable him the better to pass his feet over uneven ground surface, which is sometimes the cause of twisting and straining the already injured parts. Another means of furthering a cure is to feed the horse from the ground. This will have the effect of throwing the animal's weight more directly over his limbs, and thus assist nature, in a manner, to retrench the enlargement in the knee bandages.

Curb.—This consists of an inflammation and swelling of the posterior portion of the tendon passing over the calcis, or hock bone (p. 36, Fig. 2–39). This is often accompanied with considerable heat, pain and lameness. The cause is an accident to ligaments at and around the hock, and is the result of hard pulling, prancing or leaping, or galloping over uneven ground surfaces, etc. The peculiar conformation of some horses renders them more likely to be attended by curbs than others; but as it is always the result of over-taxation, and does not admit of much labor in the affected part, it should be remedied as soon as possible. Fig. 73 shows an extreme case of curb, such as may come from the hind feet and legs standing too far under

LAMENESS AND DISEASES, ETC.   179

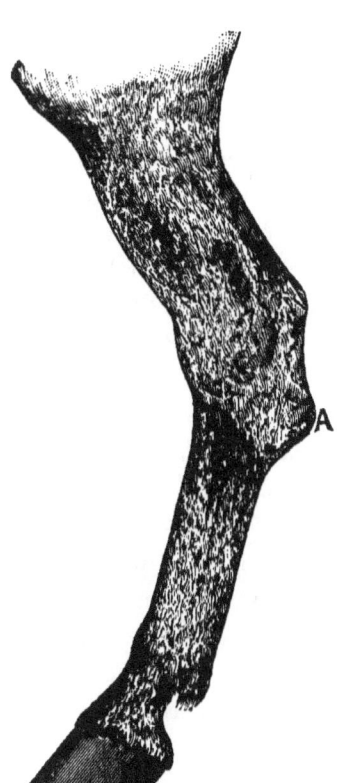 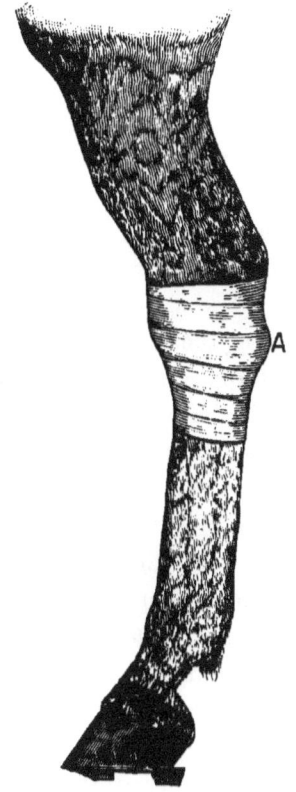

FIG. 73. HIND LEG, SHOWING CURB.   FIG. 74. LEG WITH CURB BANDAGES AND FOOT SHOD.

the body (see p. 200, Fig. 94), the result of a bent or cycle hind leg formation. In these cases use four calkin shoe (p. 213, Fig. 101). The heel calkins should stand higer than the toe calkins, thus placing the foot further back, and the changed position, together with the elevated heel, will support the leg and relieve the strain upon the affected weak joint. Bathe the curb frequently in warm water, almost hot, and bandage in four or five thicknesses (Fig. 74). After the inflammation has subsided, apply liniment described in Recipe 3, page 294, for a week or more. If any callous remains, paint the surface with iodine until it disappears.

Bone Spavin.—This disease takes its name from an enlargement of the inner side of the hock, creating a bony excrescence about the hock joint and resulting oftentimes in lameness. It can not be treated with uniform success, for it often proves very obstinate and not infrequently incurable.

I would invariably recommend that the affected horse, after being shod, be placed under a most skillful and experienced veterinary surgeon. In many instances, special shoeing alone will relieve the trouble. The shoe I have found to be the most satisfactory and disposed to give ease and comfort is the four-calked hind-foot shoe (p. 249, Fig. 145). It is obvious there can not be two cases of spavin similar. A four-calked hind-foot shoe, therefore, designed for any one case, will not be effective in another. Every case must have its own diagnosis, and thereupon the paring of the foot and the making and setting of the shoe must be determined, bearing in mind always the balancing of the foot. But, as I say above, the shoe most satisfactory all around, to give ease and comfort, is the four-calked hind-foot shoe, as above described, with the toe and heel calkins placed to suit the case in hand. I very often have found it advisable to place the inside toe calkin back from the center of toe of shoe fully three-quarters to an inch farther than the outside toe calkin, making the inside toe calkin one-quarter of an inch lower and the outside toe calkin one-quarter of an inch higher. Bevel the front toe calkins as shown in diagram above mentioned, so as to allow the toe to roll over more easily in the forward movement. Having the outside heel and toe calkins higher than the inside heel and toe calkins will cause the weight to fall upon the outside of the hock joint, and in many cases the result will be surprising.

Bog Spavin.—Is a dropsical condition of the joint, which becomes so either from a loss of power in the absorbent vessels, or an increased action of the sacs which secrete the joint oil. Perhaps both these causes may concur in producing the disease, the more remote cause of which is hard work—that is, too great or too long continued action of the joint.

The bog spavin does not so often occasion lameness as the other, except when a horse is worked hard, which generally causes a temporary lameness, removable by rest; but it does not always admit of a radical cure, for though blistering is of likely service, the trouble generally returns with any considerable exertion. Much may be done, however, to assist the horse in his movements, by properly balancing the foot and suitably adjusting the four-calked hind-foot shoe above described, shown in Fig. 145, page 249.

Canker.—This is a local disease most frequently arising from the thrush, and attacking the front feet. It consists at first of an ulcerous sore in cleft of frog, when the inflammation of the parts is severe and they are quite tender—often making the horse quite lame. The parts affected become very soft and rotten, with a discharge of purulent matter. By early attention and proper treatment the disease is easily cured, but if it continues its ravages it not infrequently destroys the horny frog and often extends to the sensitive sole and other parts of the foot. The simplest treatment I have found to be the quickest and the best: First, dress the foot, as per Fig. 23, then take three or four old rasps, sharpen one end of each and heat to a white heat, and while in that state apply to cankered part of frog, holding the iron at an angle of about 45 degrees, and giving it a quick downward stroke along the side of frog from upper edge down and forward, and continuing with the other heated irons until bottom of soreness is reached and burnt away.

Sometimes this disease attacks the inner and outer quarters, and I have operated on chronic cases where excrescences had been thrown up over the diseased parts like finger stumps, standing out from one-fourth to three-fourths inches, and by this burning process have permanently cured them. Give the horse a hot water foot bath for three hours after burning, and as the open state of cells of foot after these operations develops granulations very rapidly, this burning and soaking treatment must be kept up daily until entirely cured. This treatment is not as severe or painful as it appears, as the horse does not jerk away under it. Do not poultice the foot, but let it remain open, and keep the horse quiet in a dry stall.

Foot Rot, or Seedy Toe.—This insidious disease occurs sometimes in the toe, and at other times around the inner or outer quarters of the foot. It manifests itself by a wasting away or drying up of the sensitive laminæ, and in slight attacks may be easily cured, as the horse seemingly does not at once go lame, seemingly requiring some little time to develop into a condition of lameness. When it becomes aggravated, however, and involves toe and quarters, it is disabling, and requires careful treatment. I have treated some very stubborn cases, where a complete separation of wall and vascular parts had taken place, extending almost from ground surface to coronet, and where only one and a half to two inches of solid horn remained. In such cases I removed all the separated parts of the wall as far as the disease extended, fairly uncovering the coffin bone. I then made a wide webbed, deeply concave shoe to cover around toe and quarters; thence gradually narrowing it to the heels, with a good wide bar across to get strong frog pressure; three nail holes to be placed on each side at the heels. Next I pulled a clip on each side of the quarters and at front toe, making the clips very long, bent up at the same angle as the wall, fitting shoe snug all around, with a light leather riveted on to hold the packing of salve (see prescription No. 2), with which the bottom of foot should be filled. After the shoe is on, take enough of same salve warmed and build on outside of foot about to the thickness of natural hoof, covering the surface to at least one inch above coronet; then encase same within a leather strap or boot, fitting neatly around foot from shoe to one and a half inch above coronet, slip the leather down inside the clips running back under the bulge of the heels, buckle on the outside, then gently drive the clips in toward the foot to make secure hold against the leather; also have small screw holes drilled through the clips, about one half inch above shoe, and insert screws to assist in holding the leather firmly to bottom of foot. After dressing in this way have the foot soaked in warm water two hours a day; this, with the salve, will assist the formation of new horn and effect a permanent cure. Horses that I have treated in this way have not only grown new, strong hoofs, but were at the same time used daily at slow work.

In ordinary cases of seedy toe, level the foot, as per Fig. 23, then with a probe or sharp instrument remove all pithy, decayed substances as deep as such extend, being careful not to draw blood. Fit shoe snug to foot, draw up clips on shoe opposite the separated parts to secure a firm brace against the weakened wall when weight of horse is resting on it; have as many clips as may be necessary for this purpose. After shoe is fitted, remove the lower margin of hoof so that no pressure can come upon the separated parts, and have the nails located to go in the sound, healthy portions of the horn. Before attaching shoe use the salve treatment as directed for the more severe cases.

The subject of seedy toe would not be complete if the accompanying illustration should be omitted. It is an admir-

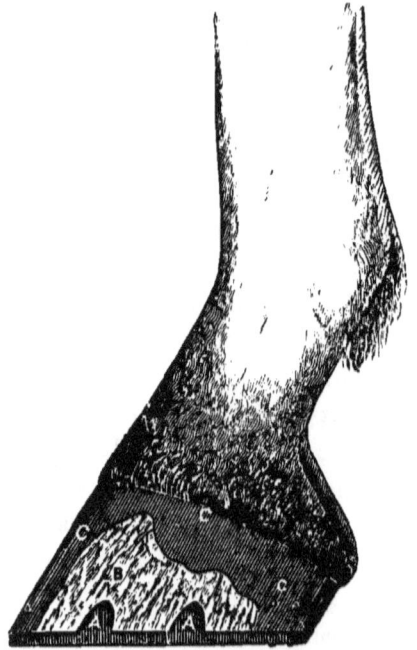

FIG. 75. HOOF, WITH SEEDY TOE—SHOD.
A, A, clips on shoe. B, diseased portion.
C, C, C, sound hoof.

able side view, showing a chronic case of foot rot, caused by the excessive wasting away of the sensitive laminæ on that side of the hoof, either by inflammation produced by a blow, or by undue dryness of the hoof. The disease of the sensitive laminæ extends as high as the sound hoof outlined by the letters C, C, C. B indicates the diseased portions contiguous to the coffin bone, and A, A, the necessary clips drawn upon the shoe, as specifically explained in the preceding paragraph.

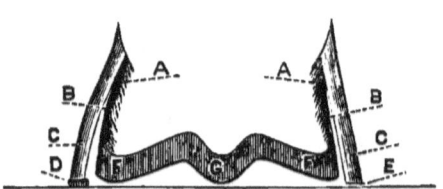

FIG. 76. SECTION OF HOOF AFFECTED WITH SEEDY TOE.

A, A, Insensitive laminæ. B, B, Outer wall. C, C, Wall separated from laminæ. D, Bulging or dishing effect of separation. E, Wall removed opposite separation. F, F, Insensitive sole. G, Frog.

Broken Bars.—This ailment is the result of an overgrowth of the sole and consequent dryness of the insensitive sole. The secretions become dry and hard, the bars unyielding and do not spring as the horse rests his weight upon the foot. This causes the bars to give way and break, making the horse very lame. If not properly treated, this disease often assumes a more serious form, difficult to cure, even in time; and if neglected its ravages will soon destroy the usefulness of the horse.

The process of treatment I use is to pare the foot, leaving a good, wide outer wall-bearing. Then commence at each side of the point of the frog and pare the commissures thin from point of frog back to the heels on the inner and outer sides of the foot; then remove all the bars and sole as deep as the soft tissues or broken bars, holding the knife at an angle of about 45 degrees, paring the sole and bars quite thin. The broken ends of the bars must be removed with the knife as deeply as they extend up into the foot. See that the foot is properly balanced, and then make and put on a suitable shoe for the work the horse has to perform. Place a piece of sole leather first under the shoe, covering the bottom of the foot. Rivet the sole leather at the heels of the shoe, trimming the leather to fit snugly to outside of shoe. Next hold up the foot, and fill the bottom with my foot salve (recipe No. 2). After the salve has become cool, lay a thin layer of white cotton over the bottom of the foot, covering the salve, and nail on the shoe. The salve will exclude the air from the affected parts, the leather will protect the bottom of the foot and hold the salve in its place. Finally stand the horse in the soaking tub for at least one or two hours in warm water. The effect of the soaking tub will be to open the pores of the wall, and assist nature in casting off the inflammation. If the foot should show signs of fever around the coronet band, keep the soaking swabs well wet with warm water, and see that they are well buckled around the lower pasterns. Keep the swabs on pastern and around the foot as long as there is fever around the coronet band. By following the above instructions I have never failed to make a permanent cure in feet affected with broken bars. This operation must be performed by a competent and skillful farrier.

Lameness and Diseases of the Foot.—One of the most common yet painful disorders of the foot is a separated wall at the coronet, which may result from any sharp instrument, such as a wire fence, the calkin of the opposite shoe, or a raised clinch of the nail. This may result in a fissure or crack in the wall, which will become permanent as the wall grows down, or it may cause a wide separation at the coronet.

Fig. 77.

The treatment should never involve the paring away the wall at the coronet, but on the contrary at the ground surface of the wall immediately below the injury, as shown in Fig. 77. Then place the shoe on the foot, having four or more nail holes immediately below the ground surface thus pared away, and draw them up gradually—first tapping one, then another—till the wall is drawn down to the shoe, and the pressure at the coronet is relieved. In order to do this effectively, the hoof should be softened by standing in warm water a sufficient length of time.

LAMENESS AND DISEASES, ETC.

If there is any foreign or detached substance in the wound it should be cleansed with warm water injected, or the wash numbered 4, on page 294.

When the wound has been thus thoroughly dressed, then apply the salve described in Recipe No. 2, on page 292. Use surgeon's cotton, saturated with the heated salve, large enough to cover the wound and the skin of the coronet above. Then retain the cotton dressing by applying a linen bandage. Then apply the iron heated, but not so hot as to burn the bandage, and close enough to open the pores. The inflammation will pass off through the pores, and the salve will stimulate a healthy growth.

In treating draft horses, have the toe well set back on the shoe, provided with a side heel calkin on the affected side. The dressing should be continued as prescribed for ten days, and the wound will slowly yet effectually heal.

There are many instances in which it is not advisable to weaken the foot by tub baths, especially where the inflammation is confined to the coronary band. An admirable substitute is found in the felt swab shown in Fig. 78, well saturated in warm water and buckled around the

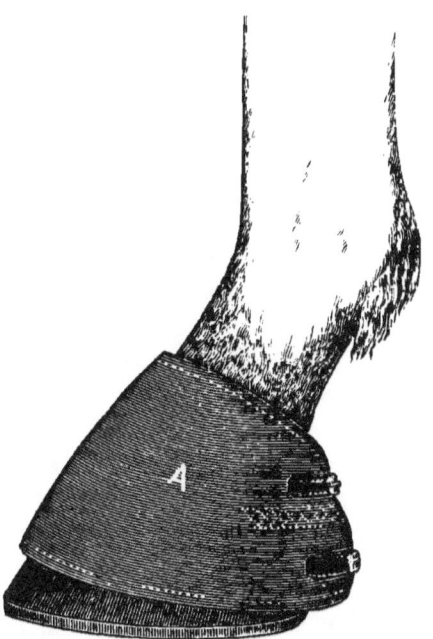

FIG. 78. HEALTHY FOOT COVERED BY FELT SWAB.

A, Swab buckled around pastern.

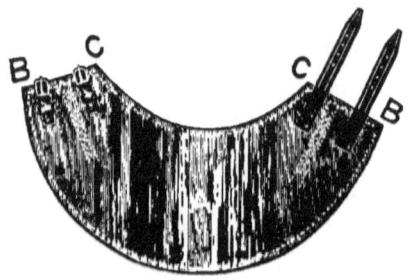

Fig. 70. FELT SWAB.
C, C, Inside of swab. B, B, Strap and buckle.

hoof, extending above the coronet. This is especially valuable in hot, dry weather, when the hoof loses the moisture from the ground and becomes brittle and hard. The swab can be made of thick felt, after the pattern shown in Fig. 79.

Abnormal Feet.—Before making an examination of faulty limbs, it is proper to present the subject of abnormal feet. The foot is in perfect poise when it is level and balanced, the heels being of the same height, so that the horse lands upon both alike, and springs from a level toe, after he has rolled over quarters of the same height. The heels must not be too high, nor the toe too long, nor the hoof out of proportion at the sides, taking the median line of the cleft of the frog as the basis of measurement.

Fig. 80 represents a perfect front foot. It is placed properly under the carcass. The vertical line, A, A, passes down through the axis of the cannon bone, and reaches the ground at the posterior angle of the wall and bar. The line B B intersects the line A A at the center of the ankle joint, and passes through the

Fig. 80. PERFECT FRONT FOOT.
A, A, Axial line of leg. B, B, Axial line through coffin bone.

axis of the coffin bone to the ground, which indicates the perfect poise of the coffin bone when the foot is at rest. This is the crucial test of a foot both level and balanced. If the coffin bone is out of position with reference to the median line, B, B, the entire foot and limb are out of balance. The journals of the joints at the ankle and knee do not articulate *in equilibrio*, and the tendons and ligaments are unduly taxed or relieved, dependent upon which side of the hoof bears an undue strain. The accompanying drawings will illustrate this point. Fig. 81 shows the proper position. Fig. 86, with the vertical dropping through the apex of hoof, is the reproduction of a perfect coffin bone, photographed from nature. The line of pressure was thrown back from its correct vertical position by an undue length and height of the wall at the toe (see Fig. 82). The reverse result is obtained by an excessive height of the heel, as shown in Fig. 85. In the one instance a preponderance of the weight is thrown upon the flexors, and in the other upon the extensors; and in both cases depriving the bone structure of the limb of its primary function of being the organic weight bearer.

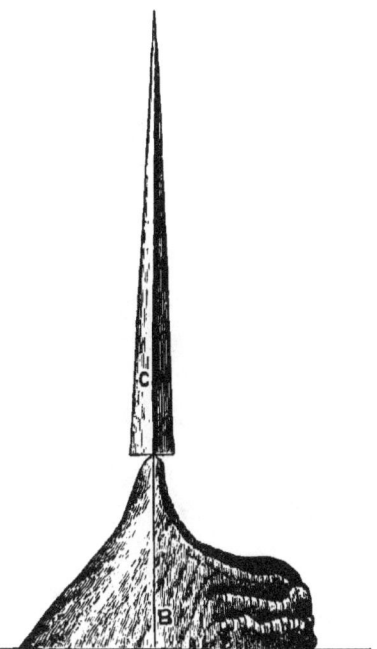

FIG. 81. COFFIN BONE.
Lateral view—correct position.

The practical result of thus placing the foot out of line with reference to the vertical position of the cannon bone, and

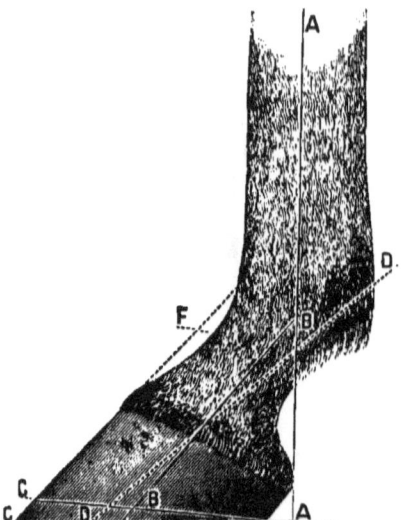

Fig. 82. HIGH TOE.
Defective results shown by lines **B, B,** and **D, D.**

the proper inclination of the pastern joint, is precisely the reverse of what is the general conclusion of the average horseman. For instance, an abnormal high toe invariably pitches the foot and limb forward, and an extra high heel (Fig. 85) has the opposite result. This is plainly shown in Fig. 84. By elevating the toe the vertical line that passes through the axis of the cannon bone reaches the ground at an appreciable distance back of the heel, thus showing the entire foot and limb are thrown forward out of their proper position. Moreover, the inclination of the pastern joint is enormously increased, as shown by the line D, D, whereas the proper inclination is shown by the line B, B. Now, if the toe is lowered the distance marked C, C, it is apparent that the vertical line A, A, will be thrown forward till it will pass through the axis of

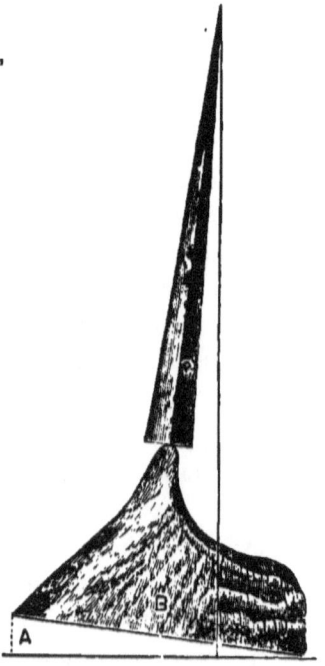

Fig. 83. COFFIN BONE, SAME DEFECT.

the ankle joint and touch the heel at the ground surface. The foot will then resume its normal position, by standing further back directly under the limb.

This investigation is so important in its practical results that the converse effect of excessive height of the heels is illustrated in this connection. Fig. 84 shows this defect in dressing the hoof for the shoe. The vertical line of pressure, A, A, is thrown forward beyond the axis of the

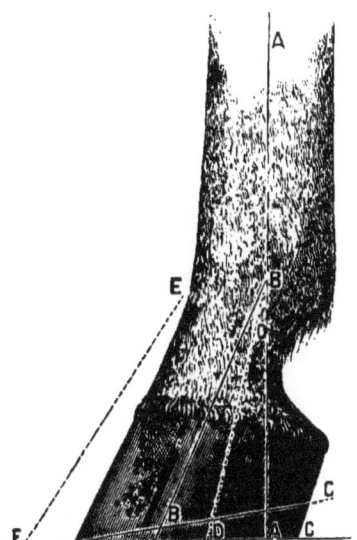

FIG. 84. SHOWS DEFECT CAUSED BY TOO HIGH HEELS.

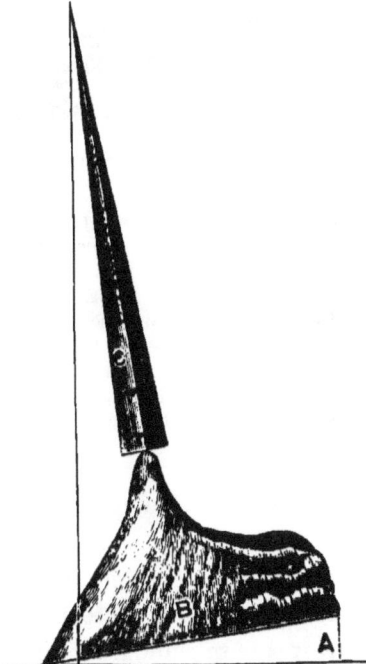

FIG. 85. COFFIN BONE, SAME DEFECT.

cannon bone, so that it reaches the ground far in advance of the angle of the heel. The inclination of the pastern is made more upright, as shown by the line D, D, instead of preserving its normal position as indicated by the line B, B. If the heels are lowered the distance indicated by the line C, C, the foot will be changed to the correct position indicated by E, E, and all the bones, joints,

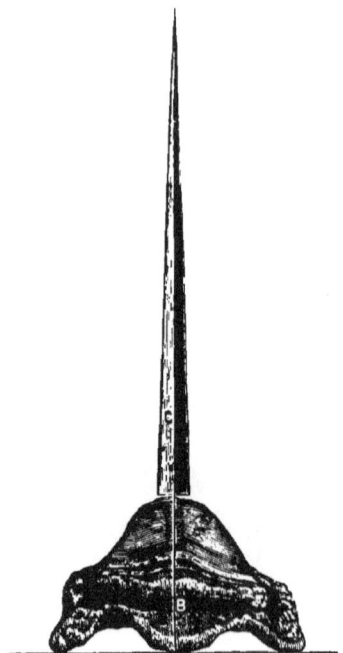
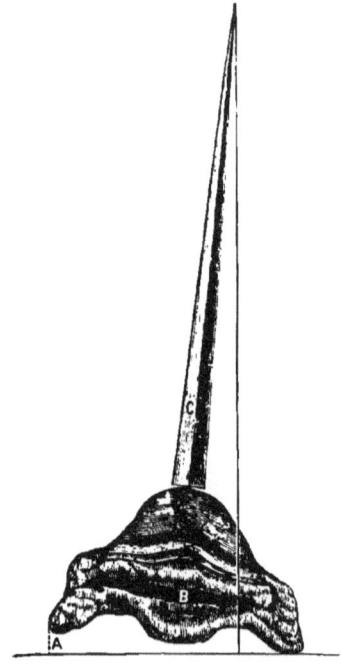

FIG. 86. COFFIN BONE—VERTICAL IN LINE.

FIG. 87. COFFIN BONE—VERTICAL OUT OF LINE.

Fig. 86 is a photograph of a perfect coffin bone, exactly level on sole bearing, with the flexor tendon cut off even with B, the navicular bone. In a well-balanced foot the vertical dropped from the center of the knee passes through the center of the apex of the coffin bone.

Fig. 87 is a photograph of a perfect coffin bone, showing the effects of an uneven height of quarters. Assuming width of hoof 4 inches on the bottom, distance from base to knee 20 inches, difference of height in quarters of ¼ inch would cause a displacement of 1¼ inches at the knee, thus unevenly distributing the weight and bearings.

tendons and ligaments will operate in structural harmony.

We are now prepared to advance to the consideration of the foot and leg in their proper positions as weight bearers.

Fig. 88 has been drawn with great care to show the perfect front limb and foot. It is correctly placed under the carcass, so

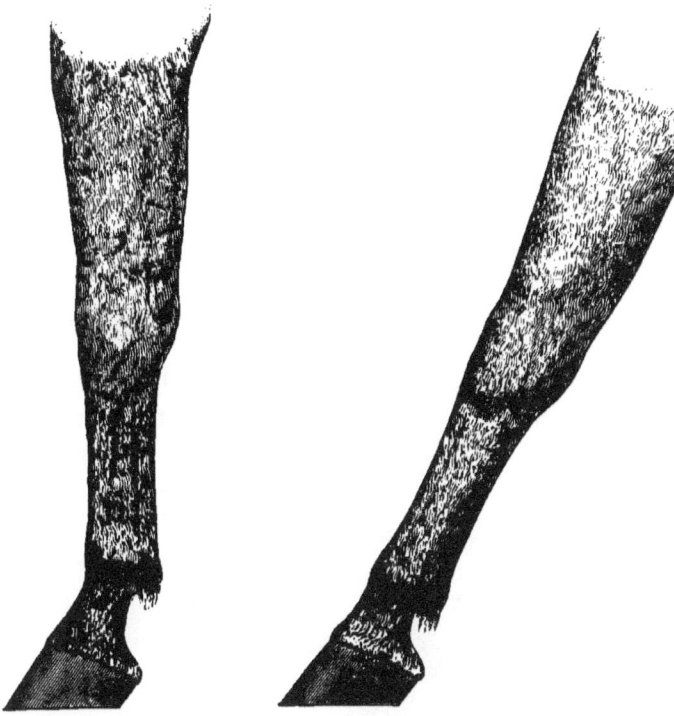

Fig. 88. PERFECT FRONT LIMB AND FOOT.   Fig. 89. FRONT LIMB AND FOOT POINTING FORWARD—HIGH TOE.

that the bone structure from the shoulder to the ground surface shall bear its exact proportion of the body, and enable all the complex actions of the joints, tendons and ligaments to operate with the greatest ease, precision and effect.

Fig. 89 shows the limb and foot pointing forward, by reason of the causes heretofore explained. The invariable result of this faulty position is soreness at the point of the frog. To relieve this painful ailment, the toe should be lowered and the wall relieved at the toe, so that no bearing will be placed upon the shoe, at least the thickness of a No. 5 horseshoe nail around the forward arch of the hoof, and the two toe nails be left out. This will give almost instant relief.

FIG. 90. FRONT LIMB AND FOOT, POINTING BACKWARD.

The opposite result, from an excessive height of heel, is exemplified in Fig. 90. The trouble, after a careful examination, will invariably be located in the heel and the flexor tendon. Gentle pressure or slight blows will indicate the sore spot. The hard, unyielding sole at the point of pain should be removed and the inflammation reduced by standing the foot and limb in a bath of tepid water. The hospital shoe to prevent lameness, if the horse is needed for immediate use, can be selected from several approved patterns. It may be necessary to cover the sole of the foot for the first shoeing with protecting leather. When this is done the best shoe to use is the bar, as shown on page 233. As a remedial shoe it can be improved by welding on oblong heel calkins, and a long toe calkin set back from the outer web of the shoe in front. If an open shoe is preferred, the four-calkin shoe illustrated on page 213 (Fig. 101) will answer the purpose. In case the lameness is severe, the leather covering may be supplied with a packing to keep the sole of the foot from becoming hard and dry. In that event, my experience has demonstrated the benefit of using fat pickled pork, just out of the brine, cut in long, thin slices and pressed well into the sore spot and into the commissures. The inflammation will be relieved if the foot, when thus packed, is placed in warm water for at least two hours, keeping up the temperature as hot as the hand can bear.

If speed is required while the horse is under treatment, the rolling motion shoe (Fig. 125), on page 235, may be used; or, if the action is already too high, the scoop-toe shoe (Fig. 121, page 232) can be substituted.

When the weight is thrown, by reason of a too high or long toe, unduly upon the flexor tendon, the result in violent action shows itself in either an inflamed flexor tendon or a complete let-down. In the latter case the usefulness of the horse is at an end, but in the former, remedial treatment, accompanied with absolute rest, insures a perfect cure. The tendon bows out as shown in Fig. 91. The foot should be dressed as shown in the illustration, and a prepared surgeon's bandage, wrung out in witch hazel, applied as therein shown, after the limb has been thoroughly bathed in the same preparation.

After the leg has thus been bandaged moderately tight, the foot should be shod with the four-calkin

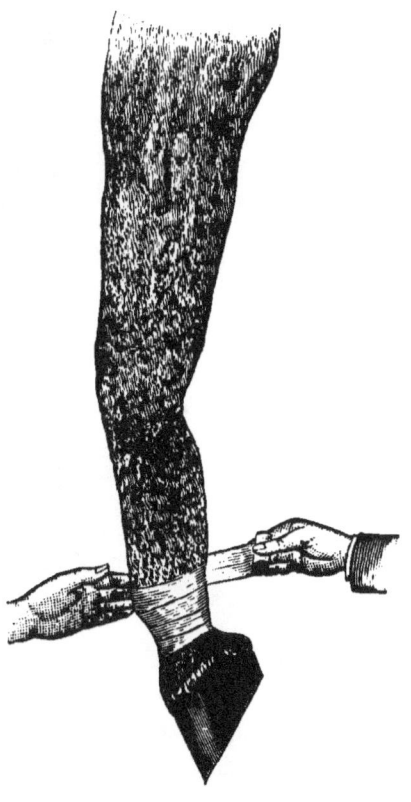

FIG. 91. FOOT PROPERLY PARED BEFORE BEING SHOD.

shoe as illustrated in Fig. 101, page 213. The heel calkins should be higher than the toe calkins. This will throw the weight forward upon the cannon bones and relieve the flexor tendons till the inflammation subsides. When this is accomplished the witch hazel may be discontinued, and the more

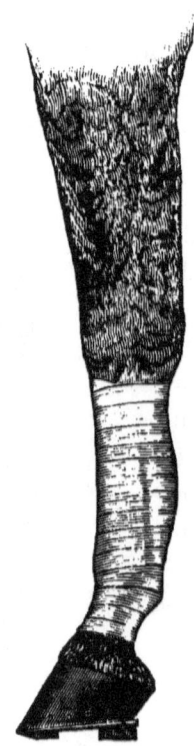

FIG. 92. FOOT AFTER BEING BANDAGED AND SHOD.

stimulating liniment described on page 294, Recipe 3, can be substituted. The liniment can be alternated with the bandage, each being applied every other day for ten days, when nature will complete the cure.

It may be useful to describe a proper soaking tub. Such a vessel is shown in Fig. 93. It should be made of hard wood, about twenty inches in height and width, with a strong bottom sufficient to stand the pressure of the heaviest draught horse. When the treatment is for inflamed tendons, the warm water should be at least sixteen inches in depth, while five or six inches of water is sufficient for the ordinary foot bath.

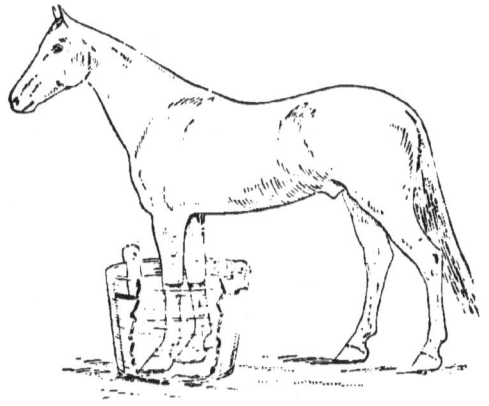

Fig. 93. Soaking Tub.

CHAPTER VIII.

FAULTS OF STRUCTURE AND ACTION.

REGULATED OR RESTRICTED BY SHOEING.

A large percentage of the horses have feet or legs which are not perfect in conformation, and as a consequence of these imperfections they are especially predisposed to certain injuries and diseases, as well as to manifest discordance of action—undesirable in itself and unpleasant in its effects according to the rapidity of motion in different gaits. Much may be learned from careful observation of the action of an evenly-balanced horse, as a standard by which to compare and determine that which is defective or undesirable in figure and gait, as previously indicated in Chapters I and V.

After examining the gait at which the horse moves, as pointed out, carefully study the poise of the legs and feet when at rest. The weak points of a horse's conformation can be better discovered while standing than while moving. If he is sound he will stand firmly and squarely on his limbs without moving them, with legs plump and naturally and equally poised; or if the foot is taken from the ground and the weight taken from it, disease may be suspected or at least tenderness, which is the precursor of disease. If the horse stands with his feet spread apart, or straddles with his hind legs, there is a weakness in the loins and the kidneys are disordered. Heavy pulling bends the knees. A kicking horse is apt to have scarred legs; a stumbling horse has blemished knees, etc.

Never buy a horse in harness. Unhitch him and take everything off but his halter and lead him around. If he has a corn or is stiff, or has any other failing, you can see it. Let him go by himself aways. Back him too. Some horses show their weakness or tricks in that way when they do n't in any other.

The vital part of a horse, as far as his value is concerned, is the foot, for it is only as an organized locomotive machine that the horse is practically the most valuable companion to man. Hence without good feet and supple, muscular legs he would be of small value, either for work or speed, and the rational care of these underlies all else in the equine economy, as any impairment of them is a matter of extreme gravity and apprehension.

It is difficult, indeed, to understand how the feet and legs of horses stand the wear and tear of work in our great cities, where every step of their iron-shod hoofs is upon a hard, unyielding road; and where, even at rest in their stables, they are, in a majority of cases, condemned to stand upon hard floors. There is no other creature living—save and excepting the donkey or mule—which can long bear the constant battering entailed by rapid locomotion over a paved surface. But if we look at the structure of the horse's foot (Figs. 3 to 15) we see how it is that the jar and vibration do not injure them more—severe as it is known to be. He is in fact mounted on springs, and it is not surprising that the intricate apparatus of locomotion, with its symmetry of movement and the perfection of its details should be admiringly termed "a living machine."

In the language of another: "His very muscles appear at every motion, not soft and flabby, but firm and distinct. His veins, like rivulets, run in an infinite number of meanders, his limbs are clean, nervous, durable and ready at every call—and of all creatures he seems to approach nearest man, both for beauty, majesty and sagacity, and his services are likewise the most noble and excellent."

The drawings on the following pages fairly illustrate the difference between well-formed and malformed legs, and good and faulty standing positions. A comparison of these may enable the reader to judge for himself as to what is the best position, and

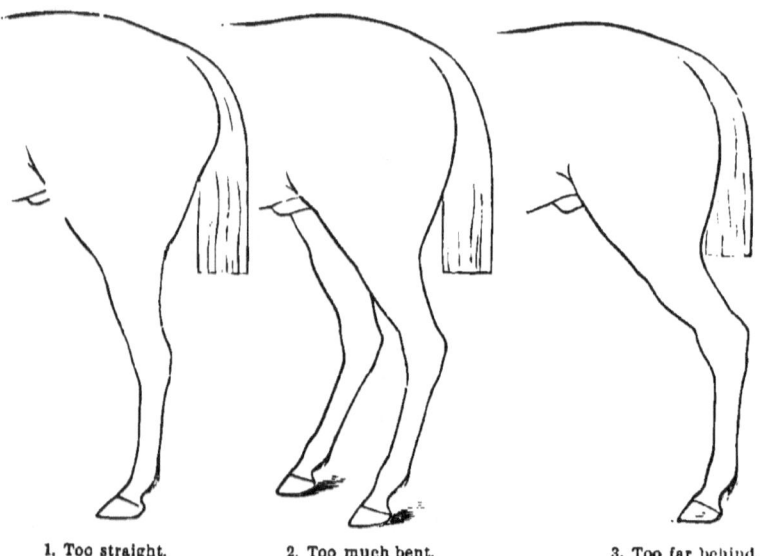

1. Too straight. 2. Too much bent. 3. Too far behind.
FIG. 94. FAULTY POSITIONS OF HIND LEGS, SIDE VIEW.

what condition or malformation of the legs causes deviation therefrom. It must be borne in mind, however, that experience is the best and only teacher in matters of this kind, and that all I can attempt within the limits of this branch of my subject, is to set the reader on the right track; the rest depends upon himself.

The character and position of the hock has much to do with the standing position of the rear part of the horse, and the numerous faulty positions in which we show this is conclusive on this point. The qualities of a good hock are that it should be clear, rigid, and well defined, without puffiness or swelling; the bones should be large and prominent, and viewed from the side should appear wide above and below. They should be neither straight or overbent. There is also a relative value to be attached to hocks malformed or apparently differing from those laid down. Horses with defective hocks may be good for one sort of work and unsuited to another. As for instance,

FAULTY CONFORMATION AND MOVEMENT. 201

hocks that will not stand violent exertions may endure for years in quiet work; but these are exceptions, and the rule stands good as before.

Comparing Figs. 1, 2, 3 (page 200), and 4 and 5 (page 201), we recognize some broad distinctions.

In Fig. 1, the hock is too straight. The legs in this position are subject to spavin and thorough-pin.

In Fig. 2, the hock is overbent and we may look for curb.

In Fig. 3, the leg is too far behind; and, therefore, does not afford the horse sufficient propelling power.

In Fig. 4, the hocks stand in and the toes stand out; and in Fig. 5, the hocks stand out and the toes stand in.

In contrast to the foregoing, Figs. 6 and 7 (page 202), represent the usually recommended position and what is considered the best position; and in connection herewith the reader is respectfully referred again to Fig. 1, illustrating the model horse, according to my 50 years' experience and observation.

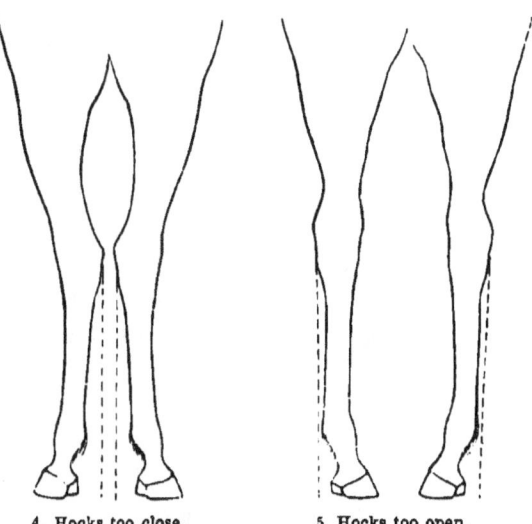

4. Hocks too close.   5. Hocks too open.

FIG. 95. FAULTY POSITION OF HIND LEGS, BACK VIEW.

202   SCIENTIFIC HORSESHOEING.

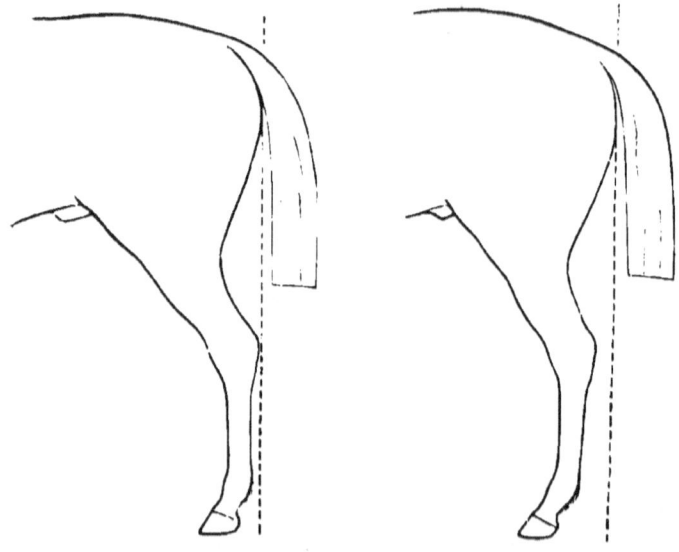

6. Position usually recommended.   7. Best position.
FIG. 96. GOOD POSITION OF HIND LEGS.

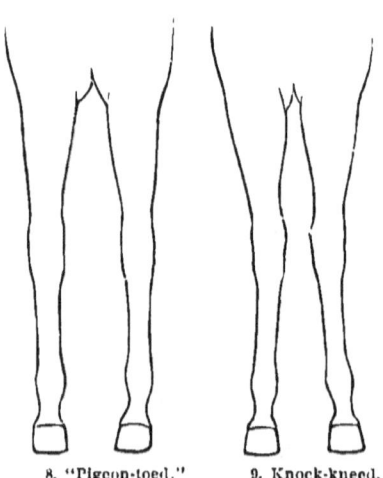

8. "Pigeon-toed."   9. Knock-kneed.
FIG. 97. FAULTY POSITIONS OF FORE LEGS.

Figs. 8, 9, 10 and 11 represent faulty positions of the fore legs. In Fig. 8, the elbow stands out and the toes stand in, commonly called "pigeon toes." In Fig. 9, the elbows stand in and the toes stand out, causing the knees to spring together.

In Fig. 10, on the 189th page, we have a side view of what is termed a "calf leg," in this the vertical line from the shoulder through the axis will pass outside of and at a distance from

FAULTY CONFORMATION AND MOVEMENT. 203

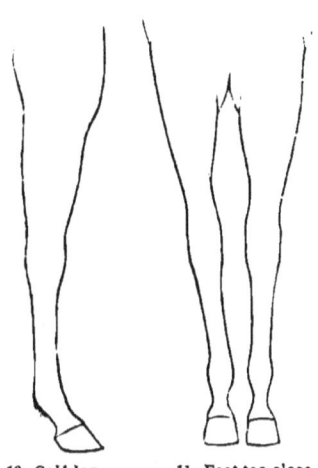

10. Calf leg.   11. Feet too close.
FIG. 98. FAULTY POSITIONS OF FORE LEGS.

the wings of the heels. This, as will be seen upon reference thereto, varies much from the requirements of a perfect horse. Such a position does not denote speed, but is not objectionable in a draft horse. In Fig. 11, the feet stand too closely together on the ground; a position not recommended in a good horse.

Finally, in contrast with these faulty positions of the forelegs, we show front and side views of them, in which the points favorable in a perfect horse are all noticeable. In the side view, the foot is well under the leg, and the axis of the bones of the leg are all in line, as indicated by the vertical dotted line that drops from point of shoulder to foot, and the foot stands upon its proper angle.

In the front view the conditions still remain the same. The shoulders are prominent, strong and well-set back, the fore arm is muscular, the fore leg tapered from elbow to foot, and the dotted line, in the vertical, passes directly through the axis of each leg and foot.

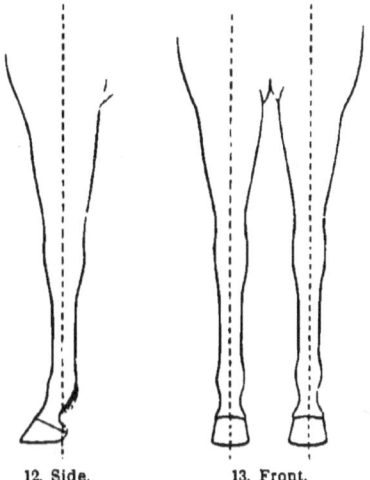

12. Side.   13. Front.
Fig. 99. VIEWS OF PERFECT LEGS.

14

Care of the Foot from Colthood.—I have often read and heard the statements of many authorities to the effect that the inside quarters of the horse's foot were weaker than the outside quarters; but from personal observation and practical knowledge, I can safely say that those statements are true only in cases of disproportionate build or where the foot has become altered or affected by mismanagement or improper shoeing. In a perfect, healthful foot, such as is shown in Fig. 24, however, the different parts are, without exception, symmetrical.

And that I might satisfy myself fully in this regard, I have for many years visited the fertilizing factories, and with a compass have closely examined thousands of green specimens after they were stripped, and measured them from the center of fissures to the union of the inner wall and floor of sole on both sides from quarters back to heels, and never found an instance of a healthful foot where the difference exceeded the sixteenth of an inch. And even when the outer wall has grown more luxuriantly upon one side than the other, have I ever found any perceptible difference in the inner part of the foot. I have also closely examined with calipers the wall upon both quarters of feet which never had been shod or tampered with, from the center of the back through the quarters to the heels, and never found any variation in the thickness. And I have gone still further to satisfy myself upon this point. I have repeated visited stock farms containing fifty or seventy-five horses and colts, whose feet never have been shod or tampered with, and upon careful inspection have found that the one-sided growth was due to the comparative length of the neck and legs. If the legs were short and the neck long, the feet would be straight; that is, if the horse was perfectly built, the legs and neck proportional, the feet were always straight in front and the growth of the foot symmetrical. If the legs were long and the neck short, the growth was more luxuriant upon the outside quarters. In some instances where the points of the shoulder were wide and the legs inclined inward, their feet would stand closely together and the growth was greater on the inside than on the outside quarter; or vice versa, if the points of the shoulder were narrow, the horse knock-kneed, and the feet apart, the growth would be larger on the outer than inner quarter.

And in fact the variation in growth at quarters may exist to a great degree. In all my measurements of the wall from the inner floors of the foot to the coronet, I did not find the quarters vary in thickness one from the other. When the old custom existed of making shoes rights and lefts, the inner quarter was made straighter than the outer, and even up to the present day the unskillful farrier, in fitting shoes, files and rasps the inner quarter straighter than the outer, to make the hoof agree with the shoe.

After all these examinations, I came to the conclusion that there was no right or left to the foot; that what will fit one foot will fit its mate. If the horse does not travel squarely on his feet, search out the cause and you will find my statements true. It is only the skillful farrier who can adjust shoes to correct malformations; the hind feet differ in shape from the fore feet; and it requires more good judgment to shoe the front than the hind feet, to keep the horse squarely upon his feet.

In conclusion, I desire to add briefly, in the light of the above facts, that in order to have perfect horses, the feet should be kept level and straight in colthood. The surplus growth should be pared and removed at least four times a year, and oftener, if necessary. For, if the feet be left to grow in a faulty position up to maturity, we may expect imperfect feet or legs. Almost any imperfect foot or leg, if treated in colthood, can be straightened; but if it be neglected to the age of six or seven years, it is then too late. A great deal, however, can be done to assist nature in restoring the malformation; and it is not to be denied that the usefulness of the horse depends upon good, solid feet and legs.

Splay Foot—Knee Hitting.—The term "splay foot" is applied to horses that point or spread their toes outward. This condition may arise from either one of two causes: first, from a fault of conformation, which may be discovered by an examination of the limb from the foot to the shoulder. If the toe turns out and the upper arm stands in close to the body, the malformation is in the "splayed" condition of the upper arm or shoulder joint. When this is the case there is no remedy to be found in any proposed style of shoeing, for the foot can not be pared to bring it straight in line with the median plane of the body without violently wrenching or twisting the jointed process of the shoulder and forearm.

Second, The cause may be referred to mismanagement or improper shoeing of the foot. In this case the arm may be normal and the fault confined to the ankle and foot—the pastern inclined inward and the toe of the foot turned outward. An examination of the hoof under these circumstances will reveal that the splayed appearance does not exist in the condition of the limb, and is therefore not real but is due to an unbalanced foot—the outside of the splay foot being too high at the toe. This defect can then be remedied and the foot straightened in line with the normal axis of the leg by proper attention in shoeing.

Sometimes this deformity is visible only in one limb, while its counterpart may be perfectly straight. An instance of this kind that came under my observation was the case of the once noted trotter, "Jo Bunker." One of his fore limbs curved inward very noticeably, with the foot splayed or turned outward, but the other limb was straight and true to the line of normal movement.

When at rest splay-footed horses always stand with their front feet slanting, wide apart, with toes out and heels in; and from this fact it is apparent that the higher the outside toe is, the farther and wider will the feet point. The longer, too, that a horse is allowed to remain in this condition, the more difficult it will be to remedy it, but much may be done in most cases to bring the feet to a correct bearing by timely methods of shoeing. Splay-footed horses are usually liable to strike or cut their knees, hence, in undertaking to shoe them for the prevention of this trouble, first examine the position of both fore and hind limbs as they stand on a level floor, and note how they are disposed. Every splay-footed, knee-hitting horse places his front feet with the outside margin of the toe first in contact with the ground, with a twist to the inside heel as it drops. The outside toe being the high point of the foot and standing out of the rectilinear way of movement, the knee of that limb can not swing out far enough to clear the other in passing. The controlling power of the muscles is exercised at the ground resistance, and if the foot leaves the ground straight it will be carried straight, but if it inclines to wind or dip in or out, the position of the foot on the ground will indicate when it is not in line with the normal axis of the limb.

To overcome knee-hitting in splay-footed horses, the directions for leveling and balancing the foot, as per Fig. 23, Chapter IV, must be observed. If there is a dished-in of the outside quarter and toe, rasp or file it to a line from ground to coronet, as shown in Figs. 17 and 18. Then, if more length is required for the ground surface, let the shoe extend over the front part of the hoof to meet the necessities of the case. The more the foot winds or twists the greater the projection of shoe must be over outside toe.

Fig. 100, on the following page, represents the pattern of shoe designed for extreme cases of knee hitting, and shows extension of web over the rim of outside toe to prevent the inward dipping of the foot as it leaves the ground, that carries it over against the opposite limb in motion. Where the inside base of the hoof can not be pared from toe to heel to bring the foot in line with normal center of limb, carefully observe if pastern

FIG. 100. FRONT FOOT SHOE (GROUND SURFACE) FOR SPLAY-FOOTED AND CHRONIC KNEE-HITTING HORSES.

A, Inside branch. B, Outside branch. C, Rivet hole, for securing leather slips when required to straighten the inside heel to place the foot level and in line with the center of limb. The dotted white line indicates extension of shoe over outside toe of foot.

still inclines inward, and if so, it must be made to conform to the right front line by building up the inside heel with a strip of sole leather inserted under the shoe, gradually tapering it off from the heel to a thin edge forward to center of toe, and then rivet on the leather and affix the shoe.

On some occasions, as where a horse cuts but one knee, it may be found that the foot on the injured limb is out of balance, and not the one that does the hitting. In such event the foot of the injured limb, after being properly leveled, may be shod with pattern, Fig. 104. The effect of this shoe will be to turn or roll the limb out of the way of the other foot by means of the outer bevel on the outside toe. Or on removal of the old shoe it can be made to answer the same purpose by welding a toe calk on the inner side, about one inch from center of toe, the calk to be one-fourth inch high by one inch long.

Forging or Clicking.—The habit of forging or clicking peculiar to many horses may arise either from disproportionate construction, or, which is most often the case, from improper shoeing; and indeed, from my own personal observation, I am led to believe that in many cases both causes may prevail at the same time. As one example, a colt, pure-gaited, never before shod, may be brought to me for shoeing, and I shoe him in accordance with my best judgment. Upon trial, he may begin to forge or click at once, or possibly not until after a lapse of time. Upon being brought back to me for a second examination and another shoeing, I may be able to detect the fault at once; possibly not, however, until after a third shoeing. It is evident, therefore, supposing that I am competent in every way in my handicraft, that if that colt continues, as we have above said, to forge or click, that we must look for the cause in the animal itself.

Upon examination it will be found that the fourteenth dorsal vertebræ (see skeleton, Fig. 2) is the pivot or axis around which the weight is poised, being the center of gravitation. It is plain, therefore, that if the symmetry of the horse be affected either by disproportionate construction, by acquired faults or by wrong shoeing, that his center of gravity is disturbed; that is, he is unbalanced. And such, in a word, is the general cause of the fault under discussion.

The horse may be heavier in front than behind; he may be too upright in his shoulders; he may be short in his pasterns. His legs may be disproportionately long in comparison with his length under the belly. He may have long pasterns and be unnaturally long in his sweeps behind, or close gaited behind, due to his stifle standing in, his hocks standing out and his toes inwardly inclined; or he may carry his head too high or too low.

Any one or more of these causes may have been present in the example above given, and were brought out upon the first shoeing. When, therefore, a horse is found to be subject to forging or clicking, the first and all-important thing is to determine how he is unbalanced and proceed to distribute equally around the center of his gravitation the natural and acquired weights he must carry. No general rule can be given for this. In the cases above mentioned, one must rely upon his own judgment and experience. I have had occasion many times to determine for myself practically the difference in weight of the fore and hind feet of horses, and having cut them off to the coronet from the same horses and weighed them, have found that the fore feet exceeded the weight of the hind feet on the average of two and one-fourth to two and three-fourth ounces. If now this difference had been a cause of forging, it was obviously my duty to adjust the difference in weight in the manner which I should deem most expedient in restoring the horse to his balance.

To treat successfully the habit of forging or clicking, it is necessary that the farrier should know first the gait at which clicking occurs, and the proportions and structure, or build, of the horse. The feet are then to be examined and the part of the shoe struck by clickings marked. A skillful farrier will then be able to determine the causes and the remedies for each.

If the horse hits the heel of the front foot, clip off the heel of that shoe on the angle of the foot on the ground surface. If he hits on the inside web at the toe, take the weight out of toe of shoe from quarters to toe on both sides, leaving the weight from quarters to heel. If he hits on the outer quarter, put the drop crease on the outside. If he hits on the inside web of shoe, concave the shoe on the ground surface at the point touched. If the head is carried low, check it up so as to lighten the front part; if too high, check down with standing martingales to add weight. If the breast collar is too low on the point of shoulders, raise it up. If the propelling power behind is too great for the front part, shoe with a five-ounce shoe heavier behind than in front. If he forges at a certain gait, drive over or under the gait. If the horse be a "dweller" with his front feet, put on a double rolling-motion shoe, highest at the quarters, gradually thinning the shoe from quarters to toe, then from quarters to heel. The effect of such a shoe will be to quicken his action in front.

The shoes designed for the hind feet should in all cases project well back at the heels, having good, long-heel calkins. The driver or farrier should be able to judge of the weight of shoes to be used. I have used four-calkin hind shoes in many cases with the best of results.

Speedy Cutting.—This is caused by the horse being unevenly balanced. Having more propelling power behind than in front—that is, the front feet not being able to get out of the way of the hind legs as they pass, the outside of the front foot strikes and wounds the inside of the shin bone in the hind leg, frequently causing much pain and soreness. It is termed "speedy cutting," from happening while the horse is in rapid action. It is an evident fact that all horses with bold, lofty knee action are not speedy cutters. Those, however, who travel with a low, gliding, forward movement, like Lady Thorne, are called "daisy cutters," and are proverbially afflicted with speedy cutting in rapid motion. To overcome this defect, it is necessary to equalize the different actions of the parts by quickening that of the front and slowing that of the hind. This can only be done in shoeing.

As there are, however, but few trotting horses that can have their toes shortened, since it would have a tendency to make them double up or shorten their stride, I use for them a double rolling-motion flat shoe, gradually thinning the shoe from quarters to heel and from quarters to toe, with dropped crease on the outer quarters. Such a shoe will allow the front foot to land on its heels, roll over the toe more quickly, and get out of the way of the hind legs. If the front feet or tendons are sore, it would have a tendency to slow the front action of the horse in landing, as he fears to hit the ground. In such cases shorten the toe of the front foot as much as safety will permit, examine the feet as well as the splint bones, for, if soreness is present, it will have a tendency to retard the action in front. If the horse is a long strider or dweller, apply the scoop-toed, rolling-motion or the plain rolling-motion shoe, which, being rolled in front, will assist the horse in getting over the toe of the foot quickly, and thus get out of the way of the other parts. In dressing the hind feet, lower the heels as much as safety will permit, keeping the front part of the toes at the natural angle, so as to have all the ground surface possible. Apply the shoe, Fig. 139. By placing long heel calkins at the sides of the heels, or allowing the shoe to extend at least one-half inch longer than the heel of the foot, the down action of the flexor perforans will be lessened, and in a relative degree, the quick-up action of the foot will also be lessened. The weight of the shoes to be worn must be determined accurately by the driver or proprietor. I have often shod this class of trotting horses with front shoes weighing eleven ounces, and with hind shoes weighing fifteen ounces, before I could get them balanced and square in their gait.

Running horses are more liable to obtain speedy cuts than trotting horses; this is occasioned principally by the carrying of weight upon their backs, the weight being placed more directly on their front legs than on their hind ones. In plating running horses to overcome this difficulty, level and straighten the front feet, having the heels and frog of an even bearing when the feet are placed on the ground; shoe with thin three-quarter tips, beveling the outside of the plate from the ground to the sole-bearing surface, so as to obviate the possibility of the leg being cut by the shoe in passing. The punishment of speedy cutting is oftentimes so severe that the race is lost by the horse being unable to withstand it without his speed being retarded more or less.

Ankle, Shin and Knee Cutting.—In ankle or shin cutting, it will generally be observed that the ankles are tilted inward. Cutting often depends weakness or leg weariness, and is liable to happen to horses when driven long distances or when they are carrying heavy shoes. Contraction and also soreness in the splint bones will cause a horse to cut, which almost always is the result of improper shoeing and bad management of the feet. All can be stopped by properly leveling and balancing the foot, and the appliance of a suitable shoe. When the position of the foot is faulty, it must be obvious that the remedy consists in altering its improper position and straightening it, as much as can be accurately done, according to the instructions given with Fig. 23, Chap. IV.

When the toe is the part which inflicts the wound use a square-toed shoe like No. 147, shown in case of shoes, page 286. This will let the foot break over the toe square, and in straight going or close-gaited horses, the foot will generally pass the knee without hitting.

FIG. 101. FRONT FOOT FOUR CALKIN SHOE, TO BE USED FOR THE RELIEF OF SORENESS IN THE FLEXOR PERFORANS, OR CASES OF QUARTER CRACK, WHERE TOE AND HEEL CALKINS ARE REQUIRED, AS WELL AS FOR SORENESS AT THE TOE AND FOR SPLIT FOOT IN FRONT.

To be beveled from A, A, to B; also from C, C, to wall-bearing surface at heel. A, A, Front toe calks to be beveled off on ground surface to front of toe at B. C, C, Heel calks to be beveled from ground surface to wall-bearing surface.

Sprains of the Tendons.—As its name implies, this complaint is an injury to the back sinew, from the effects of overtaxation. Work-horses are liable to become so affected, though it occurs more frequently in the running and trotting horses, by reason of their immense strides, the force of which has a tendency—when prolonged to a certain extent—to cause the tendons to become swollen and inflamed.

For horses suffering with sore tendons, the four-calkin rolling motion shoe, illustrated on the preceding page, will be found a successful remedy.

The shoe should extend well back at the heels, the calkins being at least one-half inch higher at the heels than at the sides of the toe, where it should be well beveled on the ground surface, in order that the horse may be enabled to "get over" the toe of his foot with but little strain on the flexor perforans.

I have also found the scoop-toed rolling-motion shoe very successful in the cases of trotting and running horses. The feet should always be well leveled and straightened, and the toes shortened as much as safety will permit. A preliminary application of warm-water bandages may be found beneficial.

Elbow and Arm Cutting.—When a horse has too much freedom in the action of the knee of his fore leg, which causes it to bend under him, when lifted, in such a manner as to strike and bruise the limb, it is called elbow or arm cutting. To overcome this difficulty, the heel of the foot should be pared as low as it can be safely done. The toe, on the contrary, should be left long. The shoe should be light, for the lighter the shoe the less liability there is of the elbow or arm being cut. The web of the shoe should be narrow, especially from the quarters to the toe. The shoe should be well concaved on its ground surface, from the heel to the toe, particularly so in the case of horses who cut or hit the arm or elbow with the heel. (It may here be observed that the greater number of horses cut their elbows with the toe.)

Adjustable Toe Weight.—The devices next shown in Figs. 102 and 103, for balancing the action of horses has many features which will recommend it to attention. I have used it for many years, and it has proven to give satisfaction in all cases. The following is the method of adjusting it to the foot:

FAULTY CONFORMATION AND MOVEMENT. 215

In case the horse's stride is short, place the weight over No. 4, as shown in diagram; by so doing, the weight is at the extremity of the toe and muscle of the arm. In case one foot is longer in the stride than the other, place the weight on the short striding foot over No. 4, and on the long striding foot over No. 3. Drive the horse, and if the stride is not equal place the weight on the long striding foot over letter 2. Drive the horse a few days, and if this does not have the desired effect, and his stride is not equal, place a weight on the short striding foot at No. 4, two or three ounces heavier than the other. The great success of this weight depends on the skillfulness of the driver to properly adjust it so as to equalize the stride of the horse.

Another great advantage of this weight is that you can give the horse foot action or take it away, by

FIG. 102. ADJUSTABLE TOE WEIGHT.
A, Ground surface of drop-crease shoe attached to foot. 1, 2, 3, 4, Points to which weight is adjusted.

FIG. 103. GROUND TREAD OF SHOE SHOWN IN FIG. 102 TO PREVENT ARM AND ELBOW CUTTING.

A, Toe calk around the curve of shoe in front to be from 1¼ in. to ¾ in. high. B, B, B, B, Bevel around inner rim of shoe and on outside at heels. C, Spur in front of shoe carrying weight, as shown on side view, Fig. 81. D, D, Inner face of toe weight.

FIG. 104. RIGHT FRONT FOOT SHOE, TO PREVENT ANKLE, SHIN AND KNEE HITTING.

C, Starting point of bevel at center of toe to a thin feather edge at B, then gradually lessening the bevel around the outside rim of shoe to A.

FIG. 105. LEFT HIND FOOT SHOE FOR ANKLE HITTING.

A, Inside toe calkin. B, Inside heel calkin.

the raising or lowering of the weights on the foot. By placing both weights over No. 1, the weights, being placed over the center of the foot, will prevent the foot from bending or doubling at the toe, and will stop the worst cases of elbow and arm cutting.

Ankle, Shin and Knee Hitting.—As a rule horses so affected, hit one leg or the other by striking it with the opposite foot from the point of the inside toe to about the heel nail. By beveling off the shoe on the outside rim, therefore, as shown in Fig. 104, from C to B, at middle of toe, to A, at last nail hole, will prevent anything like an inward dip as the foot leaves the ground, and will cause the ankle and knee to be carried outward from the opposite foot and thus avoid becoming bruised or cut.

Fig. 105 shows a hind foot shoe intended for extreme cases of ankle hitting, where the horse hits with the inside point of the toe. This occurs with horses that stand in the faulty position illustrated in Fig. 95, No. 5, having their hocks turned outwardly and consequently their toes turned in. In this case, a toe-calk should be placed on the inside, at the striking point of the foot, and also a side heel calkin. This will prevent any thing like an inward dip as the foot leaves the ground, and sufficient to carry it beyond the ankle of the opposite foot.

Speed Shoes.—This variation from the ordinary bar shoe was designed to close up the hind action, where the movement was so wide that, at full speed, the horse frequently would strike his hocks in passing, and more frequently tear off the hind hock boots. When shod with this shoe, the shoe being on the inside of the wall, this excessive straddling was obviated and the hocks were at once relieved of their boots. The more the foot is raised on the inside, the closer becomes the hind action. A, shows the bar across the frog, from heel to toe. B, B, B, shows rivet holes, through which to fasten the leather padding between the shoe and the wall. C, indicates the heel calkin, and D the outside section of the wall. The shoe may be forged as light as the hind action may require, and it makes a neater finish to cut the leather padding to the inside and outside margin of the shoe and bar, after it has been nailed to the foot. When made and fitted according to these instructions, not only will hock interference be avoided, but the

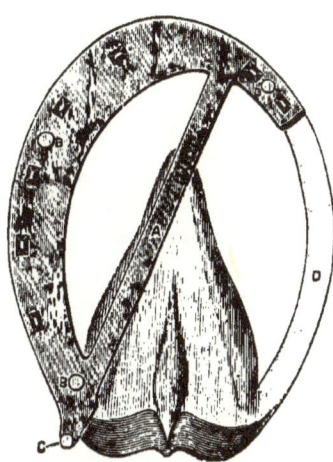

FIG. 106. BAR SHOE—VARIATION FOR CORRECTING WIDE MOVEMENT.

A, Bar across frog.

speed of the horse decidedly increased and his endurance greatly extended.

This shoe has been so beneficial to speed that I have termed it the "Record Breaker." As the horse increases his speed, he changes his gait, and as no one style of shoe was known which would be suitable to all gaits, I invented this shoe for a low-gaited horse such as Nancy Hanks. My theory is that the thinner the shoe is, the longer will be the stride; the lighter the shoe, the lighter the footfall. The wider the web, the less

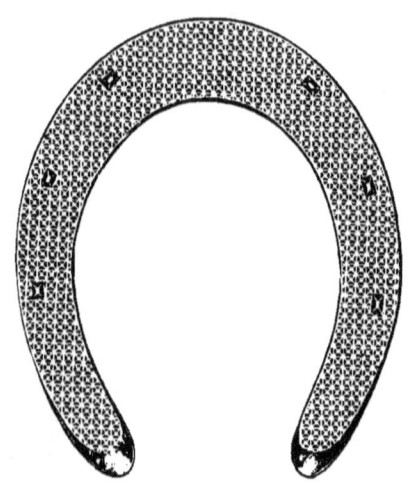

FIG. 107.   RECORD BREAKER—FRONT SHOE.

FIG. 108.   RECORD BREAKER—HIND SHOE.

the shoe sinks in the ground, and the less liable the foot is to cup and slip back as it leaves the ground. This shoe is cut in grooves straight from toe to heel, about three-sixteenths of an inch deep. This will prevent the foot from slipping sideways. The grooves cut sideways and at right angles to the former will prevent the foot from slipping backward as it leaves the ground. Judging from my experience in shoeing speed horses, slipping sideways is very tiresome, and

FAULTY CONFORMATION AND MOVEMENT. 219

therefore in affording a horse a firm foothold, as the foot lands upon and leaves the ground, he is inspired with great confidence, he can hold his speed from start to finish more uniformly, and he will win many a race which he would have lost when wearing the common, old style of flat shoes.

With this style of hind shoe, it will be impossible for the hind foot to slip backward or sideways, as it lands upon or leaves the ground. The hind legs are mainly the propelling powers of the horse. This shoe, as will be seen, is cut in diamond shapes on the ground tread. The cuts are to be made three-sixteenths of an inch deep. This style of shoe is adapted to horses with long pasterns. In my experience I have found it to be of decided advantage to the horse with long pasterns to shoe him behind with a long extension of a shoe backward. The shoe then serves as a brace or stay to support the back tendons.

In shoeing a speed horse, we must be governed by the length of the pastern, and use such a shoe as will suit and assist his gait and footfall. If the pastern is long, let the shoe extend back of the heel; if it is short and upright, let the shoe extend just the length of the heel.

This shoe (Fig. 109) is designed for a horse with a long pastern. In some cases small heel calks can be turned upon the heels, as slipping sideways when he lands, or backward when the foot leaves the ground, is very tiresome. The scoop commencing at the toe, as

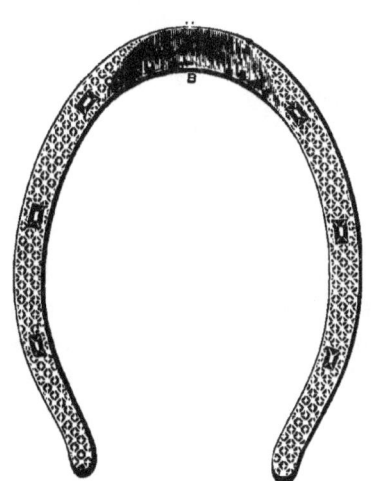

FIG. 109. RECORD BREAKER—HIND SHOE, WITH GRAB TOE.

A to B, Scoop.

A, should be gradually thinned down to the inner edge, B, thus leaving a sharp catch at the toe. I have used this shoe on hard tracks with the best of success; have known the slipping defect, generally confined to the hind feet, to be reduced to a minimum, and the speed on a hard track increased from one to three seconds.

The importance of this shoe can not be overstated. Its use is to prevent the foot from slipping backward, thus tending to strain the tendons as well as to produce the knee-sprung troubles. The toe of this shoe is gradually beveled to a thin edge from the outer to the inner surface of the shoe, and when this shoe is worn by speed horses it prevents the front foot from slipping backward as it leaves the ground. I use this style of shoe on speed horses for sore tendons and the knee-sprung defect.

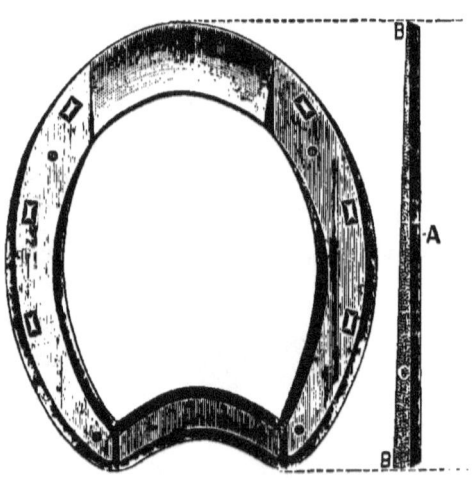

FIG. 110. IMPROVED GRAB SHOE. A, Ground tread of shoe. B, B, Tips of leather-heel of toe.

This shoe can be made as light as the foot requires, as well as the leg and the gait of the horse. All horses that are sore in the back tendons require elevation at the heels to relieve the sore tendon at each footfall. Take thick sole leather and rivet on shoe where rivet holes show in shoe, at heels and quarters. Then cut the leather out on inside of shoe, thus lightening its weight. Afterward gradually remove the leather by commencing to thin it from the heels down to a feather edge at the toe, on each side of quarters. By so doing the heels will be elevated and the sore tendons greatly relieved. B, B, shows how leather is to be tapered from heel up to toe; C, shows the leather and ground tread of shoe. The use of this shoe will afford the greatest ease and comfort to the horse at each footfall, when up to speed. The elevation with the leather must be governed by circumstances, some inflamed tendons requiring more than others.

Shoes for Quarter Crack.—The illustration herewith is a side view of foot and pasterns, with lower part of cannon bone, the foot properly balanced and the bar shoe illustrated in Fig. 112 nailed to the foot. This style of bar shoe I designed for quarter crack where toe and heel calkins were required. Quarter crack is one of the many diseases which horses are subjected to who travel day in and out upon artificially paved streets and roads. The illustration of this particular case would not do for all cases, of course. This style of shoe, however, will illustrate this case, and be a guide to any others which may come to the attention of the reader.

In this instance, the reader will turn his attention first to the Fig. 111, showing side view of the shoe shown on the

FIG. 111. SHOE FOR QUARTER CRACK, SET ON WELL-BALANCED FOOT.

A, Toe calk. B, B, Heel calkins set to break the jar.

foot. Second illustration shows the shoe, ground tread and toe calkin, and third shows the wall bearing and where shoe is beveled to avoid the quarter crack.

The rule of making the shoe is to bevel it from wall bearing wherever it comes opposite a quarter crack on the foot. This will prevent dirt from wedging in between the shoe and the wall of the foot, and at each footfall the dirt will jar out. A clip is required for draft horses.

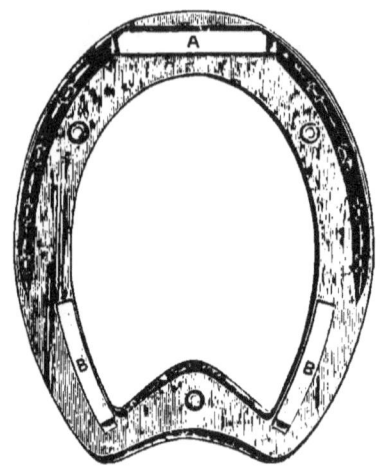

Fig. 112.

In paring the foot, bear in mind always to pare the outer edges of the quarter crack as deep as the sensitive laminæ. After paring the foot and fitting the shoe, rivet a piece of sole leather to the shoe, covering bottom of the foot, at three rivet holes, as in illustration (Fig. 113). Before nailing the shoe to the foot, take fat pickled pork, fill the bottom of foot with long slices thereof, pressing them well into the commissures with the hand. After nailing the shoe to the foot, take Recipe No. 2 made warm; dip cotton into the salve, cover the affected parts well with the salve and cotton. Then

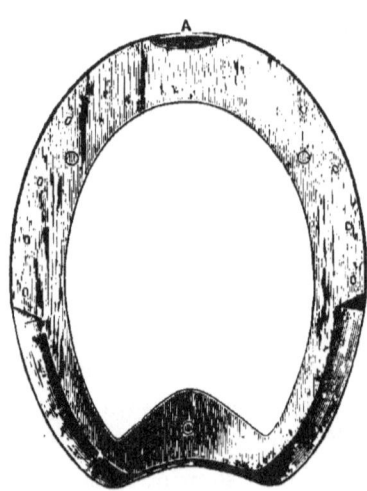

Fig. 113. **A,** Clip on point of shoe.

FAULTY CONFORMATION AND MOVEMENT. 223

bandage the cotton to the foot and stand the feet in the soaking tub, with warm water six to eight inches deep, for one or two hours. After taking the horse out of the soaking tub, better apply the soaking swabs around the pastern, kept wet with warm water, for a few days. I have cured the worst cases with this shoe and treatment, and worked the horse daily.

Fig. 114 shows a special shoe for quarter crack for running horses. I have been very successful with this, using it upon running horses where, in their early stages, they can not run up to their full speed, shod with bar shoes. The shoe is very easily made, as can be noted in the illustration, by bending, as at C. In paring the foot, the wall or horn should be removed so as to allow the shoe to set snugly up to the foot, as shown in the diagram. Placing nails in the heel of shoe will hold the wall of the foot permanently as the horse springs over the toe in his forward movement. Fig. 114, open shoes; A, A, ground tread; B, B, wall bearing; C, set-off in shoe. Side view of foot shows: A, quarter crack; B, shoe set off in front of the ground tread of quarter crack. A full front view of this shoe is given in the illustration in case of shoes, page 284, No. 103. After placing this shoe upon the foot, use my foot salve, white cotton being

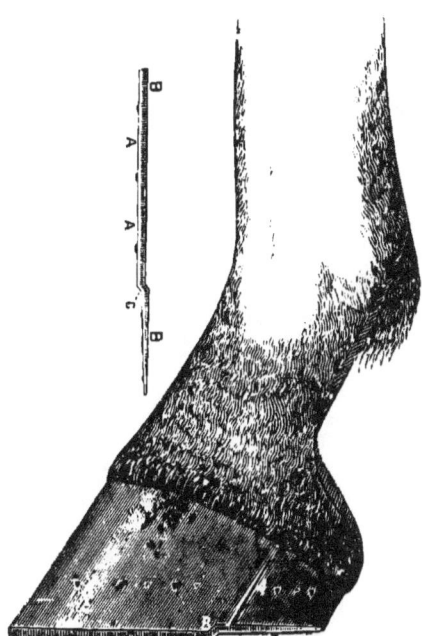

FIG. 114. SHOE FOR QUARTER CRACK.
A, Quarter crack. B, Shoe.

saturated with it, large enough to cover affected parts, warm and apply the salve. Place also a good linen, bandage around the coronet and under the heels, so as to hold the dressing firmly to the affected parts, and heat in well with a warm iron. Stand the foot in the soaking tub filled with warm water six inches deep, for one or two hours, and afterward use the soaking swabs around the pasterns and foot. Keep well wet with warm water for a few days, or until the soreness disappears.

This shoe is designed for quarter crack, where neither toe nor heel calkins are required. This treatment I have used with unvarying success in the case of speed horses that have been driven over hard tracks and roads. If horses' feet are kept properly balanced, the wall pliable and flexible, and the hoof shod with shoes suited to the work required, there will be little danger of quarter crack. The treatment is as follows: In old, long-standing cases, one side of the wall will overlap the other. In such instance, remove all the fractured and loose wall as deep as the podophyllous tissues. Be careful not to draw blood. The shoe is set down to half its thickness in front of the crack, being gradually drawn thinner as the heel is approached. Then

FIG. 115. SIDE VIEW OF HOOF PREPARED, BALANCED, AND SHOD FOR QUARTER CRACK, WHERE NO TOE NOR HEEL CALKINS ARE REQUIRED.

A, A, Wall removed under crack. B, Quarter crack.

FAULTY CONFORMATION AND MOVEMENT. 225

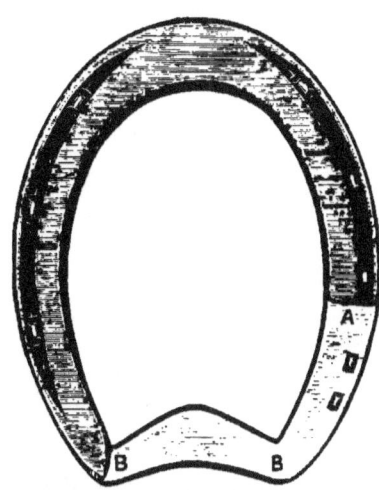

Fig. 116. SHOE FOR QUARTER CRACK.
A, Set-off, one-half thickness.

punch two small nail holes in heel of shoe, as shown in diagram. The shoe should lie easily on the wall back of the quarter crack. After the foot has been shod apply the foot salve and remedy as heretofore prescribed. Cover the quarter crack and the coronet with the white cotton thoroughly saturated with the salve. Apply the linen bandage well around the whole foot, so as to hold the dressing to the wounded parts. Warm the salve in well with the iron, made warm for this purpose. Observe these instructions and a permanent cure can be effected.

Fig. 116 is a front view of a shoe which I have used in a great many cases of quarter crack with most satisfactory results.

Rate of Speed of Trotters and Pacers.—I give here a table showing the distance covered per second by a horse when going at speeds varying from a 2:00 to a 2:30 gait. The table given is believed to be a substantially correct compilation of the figures.

It will be noticed that in the distance covered by the horse when going at a rate of speed of from 2:30 to 2:20 there is an approximate increase of three inches per second for each additional second's lowering of the speed rate, while in the speed rate between 2:10 and 2:00 the increase amounts to four and one-tenth inches per second. A horse going a mile in two minutes would distance Martha Wilkes, Palo Alto and Maud S.,

Rate of Speed.	Distance per Second.		Rate of Speed.	Distance per Second.	
	Feet.	In.		Feet.	In.
2:30	35	2	2:15	39	..
2:25	36	5	2:14	39	4
2:24	36	8	2:13	39	8
2:23	36	11	2:12	40	..
2:22	37	2	2:10	40	7
2:21	37	5	2:08¾	41	..
2:20	37	8	2:08	41	3
2:19	38	..	2:05	42	3
2:18	38	3	2:04	42	7
2:17	38	6	2:00	44	..
2:16	38	9			

and have something to spare, and would leave Nancy Hanks and Mascot, the fleetest of the present day, about seven lengths to the rear. Railroad express train, one mile a minute, eighty-eight feet a second, is a good comparison.

CHAPTER IX.

SPECIFIC AND REMEDIAL SHOEING.

ITS PURPOSE AND SCOPE DELINEATED.

The special purposes of shoeing will be considered under this head as applying to "all sorts and conditions" of feet—especially defective and diseased conditions—for which certain merits are claimed for many different styles of shoes, in remedying or curing the special defects against which they are directed. No one need be told that in operating upon feet of this kind, the highest discretion of the farrier is called upon, for it is not the application of a given style of shoe to the foot in a given way, but it is the scientific adaptation of a special kind of shoe, varied for special purposes, to suit different conditions of the foot, with a view of securing certain beneficial results. Thus regarded, this section of my subject becomes withal one of the most interesting phases of all the branches of shoeing.

There are a large number of artificers who make horseshoeing a profession, who offer convincing testimony of having mastered the principles of their art (as proved by their skill in this department of it), that I should doubtless have made an exception in their favor in my strictures on the careless bunglers who belittle the importance of the profession and unmake the well-deserved reputations of the more finished artists in the business.

In the development of that "paragon of horseflesh"—the trotter—the matter of shoeing for specific purposes has received more attention at the hands of all classes of men, and has made more progress and achieved greater triumphs in American than in any other land.

This is a department of the farrier's art that ranks with the best and most ingenious of other mechanical arts, and is justly entitled to the highest praise that can be bestowed upon it.

I have devised many different styles of shoes admirably effective for leveling and perfecting the action and the gait of horses, as well as for removing the cause and thereby healing the effect of various foot ailments, but as many of them are applicable—in a large measure—to horses used solely for speed purposes, any attempt at a complete classification at this time is precluded by the limits assigned for this work. I will, therefore, confine myself to a selection of such patterns as may be regarded the most useful for the purpose in view, though the next succeeding chapter will contain an assembly of one hundred and seventy other forms of shoes, all enumerated and described for convenient reference.

When rightly made and applied as directed, any of these shoes will prove potent auxiliaries in assisting to relieve the faults or troubles for which they are especially designed or intended, as explained in each instance—and this applies to the higher breeds of horses, as well as to others whose lot is cast in the humbler, if more useful walks of life.

Any correspondence or inquiries addressed to me relative to the matters in question, will receive prompt and careful attention at my hands.

SPECIFIC AND REMEDIAL SHOEING. 229

FIG. 117. ORIGINAL CENTENNIAL SHOE, DESIGNED BY S. T. HARRIS.

Centennial Shoe, No. 1.—Fig. 117. is one of the many I exhibited at the Centennial Exposition at Philadelphia in 1876. It was designed by Mr. S. T. Harris. of Cincinnati. The shoe derives its name from the year in which it was invented and exhibited, and it has been in use a long time. with very gratifying success.

It conforms more to the shape of the foot than any shoe ever used. The wings, A, A, bear evenly on the bars of the foot, affording the greatest possible bearing surface to the heels, and serve to distribute equally over the whole ground surface of the foot the concussion sustained, which, by reason of the position of the heels, is greatest at this point.

After the Centennial shoe has been worn for a few days and then removed from the foot, the inclination and position of the wings afford a useful and valuable deduction. The question has long been mooted among writers and farriers, what part of the foot expands the hoof, whether the wall, the bars, or the frog. Eminent authorities have given this active agency in turn to each one of the members I have mentioned, but the inclination of the wings of a worn Centennial shoe indicates an active agency of the bars in co-operating with the other parts of the foot that have not heretofore received adequate consideration. The wings of the shoe not only fall out in their bearings to the extreme points of the bars, but they are careened outwardly, the inside branches being higher than the outside branches, thus showing by their outward inclination that the bars have an active and constant agency in keeping the foot normally expanded.

As a hoof expander, therefore, we derive from the Centennial shoe one of its most valuable uses.

Centennial Shoe, No. 2. —Fig. 118. This shoe, also exhibited at the Centennial Exposition, conforms as closely as possible to the natural shape of the hoof, and places the pressure just where nature demands. Especially is it beneficial to the trotting horse that requires toe weights to balance his actions, because it is heavy in front and operates powerfully in assisting the extensor to lengthen the stride. When a shoe of this pattern weighing sixteen ounces is lifted by the heel, it seems to weigh at least two pounds. The inner rim on ground surface is to be well concaved, as shown by letters, A, A, the heels to be swedged out with a round, blunt, fullering tool, as shown in B, B, so as to get good heel and bar pressure.

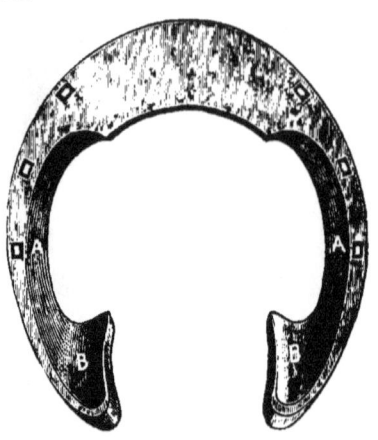

FIG. 118. MODIFIED FORM CENTENNIAL TOE-WEIGHT SHOE, DESIGNED BY S. T. HARRIS.

A, A, Bevel around inner rim of shoe on ground surface. **B, B,** Grooves at heels to obtain bar pressure.

In applying this style of shoe to a horse inclined to mix and shift his gait, bear in mind to leave a long toe. Three nails in each quarter is sufficient to hold the shoe to the foot. This shoe will produce most satisfactory results, if properly applied.

Centennial Shoe, No. 3.—Fig. 119, on next page, is another modified form of the Centennial shoe before described, and with the others was exhibited by me at the Centennial Exposition. It is more easily made, yet embraces the same principle of bar pressure. It can be made from any ordinary flat shoe, the wings to be swedged out solidly by means of a blunt, round, fullering

SPECIFIC AND REMEDIAL SHOEING.

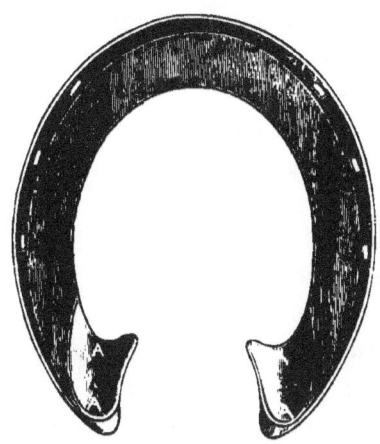

FIG. 119. ANOTHER MODIFIED FORM CENTENNIAL SHOE, DESIGNED BY S. T. HARRIS.

A, A, A, A, Grooves deepening and widening toward sole-bearing surface.

tool, until they extend over the bars, as shown at A, A, A, A. This style of shoe I consider to be of especial advantage to recover the wiring-in of the crusts at the heels. By following the wall close up to the sides of the frog, it obtains strong bar pressure, and gives the frog free access to the ground. If the sole of the foot evinces a tendency to be flat and tender, it is quite necessary to protect it from injury until it becomes strong. The only way in which this can be done is by adding to the web in the shoe. As the sole gradually renews itself and becomes thicker, reduce the width of the shoe. In two or three shoeings, the foot will become strong, when the narrow-webbed shoe may be resorted to.

Fig. 120. To make shoe, take a steel bar 1¼ by ⅜ inches, of twice the length from center of the toe to either heel—otherwise sufficiently long to extend the required distance round the foot. Strike a center at a point half the length from toe to heel on each side. Then with a chisel, cut down through the middle of bar each way—

FIG. 120. RAISED SPRING BAR SHOE, TO REDUCE CONCUSSION AND SOFTEN THE STROKE OF FOOTFALL.

stopping at a point to leave material enough where the ends of the wings unite with the shoe, then cut off the surplus stock in center to leave the wings of the desired length, beginning at a distance from each end, equal to the length of the wings desired, and continue to the required distance from the ends of the bars.

Taper the wings from heels to points and bend the shoe to the form of the foot. Make the wings conform to the shape of the frog. Then fit the shoe to the foot, springing the wings gradually from heels to points and leaving them standing one-half inch below face of shoe. I have tested this shoe on horses that were quite sore and lame, the shoe being made of cast steel, the bars being sprung down from the heel to their points on the ground surface about one-half inch; this will soften and mellow the jar. The shoe, being well tempered, will allow the bars to spring with the horse's weight, and will be found one of the best devices possible to soften and relieve the effects of concussion when the horse is tender in foot or tendons, as well as to quicken the action in trotting, leaving the frog free and unimpeded to perform its important functions of cushioning the foot and shielding the sensitive parts from injury.

The benefit of this shoe can only be obtained on hard roads or tracks.

Fig. 121. This shoe can be readily made. It begins to be gradually thinned on the face at A, A, until the centers at

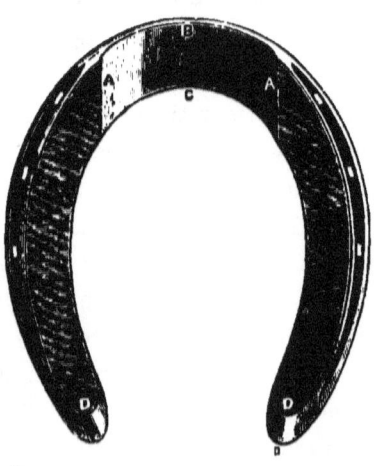

FIG. 121. FRONT FOOT SCOOP-TOE, ROLLING MOTION SHOE.

A, A, Commencement of scoop on each side of toe. B to C, Direction of scoop from out to in. C, Point where scoop is deepest. D to D, Bevel from ground surface to wall-bearing surface on each heel.

SPECIFIC AND REMEDIAL SHOEING.

FIG. 122. FRONT FOOT SHOE, KNOWN AS THE "GOLDSMITH MAID BAR SHOE," HEART-SUNKEN AND DROP-CREASED.

FIG. 123. FRONT FOOT SHOE, TO LESSEN KNEE ACTION, SHORTEN THE STRIDE, AND TO PREVENT FORGING.

A, A, Concave on ground surface around toe. B, B, B, B, Concave on ground surface around quarters. C, C, Outer ground surface to be kept flush with face of shoe.

B, C, are reached, when on its outer edge, it should be not more than two-thirds its original thickness, dipping deeper inwardly toward C, where it should be quite thin. The effect of this will be to lessen the ground surface of the foot, and quicken the action of the fore legs. This shoe will also be found beneficial for horses sore in the toes and tendons.

Fig. 122. This shoe is applicable for a number of diseases of the foot, such as weak and bruised heels, quarter cracks, etc. It is also used extensively among trotting horses, the shoes being reduced down so light, they serve to keep the shoe from spreading on the foot, when the horse is in violent action. By having the bar set down below the face of the shoe, it serves the same purpose as an open shoe. This style of shoe is quite beneficial for long-striding horses, as they land mostly on the heels, and by having the shoe thinned well back at the heel, it will prevent the foot from becoming bruised. I believe that an occasional change to the open shoe will be beneficial in giving the foot more active use of the frog.

Fig. 123, on the opposite page, illustrates a front foot shoe designed to prevent forging, to lessen knee action and shorten the stride.

1. For forging, if the hind foot hits under the toe, clip out in the toe as shown in the foregoing diagram. Lessening the weight from quarters to the toe will allow the horse to get his foot quicker out of the road of the hind foot, thus preventing this defect.

2. If the horse has too much knee action and stride, taking the weight from toe, as shown opposite, lessens the stride and knee action and serves to equalize the gait.

In either case the shoe is to be gradually thickened from A, A, to the heels. By so doing the front foot will be assisted in getting out of way of the hind foot, and where the hind foot hits up under the toe, forging will be prevented.

Fig. 124. Horses that paddle do so by reason of the faulty position of the leg and foot. Paddling consists in springing from the inside toe when the foot leaves the ground, causing it to swing out from the body. The shoe (Fig. 124) was designed to assist nature in equalizing the weight, through the axis of the leg and foot, and is shown here from the ground side.

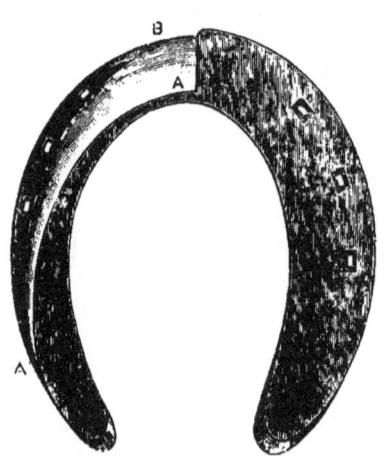

Fig. 124. IMPROVED NON-PADDLING FRONT FOOT SHOE, DESIGNED BY S. T. HARRIS.

Bevel outer rim of shoe from inner A to a thin edge at outer B, gradually diminishing the bevel to outer A, back of the quarter.

To prevent paddling, place as wide a web upon the inside branch of shoe as the foot will admit of. The inside branch of the shoe to be beveled from the ground surface on the angle of the foot from toe to heel. The outside branch is to be made as light as possible. Commence to bevel from A to B, to be carried to B to a thin edge, as shown in diagram. This shoe has given uniform satisfaction wherever used as I have directed.

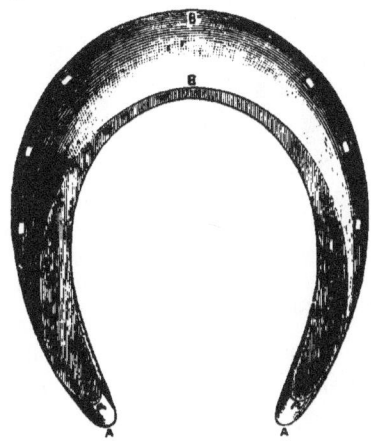

Fig. 125. ROLLING MOTION SHOE NO. 1. FOR KNEE SPRUNG AND SORE TENDONS.

A, A, A, A, Bevel on heel of shoe from ground surface to wall-bearing.
B, B, Bevel from inner to outer surface of ground-bearing, as shown.

Fig. 125. I use this shoe for knee sprung and sore tendons. It can be made of any thickness or width to suit. Inasmuch as elevation gives relief to knee sprung and sore tendons, thickness at the heels must be judged of according to the necessities of the case. Select the bar required and bend it around center, shape both sides of toes and quarters, gradually narrowing the bar edgewise from center of toe to heel.

As the bar diminishes in width it increases in thickness toward the heels. Then commence at inner B, gradually beveling to outer B, extending as far back as shown in diagram on both sides of quarters. As the web at the toe shortens on the ground surface, the thickness at the heels gives elevation. The beveling from inner to outer web lessens the ground surface of the shoe. This shoe, when properly made and adjusted, is the best I have ever used for sprung knee and sore tendons.

Fig. 126. The shoe on the opposite page I use for laminitis, quarter crack, split hoof, bruised heels, contracted feet and tender-footedness; and it has always given the best satisfaction.

The shoe is made in this way: Take a bar of the required width and thickness and bend it. Shape both sides from toe to heel. Commence beveling on outer surface, the bevel gradually diminishing at the inside web of shoe. Extend this operation from toe to heel on ground surface. Increase the web of shoe in proportion as the ground surface requires to be shortened.

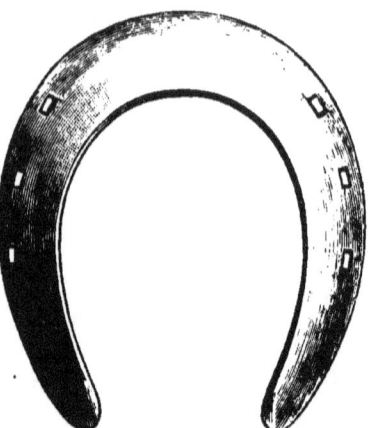

FIG. 126. ROLLING MOTION SHOE NO. 2, FOR VARIOUS PURPOSES, AS DESCRIBED. To be beveled all around on ground surface, from inside to outside of web, as shown.

The effect of this shoe on the foot will be to lessen the ground surface, breaking the jar at each footfall, bringing the foot more under the leg, and allowing it to roll easily, in the forward movement at point of toe.

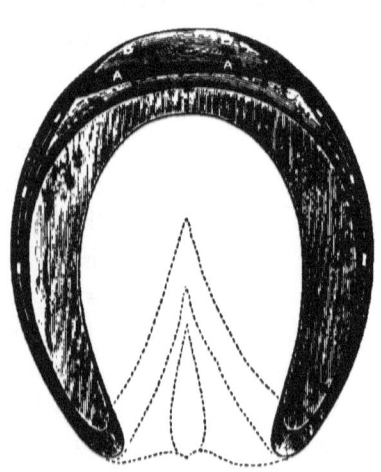

FIG. 127. FRONT FOOT SHOE, TO PREVENT STUMBLING AND GIVE GRACEFUL KNEE ACTION.

Fig. 127. Although rolling-motion shoes Nos. 1 and 2 will prevent tripping and stumbling, all horses can not travel with ease and comfort when wearing a full rolling-motion shoe. For such cases, therefore, I designed shoe, Fig. 127. I have elsewhere stated that stumbling will arise from straight shoulders, short, upright pasterns, high heels and carrying the head low. The more stiffness and soreness there is apparent, the higher the foot is to be raised from the ground to prevent the toe tripping or stumbling.

To make the shoe, cut a bar of the required width and thickness, and shape the shoe from toe to heel, making quarters the same as an ordinary shoe. Next, take a round, blunt fullering tool, and scoop out at points A, A, gradually thinning from inside web to outside web. After swedging, clip off with a chisel the surplus to the circle of the foot; then hot-rasp the outer rim of shoe, leaving the ground surface as seen in the preceding diagram.

If Fig. 127 is properly made, and the foot placed on its natural angle, the worst cases of tripping and stumbling can be prevented.

If calkins are required for winter use, set the toe calk well back from the front of shoe, and weld on side heel calkins.

This style of shoe can be successfully employed in giving the horse graceful knee action, as it will allow the toe to break over quickly and an increase of weight will cause the muscles of the limbs and shoulders to be brought more into play in lifting the feet from the ground.

Another shoe to accomplish the same result is the four-calkin shoe, made as described and shown in Fig. 101; both shoes will give a sprightly down grade style of action.

To increase hock action, if front shoes weigh 20 ounces each, make hind shoes 18 ounces or in that proportion, for increased or diminished weight. Any ordinary shoe will answer the purpose for the hind feet, by having increased weight in shoe the reflex action of picking up the foot is increased, which causes the hock to bend more and lift the foot higher from the ground, and the graceful effect is heightened with increase of speed.

Fig. 128. By shoeing with the style of shoe on the opposite page—properly made and applied—the weight being principally in the toe, at the extremities of the muscles, the action will be squared and balanced. In order that the shoe may have the desired effect, the quarters must be well concaved from the ground surface. In proportion, then, as the weight is lessened in the quarters, the toe of the shoe will be relatively heavier. This shoe can be used to quicken the horse's action by being rolled on the ground surface. I have used it with the most satisfactory results.

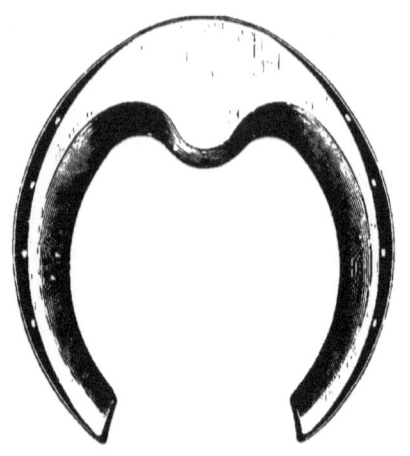

FIG. 128. FRONT FOOT SHOE, FOR BALANCING AND SQUARING THE ACTION AND GAIT OF HORSES, WHEN INCLINED TO RACK OR PACE AND SHUFFLE.

Fig. 129. This shoe is intended only for slow work in gaiting horses. If the shoe be made according to the instructions following, and head checked down with standing martingale, as described in Chap. V, page 110, balancing the action of horses, a pacer that never struck a trot will trot at once.

To make the shoe, select a bar of iron one-half inch thick, and shape the toe and quarters, then with a chisel cut from center of quarters, leaving one-half inch thickness at toe. Gradually draw the shoe thinner from toe to heel; cut at A, A, to allow for the frog. The inner edges, B, B, B, B,

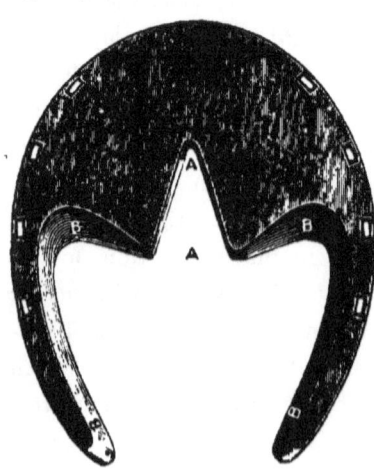

FIG. 129. IMPROVED TOE-WEIGHT SHOE.

A, A, Insertion for the frog. B, B, B, B, Concave on ground surface.

are to be made concave on ground surface, and just in proportion as the quarters and heels are lightened, weight is to be added to the toe. A shoe of this pattern will assist the horse in the extension of his stride more than any other shoe made in the ordinary way and weighing thirty ounces.

I have never failed to make a pacer trot, if shod in this manner.

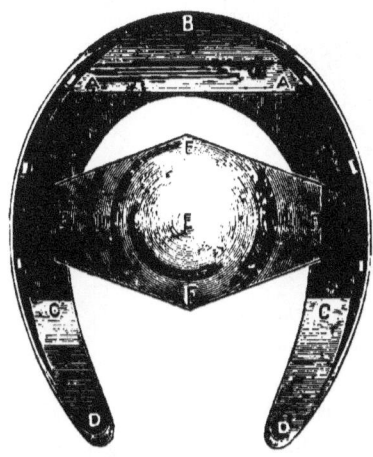

Fig. 130. Front foot turn-table shoe, for anchylosis, laminitis or founder, villitis, and ringbone.

A, A, Bevel of toe to B. C, C, Bevel from quarters to heels, D, D. E, Center of plate, 1½ in. wide by ½ in. thick, welded on center of quarters and tapering each way to F, F, F, F, the center at E being the highest point by ⅜ in. to ½ in., on which the horse must stand squarely poised.

Fig. 130. I use this shoe for founder, laminitis, ringbone, and anchylosis.

For founder, the bottom of the foot should be pared quite thin; and after the shoes are nailed on, stand the horse in soaking-tubs filled with warm water, for half a day, then apply hot poultices to the bottom of the feet.

For laminitis, bear in mind to keep all pressure from the toe, and keep up the hot water treatment same as recommended for founder.

For ring-bone, keep the foot pared as low as can be safely done. Ring-bone causes the horse to walk on his heel, and this shoe will greatly assist in getting over the toe as well as turning around—allowing the foot to roll with an easy sort of rocker motion, and with but little strain on the affected parts. I have never failed to make a horse travel well on hard roads. The horse can turn himself around as easily as though on a turn-table.

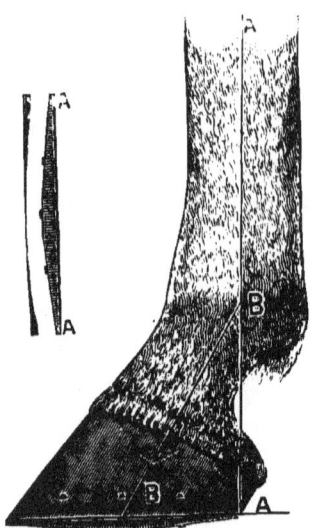

FIG. 131. DOUBLE ROLLER SHOE.
A, A, Sole bearing of the shoe.

Closely connected with the turntable shoe described elsewhere, and in chronic cases of anchylosis of the ankle joint, is the rolling motion ball shoe illustrated in Fig. 131. The practical result is the freedom of motion it permits to all the joints of the foot and limb, to compensate for the stiffness of the joint affected. This freedom of movement takes the strain from the stiff joint and enables the horse to twist and turn to find the necessary relief. The ground surface of the shoe is solid metal, the center being the highest and gradually rolling or curving to the wall on all sides. It is the shoe that the late trainer of trotting horses, Ben Mace, used with great benefit on Sensation in all of his successful trotting races.

Fig. 132. In nearly all cases, horses that cut their ankles in front place the outer side of the foot to the ground first, then the foot drops quickly to the inside heel. As it drops, the ankle is thrown inwardly toward the opposite foot, and in passing the ankle the foot hits against the ankle of the stationary foot. This will be observed if a horse with this habit be walked and his front action be carefully noted.

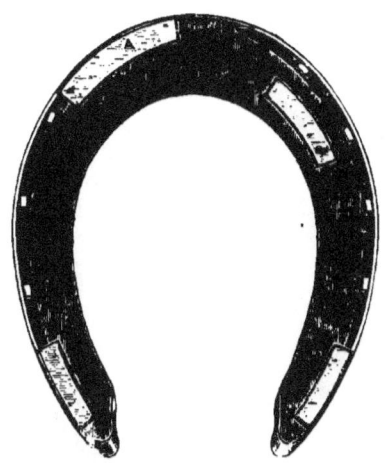

FIG. 132. COMMON SENSE SHOE, TO CORRECT ANY FAULTY MOVEMENTS.
A, Inside toe calkin.

In shoeing a horse of this character, therefore, it should be the custom of the farrier to walk the horse up and down on level ground to ascertain how he steps on his feet. If he steps on the outer toe, first carefully pare the foot level and straight, as directed. After which apply the above shoe, with inside toe calkin. Then set the outside calk, thus shortening the ground surface, and place side heel calkin on the shoe. This will allow a broader tread and prevent twisting of the foot as it leaves the ground. In the forward movement, the foot will turn over the outside toe quickly and carry its ankle out of the reach of the cutting ankle. Place the shoe on the foot, corresponding with the ankle hit, the toe calkin, A, always on the inside.

This shoe can also be used to correct any faulty step, as the ground surface can be increased or diminished without destroying the shape of the foot.

242 SCIENTIFIC HORSESHOEING.

FIG. 133. FRONT FOOT SIDE WEIGHT SHOE, TO PREVENT ANKLE OR KNEE-HITTING.

A, A, Inside rim to be beveled on the ground tread.

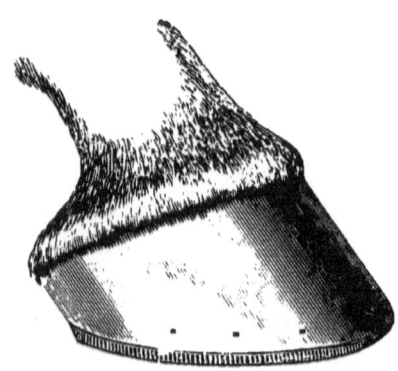

FIG. 134. SIDE VIEW OF FOOT, WITH A ROLLING MOTION SHOE.

Fig. 133. When using shoe, if the horse toes out, place a wide web on the inside; if he toes in, place the wide web on the outside. If he brushes his ankles, shins or knees, when the foot is directly under the axis of the leg, close up the nail holes in the toe on the inside, and place them in back of quarters, as shown in diagram. The inside is to be beveled on ground surface as shown at A, A. If the shoe is properly placed it can not fail to be of great service to the horse, and do all that is claimed for it.

Fig. 134. This style is known as the rolling-motion shoe, and is used to quicken the action of the horse in front, showing the length of the shoe at the heel and the roll at the toe, with the nails driven in the quarters.

Fig. 135. The shoe on the opposite page is intended for draft horses. If the horse pulls from the outside toe, the outside quarter and heel will wire in. To overcome this tendency, I designed this style of shoe. Any ordinary shoe may be used, on which the toe-piece at "A," may be welded, which should extend from the outside rim of the shoe, say from one-half inch to an inch. Stave up the outside heel of the shoe sufficiently to get good broad covering for the narrowed-in heel and quarter. Use the round fullering tool to swedge the shoe wide enough to obtain good bar pressure. Turn up heels and weld a calk on the outside heel, and fit the shoe snugly to the wall up to both sides of the frog.

The effect of the projecting toe-piece is to brace or stay the weak part of the ankle and foot, and in two or three shoeings the foot will become natural in its movements, and fairly returned to its normal state.

Fig. 136. This is another style of shoe for draft horses, as explained by the references under the cut.

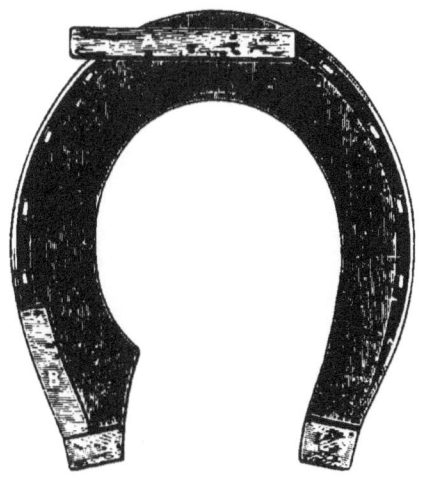

FIG. 135. FRONT FOOT SHOE, FOR DRAFT HORSE.

A, Outside toe calk. B, Side-heel calk.

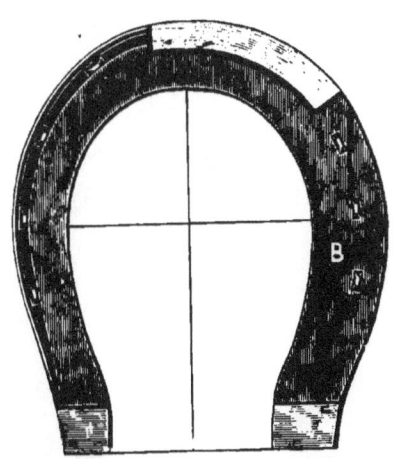

FIG. 136. FRONT FOOT SHOE, FOR DRAFT HORSES THAT WEAR HARD ON THE OUTSIDE TOE AND HEEL.

A, Outside toe calk. B, Indicates the location of a clip to be turned up on the outside rim of the shoe to hold it more firmly to the foot.

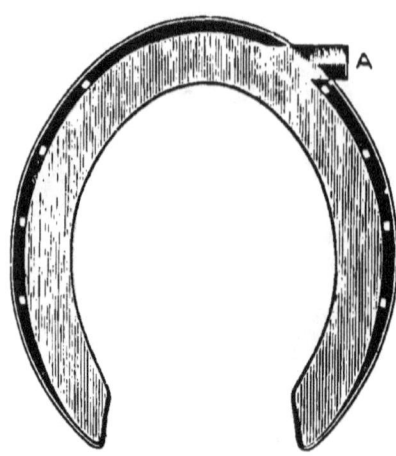

Fig. 137. FRONT FOOT SHOE, TO PREVENT PADDLING, ANKLE AND SHIN CUTTING.

A, Projection at side of toe, to be placed on the outside to remedy paddling, and on the inside to stop ankle or shin cutting.

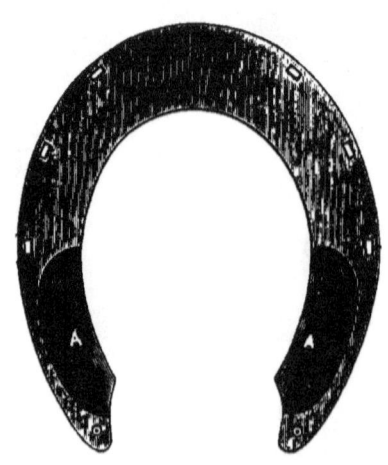

Fig. 138. FRONT FOOT SHOE, DESIGNED FOR BRUISED AND ULCERATED HEELS OR CORNS, SHOWING THE WALL-BEARING A, A.

Fig. 137. When the foot has an outward dip over the inside toe it is called padding. Use shoe, Fig. 137, placing the projecting toe-piece, A, on the inside of shoe. If the foot has an inward dip in leaving the ground, it is liable to hit the ankle or shin on the opposite leg. For such cases place the toe piece on the outside of the shoe as this will make the foot break straight over the toe. The toe-piece to extend one-half to three-quarter inch beyond the rim of shoe.

Fig. 138. This shoe is easily made. Take a shoe stiff at heels and cut it out from wall-bearing surfaces to the inner rims, as shown at A, A. If only one heel is affected, concave on that side, at the place of bruise. Pare the commissures and bars all around the diseased part as thin as the safety of the foot will permit. Then punch holes in each heel with a round punch, large enough to receive a one-sixteenth inch rivet. Then rivet a leather on the shoe, covering the bottom of the foot. Fill the bottom of the foot with fat pork out of the brine, and nail the shoe on lightly.

Soak the feet in warm water for two hours. The pork will draw and assist in removing all soreness from the part. If these instructions are closely followed, I will guarantee that the worst case of corns can be cured in thirty days. They have never failed me.

Fig. 139. This shoe was designed by the late Mr. Dan Mace for the noted mare, Lady Thorne. Great skill was required in adjusting to her feet shoes of suitable weight to balance her action. This was effected by Mr. Mace by fitting her with shoes as shown herewith, weighing 12 ounces each in front, and 14 ounces each behind; after which, her action was as regular as the pendulum of a clock.

This shoe should fit snugly on the foot up to both sides of the frog, the heels inclining outward. The shoe being longer than the foot at the heels, destroys the down action of the flexor perforans, which serves to lessen the quick up action. The length of the heels also gives more ground surface to the foot, which requires a longer interval for the horse to get over his toe. I have used this shoe with satisfactory results.

FIG. 139. HIND FOOT SHOE, TO BALANCE AND SLOW THE ACTION OF THE TROTTING HORSE, DESIGNED BY DAN MACE.

A, A to B, shows gradual bevel of front part of shoe to ground surface. C, C, Heel calkins gradually lowered toward quarters.

Fig. 140. HIND FOOT SHOE, FOR TRACK AND ROAD HORSES.

Well beveled on ground surface, as shown by letters **A, A, A.**

Fig. 141. HIND FOOT SHOE, FOR ANKLE HITTING.

A, Inside toe calk. **B,** Inside heel calk.

Fig. 140. This shoe is made of steel, and is well beveled on the ground surface. If the horse is a long strider, turn up small heel calkins so as to serve as a check to the foot in landing; if a short strider, heel calkins are not required. Fit the shoe the same length as the foot (as shown in this figure), so as not to retard the down action of the flexor perforans. By following the above directions the speed of the horse will not be retarded.

Fig. 141. This hind foot shoe is intended for an extreme case of ankle hitting, where the horse hits with the inside point of the toe. This occurs with horses that stand in a faulty position having their toes turned in. In such cases a toe-calk should be placed on the inside, at the striking point of the foot, A, and also a side heel calkin, B. This will prevent any thing like an inward dip of the foot, as the horse starts, and will cause an outward dip sufficient to carry the foot beyond the ankle of the opposite leg without striking it.

Fig. 142. This shoe, if properly made and adjusted to the foot, will not fail to do all that is claimed for it. Trotting horses vary so greatly that no rule can be laid down applicable to all, beyond the general observation to shoe each horse in accordance with his shape, build and gait, with differently weighted and constructed shoes.

The shoe in question should be used only on horses with their hind legs inclined to stand under the body. On close examination of the hind legs from the hock, we find the two hind feet close together, and the legs open between the hocks; we notice the pasterns from the union of the upper pastern to the lower portion of the cannon-bone leaning outwardly. Dropping plumb lines from the inner and outer sides of the hock to the ground, we observe that both will hang, the one on the outer and the other toward the outer side, and that the weight does not pass through the axis of the leg and foot. In proportion, therefore, as these lines are distant from their normal position, the outer branch of the shoe will require to be turned outwardly to meet the vertical, and as the inside heel calkin of the shoe is lowered, just so much will the upper pastern be brought near the center line through axis of foot and leg.

The inside branch of shoe is to fit snugly to the inner wall of foot. The outside branch of shoe, extending well back of heel and leg, will serve as a brace to support the upper pastern

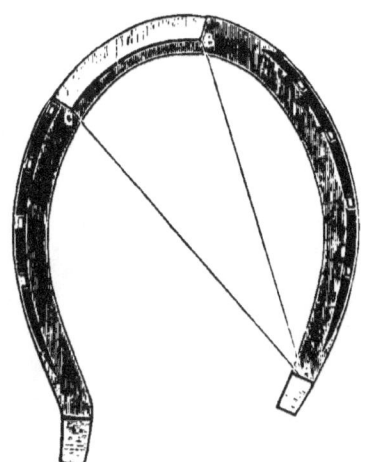

Fig. 142. HIND FOOT SHOE, TO WIDEN THE ACTION.

A, Inside branch. B, Ending of inside toe calk. C, Ending of outside toe calk. Lines A B, A C show circle of toe.

and the shank or cannon-bone. When the horse in motion lands his foot upon the ground, the heel of the foot on the inside being the lowest, the inner muscle will bear the greater strain; and as the foot leaves the ground, the outer muscle will spring back, carrying the foot outwardly over the outside part of the toe, thus widening the tride as the foot leaves the ground, and allowing the hind leg to pass the fore foot and avoid speedy cutting.

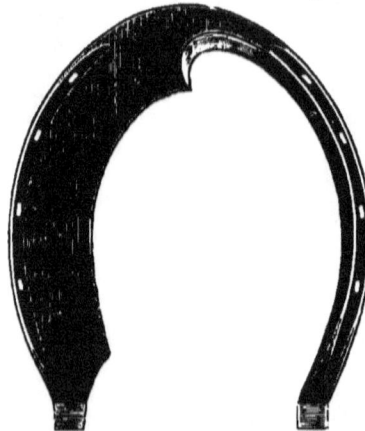

FIG. 143. HIND FOOT SIDE WEIGHT SHOE.

FIG. 144. HIND FOOT SHOE, TO PREVENT ANKLE CUTTING.

A to **B**, Inside heel calkin gradually thinned.

Fig. 143. To equalize the wearing.—This represents a style of shoe adapted for horses that wear heavily on one side of the foot. This often occurs from an inclination of the pastern to lean in or out, thus causing the shoe to wear more on the side to which the foot and pastern leans than on the other. If the wear is greatest on the outside, place the wide branch of the shoe on that side; and, similarly, if greatest wear occurs on the inside have the wide web of the shoe on that side. In this way the wearing of the shoe will be equalized and the foot and limb will be correspondingly benefitted.

Fig.144 represents a pattern of shoe to prevent ankle cutting on horses with long oblique pasterns leaning inward and the toes standing outward. The heel calk shown is to be on the inside branch of the shoe gradually tapering toward the heel from A to B, as this will tend to straighten the pasterns by raising the inside of the foot more directly under the leg. Usually it is found that with pasterns of the kind in question, the inside heel is shorter on the ground tread than the outside, and this shoe will supply the deficiency and thus avoid the striking or cutting of the ankle as stated.

Fig. 145. This shoe is made as light as can be conveniently worn, and extends well back at the heels, the calkins behind being slightly higher than the front toe calks. The shoe, being well rolled on the ground surface, will allow the horse in his forward movement to get over the toe with but little strain on the affected parts.

FIG. 145. HIND FOOT SHOE, DESIGNED FOR CURVE, SPAVIN AND SORE TENDONS.

A, A, Bevel from front of toe calks to outer rim of toe at B.

In shoeing for spavin, the heel calkins are to be made to suit the emergencies. For this trouble, first pare the foot according to directions given in Chapter IV. Place the foot on the floor and pick up the other foot. If the horse does not stand down at the heel, the heel calkins must be left high enough on the shoe to make up for the deficiency; for in a spavined leg the foot always has two motions, first the horse drops on toe, then back on heel. It is therefore plain to see that the heel calkins behind should be higher than in front. Again, if a horse is restless on his hind feet, or stands with one foot twisted in and placed with the heel on the coronet of the other, it is clearly indicative of a spavin of some nature, whether obscure or visible. I have used this style of shoe with admirable success.

FIG. 146. HIND FOOT SHOE, TO PREVENT BRUISING OR CALKING THE CORONET.

A, Front toe calk B, Inside heel calk.

FIG. 147. HIND FOOT SHOE, FOR HORSES REQUIRING TOE AND HEEL CALKINS, TO PREVENT TWISTING EITHER WAY, IN OR OUT.

A, Toe calk, extending over the side, as directed below.

Fig. 146. refers to calking of the coronet. This is often done by horses treading on the coronet with either or both heels of their shoes when standing in the stall, cutting and bruising it, oftentimes producing serious lameness. When toe and heel calkins are required, apply this shoe.

The inside heel calkin is welded lengthwise on the shoe, and set back from the heel fully an inch, the ground surface being beveled to a thin edge. If both heel calkins are placed on the coronet, weld a side heel on each side of the shoe, beveling the heels as before. By so doing, all danger of cutting or bruising the coronet is overcome. If plain shoes are used, bevel the heels on the ground surface and shoe short.

Fig. 147. A great many horses are in the habit of twisting their feet when lifting them from the ground, which makes them liable to interfere and strain their ankles or foot joints. Some will twist their foot in; others will twist it out.

By applying the shoe seen in the diagram, if the twist of the foot is in, let the toe calk, A, project over the outside; if vice versa, change the projection of the toe to the inside. This style of shoe will prevent the twisting of the foot, and enable the horse to get straight over the foot in front.

Fig. 148. This shoe I use for wheeled feet. Taking the weight from front of shoe lessens the weight on the extensor. In the flexing of the foot, changing the weight from quarters to heels, the foot will be easily lifted. The web of shoe will cover the quarters and wired-in heels, gradually restoring them to their natural condition.

I have successfully used this shoe for preventing forging. It will be readily admitted that if weight in the toe of a shoe will lengthen the stride, reversing the weight will shorten the stride.

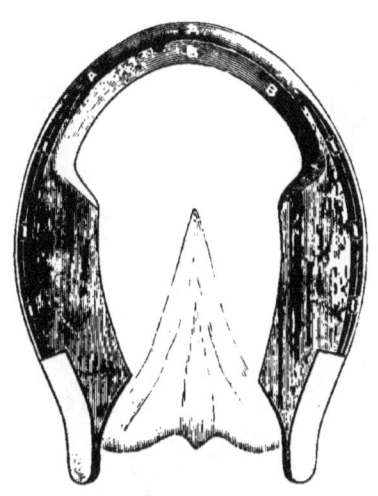

Fig. 148. HIND FOOT SHOE FOR WHEELED FOOT.

A, A, A, Outside bevel at toe.
B, B, B, Inside bevel at toe.

Fig. 149. The shoe on the following page is designed for trotting horses that carry their feet close to the ground. Many horses shod with this shoe have won races which would have been lost to them had they worn the ordinary shoe.

It is plain that just in proportion as the thickness of the shoe increases at the toe, the stride will be lessened; and in proportion as the scoop is deepened, the stride will be lengthened. A great advantage gained in the use of this shoe is, that as the foot lands, it slides forward and hardens the earth. In the act of springing from the ground, the outer rim at letter B,

17

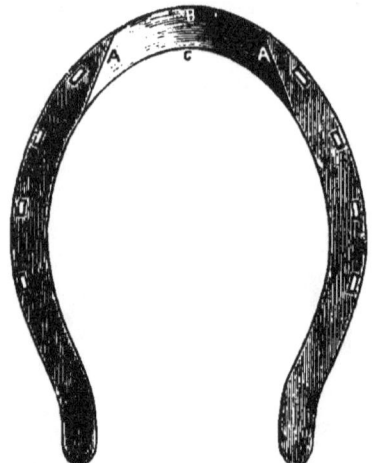

Fig. 149. HIND FOOT SCOOPED-TOE ROLLING MOTION SHOE, TO PREVENT SLIPPING WHEN SPRINGING FROM THE GROUND.

A, A, Width of scoop at toe. B, Scoop to be beveled inwardly to C.

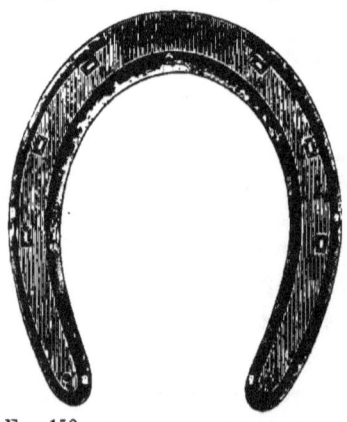

Fig. 150. FRONT FOOT SHOE FOR LINE TROTTERS, TO PREVENT SCALPING.

A, Bevel around inner rim to B, extending around the heels and quarters, B, B, and carried forward to near front toe nails. The heels of shoe also to be beveled at B, B, on ground surface, with the angle of the foot.

the high point gives a solid catch; and it is evident, therefore, that the advantage gained in landing is not lost in springing off the ground. This backward and forward friction is very tiresome to the horse, and may be compared to the resistance experienced by the human being running over sand and snow.

This shoe is easily made by laying the center of the toe on the horn of the anvil with face downward and hammering the scoop out, letting the heel of shoe project well beyond the break of heel. It affords great bracing or stay to the back sinews.

This shoe is designed for use upon horses with long pasterns. Short upright pasterns can be shod shorter, as there is less strain on back tendons. If the back sinews are sore, put on heel calkins.

Fig. 150. This is a pattern of front foot shoe for line trotters. Horses of this class, when up to speed, carry their hind limbs in line with the fore, and great care is required in shoeing them lest they scalp the hind shin or coronet as it passes under the front foot. The thinner the front shoes are

SPECIFIC AND REMEDIAL SHOEING.

the less liability there will be to injury in this way. The shoe must also be beveled at the heels on the ground surface with the angle of the hoof, as indicated in diagram 150, and as explained with Fig. 28. The weight of the shoes must be determined by the driver, as some horses require more weight than other in order to balance their action.

Fig. 151 represents a bar shoe for the same general purpose as described for Fig. 150; but as some horses are more tender in the heels than others, this style of bar shoe may be substituted for the open shoe.

Fig. 152 indicates the pattern of shoe recommended to prevent side or back slipping on hard tracks. Whatever is gained by a forward slide is not lost, for the purchase obtained by the use of this style of rasp-cut shoe will enable the horse to land and spring with better confidence, speed and endurance than by any other form. This shoe should be made of steel and after the teeth are cut, they are to be tempered in oil.

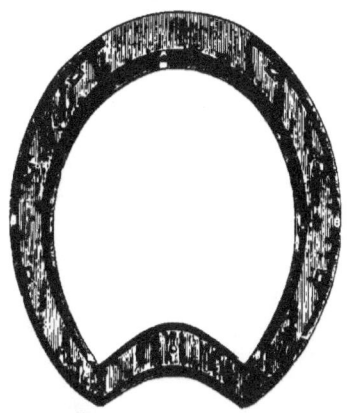

FIG. 151. FRONT FOOT BAR SHOE, TO BE USED WHEN REQUIRED ON LINE TROTTERS.

A to B, Bevel around inner and outer rim same as in Fig. 117. The dot shown in center of bar is rivet hole for leather when used under the shoe.

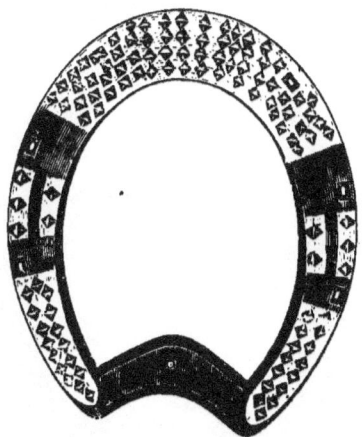

FIG. 152. FRONT FOOT RASP CUT BAR SHOE, TO PREVENT SLIPPING ON HARD TRACKS.

The dot in center of bar is rivet hole to secure leather when required.

254   SCIENTIFIC HORSESHOEING.

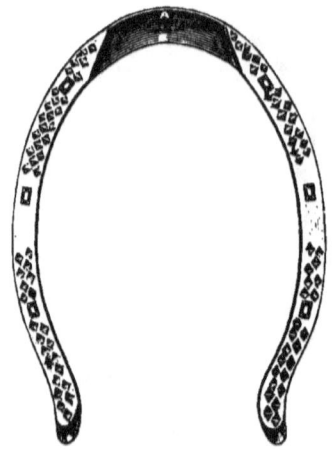

FIG. 153. HIND FOOT RASP CUT GRAB SHOE, WITH DEEP SCOOP AT TOE.

Scoop from **A** to **B**, as shown, the outer rim at **A** to be flush with face of shoe.

FIG. 154. FRONT FOOT RAISED SPLIT BAR SHOE, FOR CONTRACTION, SORE TENDONS, SIDE BONES, CORNS, BRUISED HEELS, ETC.

Fig. 153 shows a hind foot, rasp-cut grab shoe, to prevent slipping on hard tracks, as explained with Fig. 152. The extra scoop at front of toe will give an additional purchase and firm ground hold to the foot when rising.

Fig. 154. Front foot raised split-bar steel shoe, for contracted hoofs, sore tendons, side bones, corns, bruised heels, etc. This shoe is to be made of steel in order that the bar may spring under the weight of the horse.

Make it in the same way as other bar shoes, and after the shoe is shaped and fitted cut the bar in center at A, A, then commence at B, B, to raise the bar say $\frac{1}{4}$ to $\frac{1}{2}$ inch, keeping both faces flat. In cases where leather is to be used to obtain frog pressure, fit the leather to cavity in bar under the shoe, punch holes in center of bar and at B, B, as shown by dots, for reception of rivets, then bevel around the toe of shoe on ground tread as shown.

With the foot properly leveled and balanced, as per

SPECIFIC AND REMEDIAL SHOEING.

Fig. 23, this shoe will be found very effective for use in any of the cases mentioned.

Fig. 155. Front foot scooped toe or grab shoe, with side heel calks for trotting and pacing horses inclined to twist or slip in landing or rising.

It is a waste of power and loss of motion for horses to twist or turn in any way out of a direct forward line, and by use of the scooped-toe in this shoe we have an excellent corrective for this tendency, as well as a valuable aid in speed getting.

Fig. 156 is a new form of double rolling motion bar shoe, designed to quicken the action in front, and thus prevent stumbling, forging and speedy cutting. By the increased knee action which this shoe gives it will also relieve soreness of tendons and feet. When used for sore tendons, after the foot is properly leveled, build up the heels to take off all possible pressure from the back of the leg, by inserting a thick piece of sole leather under the shoe to cover the bottom of foot, gradually thinning the leather from

FIG. 155. FRONT FOOT BAR SCOOPED-TOE GRAB SHOE.
To prevent slipping, scoop the toe from **A** to **B**, around to **C, C**. **D, D,** Side heel calks. Dot in center of bar, rivet hole for leather when required.

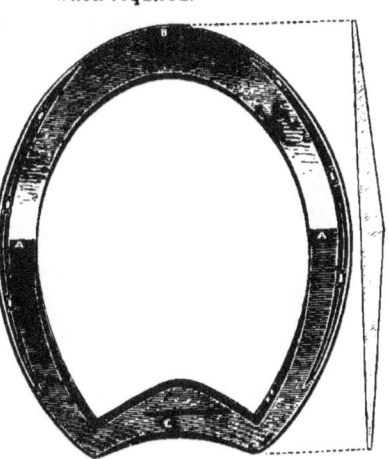

FIG. 156. FRONT FOOT CENTER BEARING, DOUBLE ROLLING MOTION BAR SHOE, TO QUICKEN THE FRONT ACTION, PREVENT SPEEDY CUTTING, FORGING, STUMBLING, ETC.

A, A, High center point in shoe, gradually beveled forward to **B,** at toe, and back to **C,** at heel bar. **D,** Side view of shoe, representing the foot-bearing face by straight line, and the ground face by the easy bevels each way from center. The thickness of center is to be regulated to suit the necessities of the case.

heel to toe. Then in case the weight is to be reduced, after the shoe is nailed on, the leather can be cut out around the inside of shoe.

Fig. 157. Hind foot scooped toe or grab shoe, to prevent speedy cutting. This is a great shoe for speedy, close gaited horses. The scoop at toe secures the foothold and prevents slipping backward when leaving the ground, while the inner and outer bevels on shoe prevent the cutting or bruising of front quarters when in rapid motion. This shoe is to be made thicker at the toe and gradually beveled thinner to the heels.

FIG. 157. HIND FOOT SCOOPED TOE GRAB SHOE, TO PREVENT SPEEDY CUTTING.

Scoop at toe to be deepened inward from **A** to **B**. **C, D,** Bevels around inner and outer rims of branches.

FIG. 158. FRONT FOOT SCOOPED GRAB TOE BAR SHOE, TO PREVENT SPEED HORSES SLIPPING ON SOFT TRACKS.

A, Outer rim of toe to be of same height on ground tread as the four calkins; the scoop to bevel in to **B,** which is thinned down a little below the web of the shoe, and extends to sides, **C, C.** Side heel and quarter calkins, **D, D, D, D,** wedge or ∧ shaped, with points upward. These calkins are to be of same height as the grab toe from **A** to **C, C.**

Fig. 158. With this style of shoe made as directed by references underneath the cut, the foot can not slip either to the rear or sides, and by being easily lifted from muddy tracks with little friction, the horse grows surer footed and less leg weary or jaded than would otherwise be the case with the ordinary toe and heel calked shoe.

Fig. 159. Any ordinary shoe may be adapted to this form by cutting off both of the branches to the required length, then by using a bar, say ⅜ in. thick by ⅝ in. wide, long enough to extend across the quarters, and welding the tongue piece on bar to reach back and cover the frog between the heels, after which weld to the shoe and put on calks at toe, sides and heel of equal height, as shown at A, B, B, and C. The cleft of frog is marked at D, and the dressed wall at E, E. In almost all cases of this kind pressure is to be kept off the frog, and

FIG. 159. FRONT FOOT THREE-QUARTER SHOE, FOR CORNS, BRUISED HEELS, SIDE BONES, QUARTER CRACKS, ETC.

A, B, B, C, C, Toe quarters and heel calks. D, Cleft of frog. E, E, Bruised heels. F, F, Lower margin of level wall.

this can easily be done by bending the broad tongue piece away from the foot. This shoe may, if desired, also be made plain, that is, without calks, and in either form will be found of valuable service if applied for the purposes intended with foot prepared, as per Fig. 23.

Fig. 160 (next page). A horse thus affected endeavors to remove the weight from the back of his foot by walking on his toe. This shoe can be used equally well for horses and mules—the heel calks to be high enough in each instance to level the heel with the ground, then as the weight can be borne on the heels, the calks will gradually be worn down and give indications in this way of returning soundness. The toe-piece or front clip is to be turned up at same angle as the front of hoof and project forward to suit the case in hand, as the higher the animal stands on his toe, the longer and higher the spur should be, varying from one to one and one-half inches. With proper attention to these points and to leveling the foot, as per Fig. 23, this shoe can be applied with success.

FIG. 160. SIDE VIEW OF HOOF SHOD FOR RELIEF OF SPRAINED AND CONTRACTED TENDONS, WOUNDS IN THE FOOT, ETC.
(For plan of shoe, see Fig. 162.)

A, Coronary cavity. **B,** Outer wall. **C,** Side of shoe. **D,** Toe piece turned up. **E,** Heel calk.

Fig. 161. The same method of preparing the foot as described for the preceding figure, is applicable to all horses or mules inclined to walk on their toes.

FIG. 161. SIDE VIEW OF ANOTHER STYLE OF SHOE SIMILAR TO FIG. 160.
(For plan of shoe, see Fig. 163.)

SPECIFIC AND REMEDIAL SHOEING.

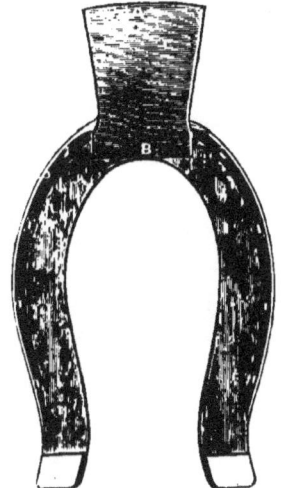

FIG. 162. GROUND SURFACE OF MULE SHOE SHOWN IN SIDE VIEW OF HOOF, FIG. 160.

A, B, Projecting toe piece.

FIG. 164. WALL-BEARING SURFACE OF SHOE SHOWN IN FIGS. 161 AND 163.

From these figures (160 to 164) a correct idea may be obtained for making and applying the shoes for the purpose named.

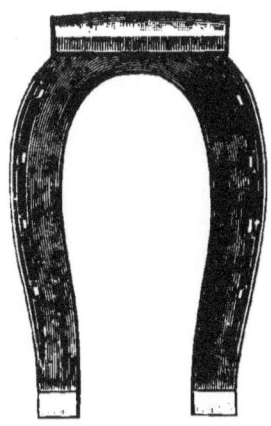

FIG. 163. GROUND TREAD OF SHOE SHOWN IN SIDE VIEW OF HOOF, FIG. 161.

Fig. 165. Ground surface of right hind foot spreading shoe, to prevent cross-firing.
A, Heel calk to be turned up at end of long outside branch. B, B, B, Ground surface of shoe, the dotted line showing its projection over the outside of foot.

Fig. 166. Wall-bearing surface of same shoe as shown in Fig. 132.
A, A, Bevel on outside rim of shoe, from wall bearing to ground tread. C, C, C, Flat wall bearing.

Fig. 165. Cross-firing is caused by unbalanced feet and improperly constructed shoes. Almost all speed horses require the sharp outside edge of their front shoes to be taken off on the ground surface to prevent scalping. By examining and comparing the stride of the cross-firing foot, it will be found that the stride of that member is shorter than its fellow by four to six inches, causing an occasional hitch or hop in the gait. In cases of this kind place a cross-firing shoe like Fig. 165 on the short striding foot, to weigh four to six ounces heavier than the one on the opposite foot. Where the horse cross-fires with both hind feet have them shod with shoes of equal weight. By lowering the inside toe and raising the outside heel on the long outside branch of the shoe, the feet will be made to stand wider apart on the ground and will be thus carried outward from the body, passing the front feet without hitting or bruising the inside ankles or shins. The success of this style of shoe is greatly dependent on the good judgment of the shoer.

Fig. 167 (on opposite page). In bad cases of dragging, the ends of toe calk should project over the front rim of shoe one half to one inch, the projection being greater in proportion with the increase of the trouble. Both ends of the calk should extend equally to a straight line across the front. The clip should be turned up on same angle with the front of the hoof.

If the foot is leveled, as directed with Fig. 23, this shoe will prevent the worst form of dragging, as when in motion the weight passes over the projecting toe calks the foot will be lifted with a quick upward movement. If the front toe of hoof is worn blunt by dragging, the line of wall must be carried down to the ground tread by making the shoe extend forward to meet the angle of the wall, and thus secure the full length of ground tread. This same style of shoe will in many cases stop forging or clicking.

Fig. 168. Hind foot shoe to prevent ankle hitting. In order to determine how this shoe is to be worn the horse should be seen both in motion and at rest. If the foot twists in as the

FIG. 167. HIND FOOT SHOE, TO PREVENT DRAGGING AND FORGING.

A, Reversed bent toe calk from inner center of web, extending over each side of toe rim. **B,** Center of clip, to be turned up in front between the projecting prongs of calk.

FIG. 168. HIND FOOT SHOE, TO PREVENT ANKLE HITTING.

A, Toe calk on outside rim of shoe. **B,** Extension of outside branch with heel calk at end. **C,** Inside branch, with heel beveled from ground tread in line with hoof.

heel leaves the ground he will hit back of inside heel nail. I have never known a horse that twisted his heels out ever to cut or hit his ankles. A shoe made as per Fig. 168 will turn the foot outward from the ankle and thus avoid any interference. The outside heel calk at B should be as high as the case may require, say from $\frac{3}{8}$ to $\frac{1}{2}$ inch. The inside branch to be gradually thinned down from last nail hole to end at C, and the shoe to be fitted snug to the foot around that side.

Use and Abuse of Tips.—Tips should not be used indiscriminately, the build and construction of a horse's legs and pasterns must be duly considered; for instance, tips will be injurious if horse has long sloping pasterns whereby the line of weight inclines forward out of the vertical. On the other hand, short upright pasterns where legs are perpendicular or inclined back under the body, have feet at such an angle (say 55°) for the successful use of tips. Such horses wear the toes of shoes more than the heels, and a toe-tip is all that is needed, therefore, to protect the hoof from undue wear. A great majority of horses, however, are adapted to the use of tips, and I think they would be better off from such use on the front feet than otherwise. By wearing tips the front feet would escape corns, bruised heels, quarter-cracks, contraction, thrush, sore tendons, leg weariness, interference or cutting and such like ills to which horseflesh is heir—more from clumsy, misfitting shoes, than from all other causes combined. In some sections of the country too, where, in wet weather, the soil is sticky, heavy clay, horses are apt to pick up "balls," which pack and wedge up in the foot under full shoes and becoming dry and hard, soon causes lameness, whereas the use of tips would avoid such results. When used, narrow tips are far preferable to wide ones, as it is well known that horses do not wear out from overwork so much as from mismanagement and overweighting of the feet. Good judgment is required in applying tips: first, examine the formation of wall and sole; if the sole is cup-form or well arched, this style of foot can be most successfully tipped. The foot should not be pared off at toe and heels so low for tips as for full shoes, as the tips have to be let in the wall flush with the ground tread. In this way the angle of foot is in no wise changed and the wear will be even all over. From two to three nails on each side of tips will suffice to hold them on firmly. Punch for a low, short, thick hold inclining the nail outwardly to avoid cramping the foot. Tips can be used to advantage on colts for first shoeings in breaking them, also on dirt roads and the natural exercise of frog pressure will develop the foot into a strong and healthy organ. The tips are to be beveled off on the outer edge of the web, so as to follow the angle of the foot.

Sharpening, or Winter Shoeing.—In many instances, winter shoeing presents fresh difficulties, for the shoes have then to do a double duty—to secure the foot-hold as well as to protect the foot. Toe and heel calkins are almost always employed as best suiting the requirements of each case. In all cases, however, these should be short and sharp, as then the foot will be kept nearer the ground, at the same time they will answer every purpose for a firm catch upon the hard or slippery ice, and the horse will be less liable to rock sidewise, thus avoiding injury or joint lameness. For ordinary workhorses, toe and heel calkins are all that are required; and, as a rule, it is better to sharpen the outside heel calk. lengthwise, or from front to back, as by so doing side slips will be avoided and strains on the joints and tendons be prevented. For speed horses, side heel calks are better for the front shoes than mere end calks, as the horse is not so apt to strike and pull off the front shoes with his hind feet when at speed; also, the feet will not slip in or out so easily this way. The hind feet can in most cases be shod with ordinary turned up heels, as this will assist in preventing the "calking" of one hind foot by the other. Side heel calks ought to be placed on the inside branch of the shoe, near the heel, as this will lessen the danger of wounding the opposite member.

All about Calks.—It should, however, never be lost sight of that the shorter, sharper and smaller the calkins are, so long as they answer the purpose for which they are intended, so much the better for the foot that wears them. High calkins, while they confer no firmer foothold, may easily become a source of injury, both to the foot itself and the limb at large. It is only from that portion of the catch which enters the ground surface that the horse derives any benefit in the shape of foothold; and it must be apparent to every one that long calkins have no advantages in this respect over moderately short ones on hard, uneven ground, while they present many other disadvantages, on which I have already laid particular stress in Chaps. IV and VI.

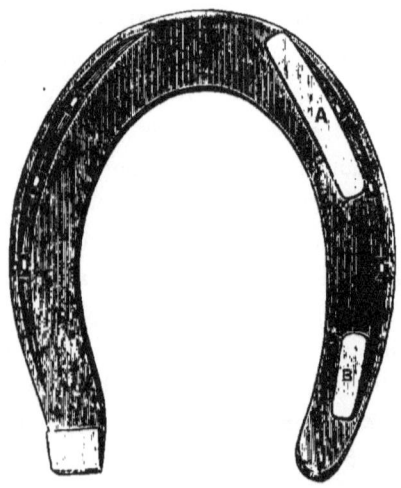

Bracing or Crutch Shoes.—Fig. 169 is a style of shoe for the right front foot, used to brace up the weak ankle or pastern that leans in, so as to prevent the horse from hitting and bruising the inside of the front leg. I have used this shoe with the most satisfactory results.

FIG. 169. RIGHT FRONT SHOE.
A, Toe and heel calkins, inside shoe.

Fig. 170 is intended for the left front foot, when the pastern leans out. As the left foot passes over the outside toe it takes an inward sweep, thus hitting and bruising the opposite leg. The projection of the toe calkin, A, beyond the outer edge of the shoe, must suit the case in hand. I have known of a toe calkin in such instance to project at least an inch. The outside heel calkin, set as at C, will materially support the outside pastern.

FIG. 170. LEFT FRONT SHOE.

A, Toe calkin. B, Inside heel calkin. C, Outside heel calkin.

FIG. 171. SPLIT BAR SHOE.

A, Outside heel calkin. B, B, Bevel around toe. C, Split bar. D, Inside heel calkin.

The use of this shoe will be found of practical benefit when outside quarters are wired under and badly contracted. Such defects cause the quarters to wear excessively on the outside. The outside heel calkin and the inside heel calkin should be set as at A and D, respectively, thus increasing the full ground tread, while lessening the inside. Beveling around the toe, B, B, according to the necessities of the case in hand, allows the foot to break over the toe more easily and prevents stumbling. Allowing the bar to remain open, as at C, gives the heels greater freedom to expand and contract at each footfall. Placing the calkins as shown in diagram tends to equalize the pressure through cleft of frog and center of leg, thus strengthening the weak joints. If the foot is pared and the shoe made and fitted according to instructions, a decided improvement both in the foot and its action will result in straightforward movement.

FIG. 172. BROAD BAR BEVELED SHOE.
B, B, Bevel—broadest at toe, lessening toward the heel.

The shoe illustrated in Fig. 172 gives through the broad, wide bar a strong frog pressure for weak heels and quarters. It is well concaved on sole bearing surface, being of greatest bevel at the toe and lessening toward the heels. Weak feet always obtain the best of protection from a stiff, wide-webbed shoe, and this style can be successfully used for quarter cracks, sore tendons and flat feet.

FIG. 173. LEFT HIND SHOE.
A, Calkin.

This form of shoe (Fig. 173) will serve as a crutch to support weak pastern

SPECIFIC AND REMEDIAL SHOEING. 267

joints—the cause of a horse's cutting defect. Before shoeing, observe both from the front and rear how much the ankle leans in, and place the side calkin as shown in diagram, high enough to straighten the pastern under the foot and leg, bearing in mind always that the main object is to strengthen the weak parts of the pastern joints.

The figure herewith (Fig. 174) represents a pattern of a bracing shoe to correct cutting inside point of toe, and is one of the most effective of the bracing shoes. Place calkin at inside of toe, as at A, to serve as a brace; another at outside, as B, and a side heel calkin on the outside branch. The effect of this shoe will be to cause the foot to drop outward and allow the opposite foot to pass the ankle without hitting or bruising it.

FIG. 174. SHOE TO CORRECT CUTTING INSIDE POINT OF TOE.

The shoe following (Fig. 175) is designed to prevent ankle hitting. The foot in its motion strikes the opposite hind ankle at B. Weld side heel calkin as at B. Gradually thin down heel of shoe from inside heel calkin to inside branch of heel. Notice the forward movement of the foot, as it leaves the ground. Place a toe calkin as at A, allowing it to project beyond the outside of the shoe from one-half to three-quarters of an inch. Turn heel calkin on at outside branch of shoe, and thus shaped it will prevent an inward dip as the foot leaves the ground, thus obviating the ankle bruising.

18

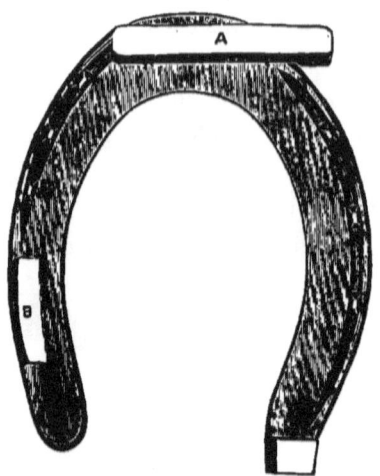

Fig. 175. SHOE TO PREVENT ANKLE HITTING.
A, Projecting toe calkin. B, Side heel calkin.

Fig. 176 is another model of hind shoe to prevent ankle hitting. If the toe of the foot tilts in, place an inside toe calkin as at A, and a side heel calkin as at B. Then turn a heel on the outside branch of the shoe. Always endeavor by studying the action to locate the cause of ankle hitting, as the same style of shoe that will stop one horse will not always stop another. I have used all the foregoing styles of shoes with the best results on different horses.

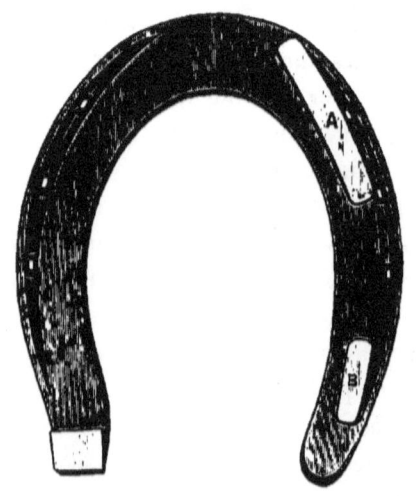

Fig. 176. SHOE TO PREVENT ANKLE HITTING.
A, B, Inside toe and heel calkins.

SPECIFIC AND REMEDIAL SHOEING.

A, Coffin bone.
B, Navicular bone.
C, Lower pastern bone.
D, Upper pastern bone.
E, Cannon bone.
F, Velvety tissue, or sensitive sole.
G, Horny wall.
H, Horny sole.
I, Horny frog.
K, Plantar cushion, or sensitive sole.
L, Horny laminæ.
M, Sensitive laminæ.
N, Front extensor tendon.
O, Perforatus (superficial flexor.
P, Perforans (deep flexor of the foot, inserted under the coffin bone.
R, Suspensory ligament of the fetlock.
S, Sesamoid bone (dotted line).
T, Branch of perforatus tendon attached to lower pastern bone.
U, line of deflection from V, caused by knuckling.

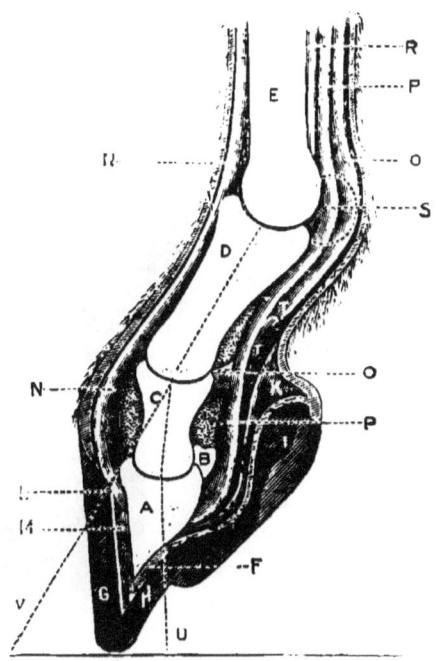

FIG. 177. SECTIONAL VIEW OF FOOT.

Knuckling Shoes.—Fig. 177 is a sectional view of foot, lower and upper pastern bones, and end of cannon or shank bone. The line from C to V shows the natural direction of the foot, when the coffin bone is in a healthy, normal condition; C to U shows the deflection from the natural course in a bad case of knuckling. The difference may be readily seen by comparing Fig. 177 with Fig. 178, after the shoe (Fig. 179; and Fig. 180, showing section of ground tread) is nailed to the foot. This shoe (Figs. 179 and 179A) is easily made by welding toe calk in front of shoe, as shown (Fig. 179A). The height of the toe calk should vary according to the case in hand. The heels of shoe should be beveled on the ground tread, as shown at B, B, Fig. 179; and Fig. 179A shows a side view of the front toe calkin on ground tread, and the point, C, at which to commence to bend the front part of shoe down from the toe. Fig. 178 shows the position of the pasterns and foot after it has been dressed and the shoe nailed to it.

I have been very successful in using this style of shoe in extreme cases of knuckling, espe-

Fig. 178.

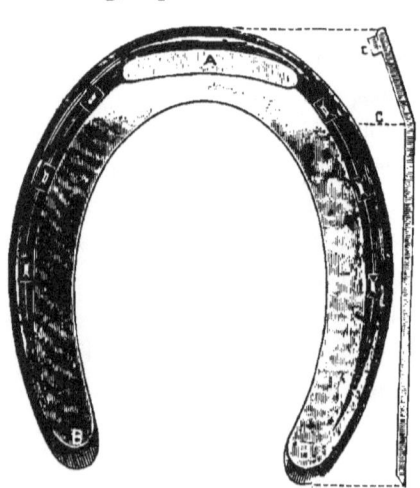

Figs. 179 and 179a.

cially in colts of various ages, from six months to two years. Even aged horses can be thus benefited. This explanation should be sufficient, as the cuts speak for themselves. By using the shoe as here illustrated, the pastern can be quickly straightened and the ground tread of foot be forced to its natural position. The tendons, ligaments and bones

SPECIFIC AND REMEDIAL SHOEING.   271

of a colt are naturally tender, and that is the time for this treatment for knuckling; for if the colt be allowed to run until it has matured into a full-grown horse, not only may it be impossible to effect a permanent cure, but after the members become contracted it is somewhat doubtful if any cure at all can be effected.

This invaluable form of front shoe I designed to remedy either an inner or outer contraction of the quarter. The ground tread is to be changed as shown at A. Punch the nail holes inclining outwardly. By doing this the nails open the foot to some extent, and have a tendency to unlock the bound quarter and give almost instant relief.

FIG. 180.   GROUND TREAD.
A, Showing change of ground tread.

Fig. 181 illustrates the sole, or wall bearing concave on sound natural quarters, as shown at A, and bevel out as shown at B, the bevel being outwardly from the inner web of the shoe to the outer margin. As the weight of the horse falls on the shoe, it will have a tendency to press the contracted quarters outwardly at every footfall and give relief to the affected parts.

FIG. 181.   SOLE BEARING.

This shoe (Fig. 182) I have always used, with the best results, in preventing toe dragging, and in many cases to stop forging. Always examine the pastern before shoeing. If it stands back, place a side heel calkin on the shoe, to raise it up on a line with the front part of the foot, which is the correct position at rest. This will cause the joints of the pastern to work smoothly and properly. To make this shoe, take an old rasp, weld on the front toe of shoe and

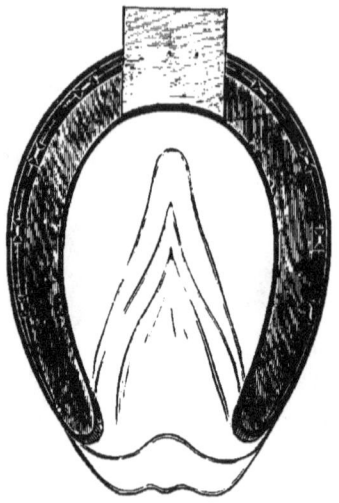

FIG. 182. SHOE TO PREVENT TOE DRAGGING.

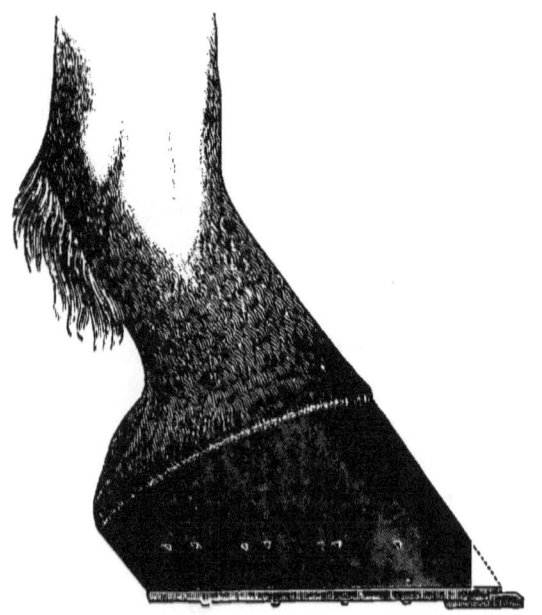

FIG. 183. SHOE TO PREVENT TOE DRAGGING—SIDE VIEW.

cut off the length to that extent which the exigencies of each case require. This projecting toe calkin should be extended, on experimental trial, till the horse no longer strikes and wears away the hind hoof at the toe, by interference with the diagonally opposite front shoe.

Fig. 183 shows the shoe, known as the shoe to prevent toe dragging, nailed to the foot, the extension of the shoe beyond the toe, on a line with the front pastern, and front wall of foot to ground tread. The dotted line shows where the front wall of foot ought to come. Making the shoe to extend over, it takes the foot longer to get over the toe and retards the action behind; allowing the front foot to get out of the way of the hind foot, will thus prevent forging. I have always found this shoe to prevent toe dragging and forging very useful.

This half bar shoe (Fig. 184) I use for contraction in the outside heel and quarters, in case the frog is pushed to one side. I place the bar of the shoe so as to rest lightly on one-half of the frog—that is, on the side of the foot wiring under. I simply fit the shoe neatly and firmly to the foot. A, A, and B, B, represent side toe and heel calkins. Then bevel the toe in front as shown in diagram. This will allow the horse to roll over the toe more easily in the forward movement. Bevel the shoe as shown in Fig. 181, on the wall bearing, for contracted and wired in quarters. This style of shoe serves as a support to assist nature in restoring the foot to its normal condition.

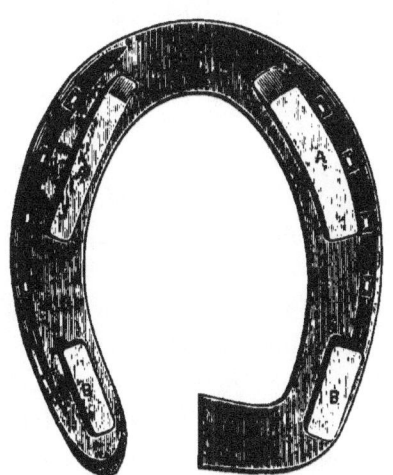

FIG. 184. HALF BAR SHOE.

A, A, Side toe calkins. B, B, Side heel calkins.

Hitching, its Causes and Cure.—Hitching and hopping are defects so common that I wish to say a word about them, inasmuch as I have been requested to do so; and while I know that no two individuals agree upon this important matter, I am glad to put forward my theory, if only to draw out others. The defect is mostly confined to the hind legs; but there are some instances—notably that of the famous trotting mare, Lida Bassett—of hitching in the front leg. As she was one of the fastest in her day, the example will be a good one. When she was up to her speed, the stride of her left front foot was some four inches longer than that of her right front foot. It was some time before the trainer knew the cause or her hitching.

When I first began to study up the causes of this defect, I assigned it to several, and later experience has borne me out. First, the feet may be unbalanced, or improperly weighted in front; second, illy made and poorly fitted shoes in front may cause the horse to scalp her coronet on the inside pastern; third, drawing too much weight when up to speed may be a source of the trouble; fourth, too long drives when out of condition may cause hitching; fifth, being overdriven when short of work; and sixth, hitching may spring from curb, ring-bone, or spavin.

It may, however, be maintained that a most frequent cause of hitching is unbalanced or improperly weighted feet. These cause a horse to lose his natural stride. For instance, taking off front shoes of fifteen or eighteen ounces, to which weights the horse has become accustomed, and substituting shoes of less weight, will make a vast difference. But whatever may be the cause of hitching behind, it will always be found by measuring the stride of the hitching leg and foot, that it is from four to seven inches shorter than the other. Curb, ring-bone and spavin often cause hitching and hopping in the leg affected with any of these disorders. An excellent method of overcoming the defect from these sources is to shoe the hitching leg with a hind-foot shoe to weigh from five to seven ounces more than the other hind-foot shoe. This added weight will carry the foot and leg longer in the stride. It will also be found, whichever hind leg hitches, the stride of the opposite front foot will be shorter. For instance, if the hitching takes place in the left hind leg, from any cause, the front right leg will have a shorter stride. By placing upon the right front foot a shoe weighing three or four ounces more than the left front foot, the former will be lengthened in its stride.

Having ascertained the uneven gait and taken its measurement, the next thing is to set about the treatment. I found Lida Bassett, for instance, hitching with her right front foot. I welded a spur to the toe of the shoe, turned up with the front angle of the foot, and slipped over it a small brass weight of three ounces. Thereupon her front strides became equal and her movement was as smooth and uniform as the pendulum of a clock. A great many speed horses act badly when up to speed, for the reason that their strides in front are not equal in length at each footfall. In such a case, I shoe the front feet with the heavier shoe on the hitching foot, the weight determined by the circumstances.

In general, to cure a horse of hitching, the farrier should first learn the weights in front and behind the horse is accustomed to when he trots squarely. Next find out at what gait he begins hitching. Notice all the peculiarities and even question the driver. But the most important is to see that the feet are properly balanced and under the body. Then, having studied the horse and learned all his defects and peculiarities, shoe him to correct them all according to the instructions heretofore given. It may become a matter of more or less experiment, but practical experience and good judgment are the handmaids of success in scientific farriery. Cultivate them.

Shoeing for Relief and Ease from Ringbone.—For the benefit of the reader, I insert here a suggestion as to some shoes which can be used for relief and ease from ringbone. In each case the shoes are to be made to assist him in the work he has to perform. The general shoe is the one described upon page 140, Fig. 35. When the subject is a general business horse, the shoe described upon page 213, Fig. 101; when speed or road horses are concerned, page 232, Fig. 121.

If scoop be taken out of shoe on the ground tread, as far around as the two front nails at the toe (see Fig. 121, page 232), the jar at each footfall will be lessened around the affected parts. An easy method of lessening the concussion at each footfall is to make an opening between the shoe and front wall of foot large enough to slip in a No. 9 horseshoe nail. This relieves the affected parts at each footfall, at the apex of the os pedis.

CHAPTER X.

A TABLEAU OF HORSESHOES,

OLD AND NEW STYLES PICTURED AND COMPARED.

To carry out the subject of this book still further and to show at a glance the progress that has been made in the whole scheme and staple of horseshoeing within our generation, covering a period of thirty-five years, a regular progressive series of different designs of shoes is here introduced in order to exhibit as clearly as possible the passing stages of advancement in the art by the several styles of shoes in use at various times for various purposes until they were gradually relegated or superseded by more modern patterns of ingenious workmanship and skill, which accomplish wonders in balancing the action and leveling the gait of horses, or are admirably effective in remedying or curing many of the faulty movements and morbid affections of the feet and legs. "Scientific horseshoeing," with all that the term implies, is thus seen to be the outcome of many previous years of experimental tests before it came to "the parting of the ways" which led it from speculative regions to the place which it now occupies—as an art built on scientific principles. The shoes and tools grouped in the cases—Figs. 186 to 190—formed part of my display at the World's Fair, at Chicago, 1893, and were awarded the First Premium, Medals and Diploma.

In addition to the shoes shown in these cases, a large number of still more recent patterns are illustrated in the preceding pages of this book—from designs which I have made since the close of the World's Fair.

278 SCIENTIFIC HORSESHOEING.

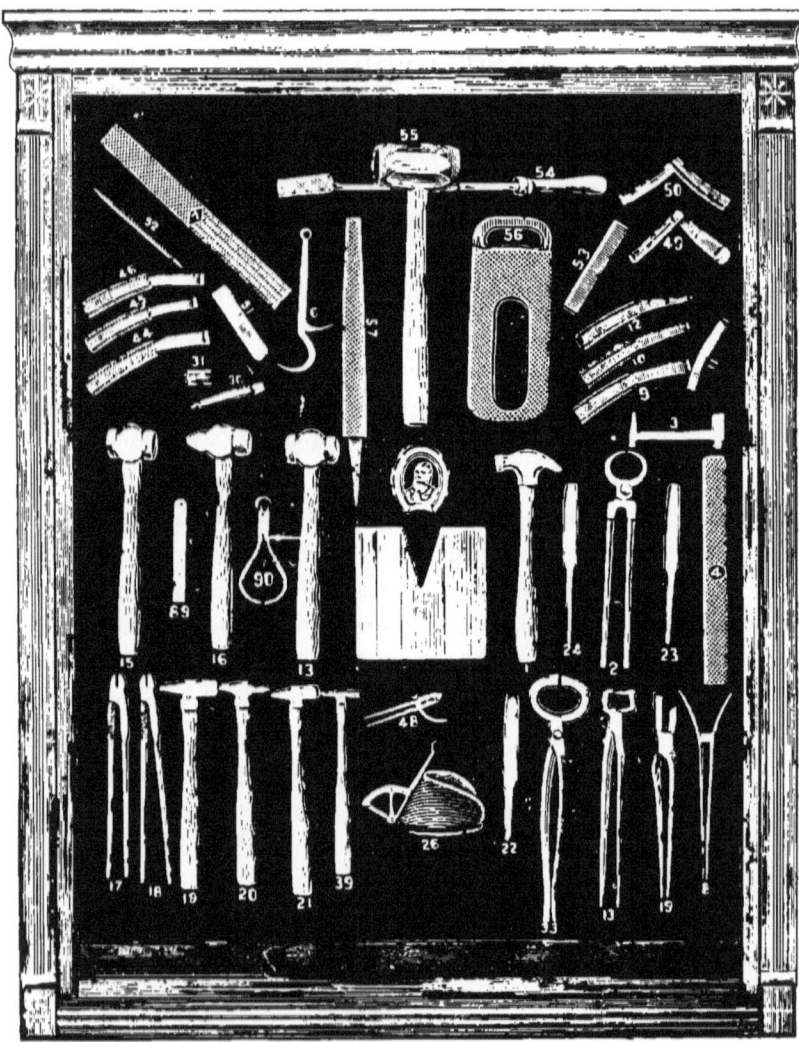

Fig. 186. Case No. 1.
Improved Tools for Scientific Horseshoeing.

FIG. 186. CASE NO. 1.

In tools, as in everything else, the best is the cheapest, and this case represents the best products of ingenuity and mechanical skill of the various articles made to serve the most useful purposes of experts in farriery. There are many shoeing smiths who still pursue the same routine of shop work that their ancestors did of old. No modern tools. No improved methods. And considering the improvements made in other pursuits are actually as much in the rut to-day as were the rural blacksmiths of generations ago. While this is so, it is a noticeable fact that better facilities for doing better and quicker work results in more trade and more popular satisfaction every time. This affords the most conclusive evidence that the best tools are indispensable to the enterprising farrier, and this case embraces everything that properly belongs to this class of goods. The list includes the following articles:

No. 1. Driving Hammer, weight, 13 ounces.
2. Pincers.
3. Clinch Cutter.
4. Horse Rasp, size, 14 inches.
6. Foot Hook.
7. Rasp, size, 16 inches.
8. Spreader, for operating on diseased hoofs.
9, 10, 11, 12, 44, 45, 46. Farriers Knives of various sizes, No. 11 an extra blade without handle.
13, 15, 16. Hand Hammers of various weights.
17, 18. Fire Tongs.
19, 21. Creasers, light and heavy bitted.
20, 39. Stamps or Punches.
22, 23, 24. Plain and Countersunk Pritchells for stamping shoes.
26. Russell's Foot Adjuster, fitted to a horse's hoof.
30. Center Punch or Prick for nail piercing.
31. Three Square Iron or Steel Cutter.
33. Foot Tester.
34. Hoof Cutting Nippers.
35. Nail Clincher.
47. Russell's Bed Plate for leveling the foot.
48. Adjustable Compass for measuring height of hoof.
49, 50. Farrier's Clasps or Pocket Knives.
51, 53. Whetstones.
52. Three Square File for dressing knives.
54. Froat to rasp teeth.
55. Sledge, weight, 7 pounds.
56. Double Rasp.
57. Half Round bastard Hot Filing Rasp.
89. Steel Rule, 6 inches, for measuring hoofs.
90. Adjustable Calipers to verify measurements around hoof.

Fig. 187. Case No. 2.

No. 1. Hind bar shoe, worn by trotter "Clementine."
2. Front four calkin shoe, see book, Fig 80.
3. Hind four calkin shoe, see book, Fig. 112.
4. Front scooped grab toe shoe.
5. Front toe weight shoe to balance action, old style, 1862.
6. Front shoe concaved on inner rim.
7. Shoe concaved on inner quarters to prevent picking stones, old style, 1860.
8. Front winter shoe with sharp toe and heel calkins.
9. Front rim shoe to prevent knee hitting, see Fig. 82.
10. Front toe weight shoe, see Fig. 97.
11. Front toe weight shoe, see Fig. 96.
12. Front toe weight shoe to make pacers trot.
13. Front shoe with toe calk for trotters, old style, 1848.
14. Front bar shoe (old style.)
15. Front concaved shoe for saddle horses.
16. Front navicular shoe, worn by "Proteine," see Fig. 63.
17. Hind shoe for curb and sore tendons.
18. Front scooped toe mud shoe, old style, 1860.
19. Front rim shoe.
20. Front heart sunk bar shoe, old style, 1861.
21. Front round shoe, old style.
22. Front shoe for flat feet, see Fig. 35.
23. Front shoe for draft horse, Fig. 102.
24. Front scooped toe shoe, see Fig. 89.
25. Front shoe for ankle and knee hitting, old style.
26. Hind shoe to lessen stride, old style.
27. Front scooped toe rolling motion rim shoe.
28. Hind shoe for draft horse, see Fig. 33.
29. Front shoe for draught horse, see Fig. 32.
30. Front concave shoe for saddle horse.
31. Mule shoe, see Fig. 56.
32. Hind shoe for ankle hitting, see Fig. 84.
33. Racing plate, see Fig. 30.
34. Hind shoe for ankle hitting, old style.
35. Front shoe for ankle hitting, old style.
36. Front side weight shoe, old style, 1876.
37. Front shoe for bar pressure.
38. Front shoe for enlarging ground tread, old style, 1861.
39. Front rim shoe, nails set for low thick hold, 1861.
40. Hind three quarter shoe for ankle cutting, old style.
41. Hind shoe to straighten foot under leg.

282   SCIENTIFIC HORSESHOEING.

FIG. 188. CASE NO. 3.

FIG. 188. CASE NO. 3.

No. 42. Hind shoe, worn by trotter "Thomas Jefferson."
43. Front side weight shoe for ankle and knee hitting.
44. Front scooped toe shoe for stumbling, see Fig. 95.
45. Hind shoe for quarter grabbing.
46. Front concaved shoe for trotters, old style.
47. Front non-paddling shoe, see Fig. 104.
48. Front shoe beveled from toe to heels, worn by "Thos. Jefferson."
49. Hind square toe shoe for ankle hitting, old style, by S. T. H., 1873.
50. Hind shoe for trotters, old style
51. Tip shoe, old style.
52. Hind scooped toe shoe, old style, see Fig. 116.
53. Front shoe for ankle and knee hitting, old style, by S. T. H., 1873.
54. Front bar shoe, worn by "Goldsmith Maid," 1871, see Fig. 90.
55. Front modified "Centennial" shoe, by S. T. H., see Fig. 87.
56. Front rolling motion shoe, No. 1, see Fig. 93.
57. Front shoe for forging, etc., see Fig. 91.
58. Front shoe for knee hitting.
59. Front raised spring bar shoe, see Fig. 88.
60. Front "Centennial" shoe, by S. T. H., see Fig. 85.
61. Front shoe for roadsters.
62. Front spring heel shoe for contraction.
63. Hind shoe for knuckling.
64. Front shoe concaved and thin at heels.
65. Hind scooped toe shoe.
66. Front shoe for knee hitting, by S. T. H.
67. Front shoe modified "Centennial."
68. Front side weight shoe for knee hitting, see Fig. 100.
69. Hind shoe for quarter grabbing.
70. Hind rolling motion shoe, old style.
71. Front bar shoe grooved for slipping, old style.
72. Front grooved center shoe, worn by "American Girl," weight, 31 ounces, see trotting record, page 118.
73. Front rim bar shoe, nailed at toe, old style.
74. Hind concaved shoe, old style.
75. Front shoe concaved quarters, old style trotters, 1862.
76. Front shoe concaved, old style.
77. Plain shoe.
78. Hind shoe for knuckling, see Fig. 71.

The center of this case is occupied by a display of medals which I have received on similar exhibits of shoes, etc., at various expositions throughout the country. See page vii-x.

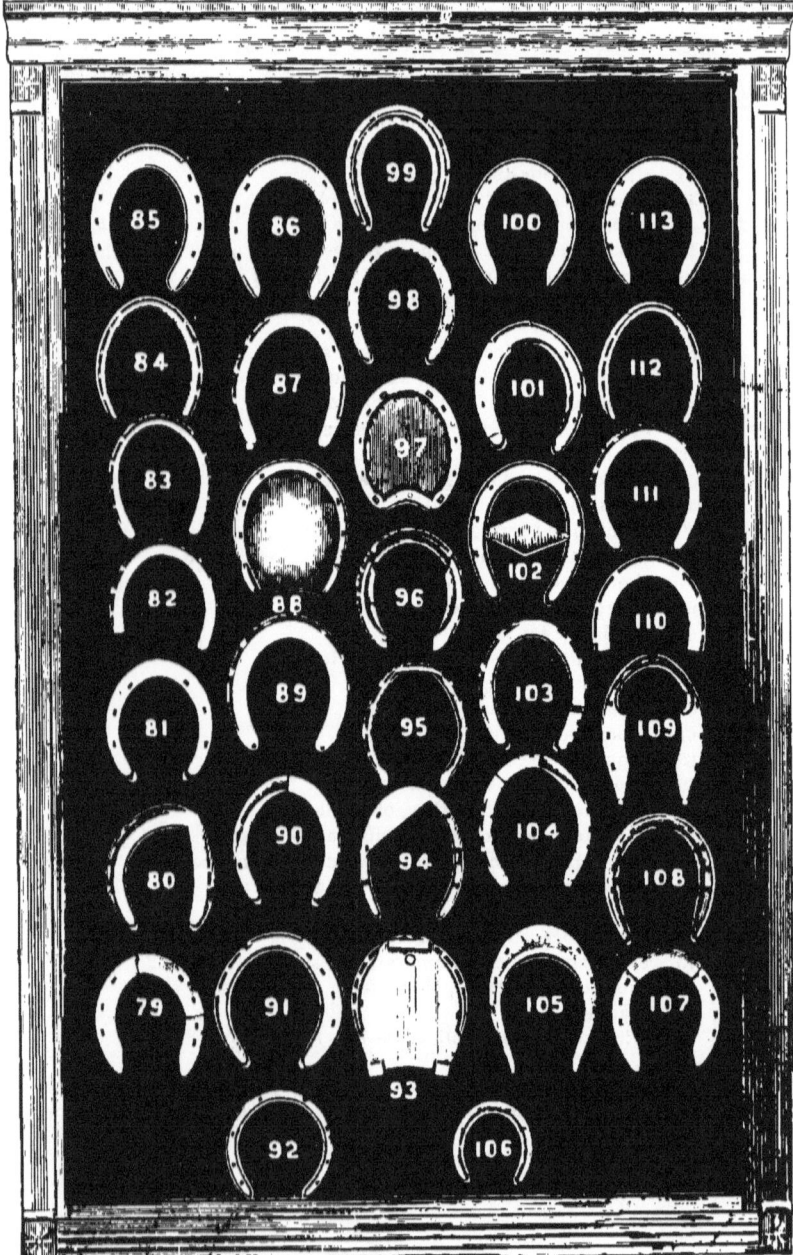

FIG. 189. CASE NO. 4.

No. 79. Front concaved rolling motion shoe to change front action.
80. Front shoe for knee hitting, worn by "Gladiator," 1877.
81. Front shoe ground tread beveled to increase its surface.
82. Front three quarter shoe for bruised heels.
83. Front shoe gradually thinned from toe to heels.
84. Hind concaved shoe.
85. Front shoe flat toe and heel calkins for trotters.
86. Same style shoe as No. 85.
87. Hind shoe inside heel calk for ankle hitting.
88. Front navicular shoe—A, high center of pad, B, heel calkins.
89. Front shoe for bruised heels, see Fig. 91.
90. Front shoe for knee hitting, see Fig. 83.
91. Front shoe for "pigeon toe," wide web outside.
92. Front racing plate, aluminum, weight, one-half ounce.
93. Front hospital shoe, adjustable center plate, for wounds, etc.
94. Front shoe for knee hitting.
95. Hind shoe concaved quarters for roadsters.
96. Front shoe for various purposes, see Fig. 91.
97. Front shoe with leather pad, four calks, etc., for slipping, etc.
98. Front shoe rounded ground surface for forging.
99. Front deep seated concaved shoe for saddle horses.
100. Front rim shoe to prevent slipping.
101. Front non-paddling shoe, toe and heel calks, and wide web inside.
102. Front modified turn-table shoe.
103. Front shoe for quarter cracks.
104. Front shoe toe and heel calks inside for ankle cutting.
105. Front "hospital" shoe for sore tendons, heels 1 inch high, tapering to toe.
106. Pony shoe.
107. Front shoe toe beveled out and quarters beveled in for stumbling.
108. Front deep seated rim shoe for slipping.
109. Hind shoe modified for wheeled feet.
110. Front three quarter tip for sore heels.
111. Front light aluminum shoe for track work.
112. Hind deep concaved shoe.
113. Front rim shoe to prevent slipping.

Fig. 190. Case No. 5.

FIG. 190. CASE NO. 5. 287

No. 114. Front rim tip, worn by trotting horse "Jack."
115. Hind rim tip.
116. Hind shoe for Shetland pony.
117. Front shoe for Shetland pony.
118. Front racing plate.
119. Hind racing plate.
120. Front bar shoe, open space outside, for interfering, etc. (Irish shoe).
121. Hind scoop toe grab shoe for track work.
122. Hind skeleton plate for racing.
123. Front skeleton plate for racing.
124. Hind shoe, elevated heel bar, for curbs and spavins on trotters.
125. Front heart sunk bar rolling motion shoe.
126. Hind scooped toe grab shoe.
127. Front center bearing shoe, see Fig. 123.
128. Hind "spreading" shoe, see Figs. 132 and 133.
129. Front rasp cut plain flat shoe, see Fig. 119.
130. Front deep concaved shoe for saddle horses.
131. Front improved rolling motion shoe, rim on inner border.
132. Front scooped toe grab shoe with bar for racers.
133. Front concaved shoe with thin heels for high heeled horses.
134. Front toe weight scooped grab toe bar shoe for track use.
135. Front bar shoe, see Fig. 118.
136. Front shoe beveled on outer and inner rims for speedy cutting, forging, etc.
137. Hind scoop grab toe bar shoe beveled on inner quarters.
138. Front scooped grab toe bar shoe, see Fig. 122.
139. Front rolling motion shoe No. 2, see Fig 94.
140. Front rasp cut plain flat shoe, see Fig. 117.
141. Front rasp cut bar shoe.
142. Front plain flat shoe.
143. Front plain heart sunk bar shoe.
144. Front plain open shoe.
145. Hind rasp cut shoe, see Fig. 120.
146. Hind rasp cut grab shoe (modified from the last).
147. Front shoe square concaved toe flat ground face for knee hitting.
148. Front shoe light weight for stumbling, see Fig. 95.
149. Front bar shoe with toe calk, worn by "Kremlin."
150. Front plain light bar shoe.
151. Hind bar shoe, long heels, for long striding horses or weak tendons.
152. Front concaved thin heeled shoe for high heeled horses.
153. Scooped toe or grab tip.
154. Hind bar shoe with long outside branch.
155. Front raised split bar shoe with leather pad, see Fig. 121.
156. Front shoe deeply concaved for saddle horses.
157. Hind plain side weight shoe.
158. Front grab toe bar shoe with side and heel calks, see Fig. 125.
159. Front heart sunk bar shoe with toe and heel calks.
160. Front shoe modified "Centennial," see Fig. 86.
161. Front rope toed shoe with heel calks for ice and mud.
162. Hind scooped toe grab shoe for trotters.
163. Front toe weight bar shoe.
164. Front scooped toe grab shoe, long branch outside, for trotters.
165. Hind plain light shoe.
166. Front scooped toe grab shoe beveled in and out for trotters.
167. Hind shoe, tapered heels to toe, worn by trotter "Harry Wilkes."
168. Hind scooped toe grab shoe.
169. Hind shoe for knuckling, see Fig. 71.
170. Hind scoop grab toe bar shoe, long heel branches, etc., for sore tendons.

Fig. 191. A CASE OF FINE HORSESHOES.—MADE BY PROF. WM. RUSSELL.

The above case of horseshoes is said to be the finest in the world. The large shoe in the middle of the case is a medal frame with fourteen medals on the inside. The weight of the large shoe is 16½ pounds. All of the shoes shown are for speed horses, and represent the most recent used by me in my system of balancing the feet so as to insure the greatest speed and endurance The fifteen medals (gold, silver and bronze) are all the highest premiums, and represent the highest honors obtained, wherever the shoes have been exhibited.

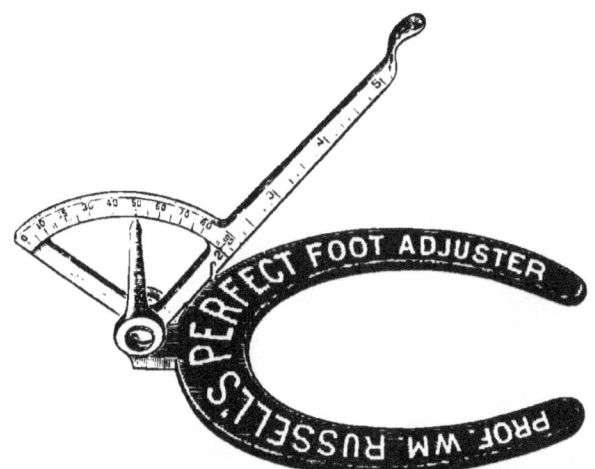

Fig. 192. Russell's Foot Adjuster.

Instructions for use given on pages 77 to 81; also see Figs. 16 to 20.

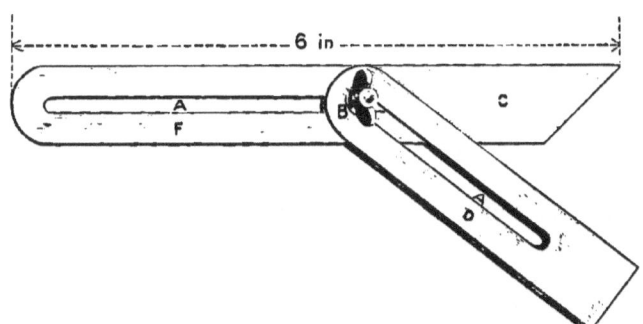

Fig. 193. Russell's Heel Adjuster, for obtaining the Angles of the Heels.

A, A, Slots in plates for adjustment to position desired.
B, Thumb screw for setting the plates.
C, Γ, Adjustable lever to obtain the angle of heels.
D, Lower bed-plate, to lay on bottom of the foot across the quarters, in equalizing the angle on both sides of the heel.

290　SCIENTIFIC HORSESHOEING.

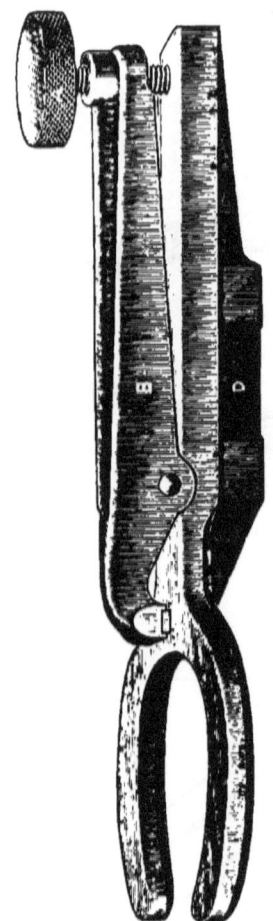

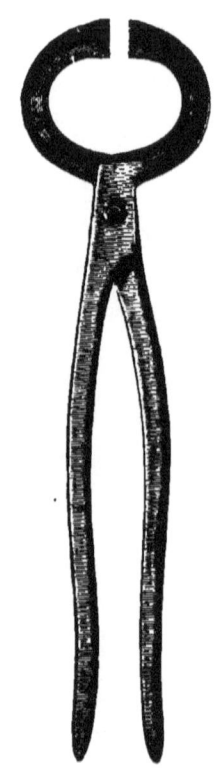

Fig. 195. Russell's Foot Testers.

Explained on page 135.

Fig. 194. Russell's Hand Vise, for Hot Rasping Shoes.

A, Set screw to fasten the jaw, **B,** on shoe.

C, Bed plate, shaped like a front foot shoe, on which to lay the shoe, to hot or cold rasp it on the bevel of the heels and quarters.

D, Lower projection, to catch in the jaws of stationary vise.

E, End of jaw to grip the shoes. Length of vise, 16 inches.

This tool is indispensable to all shoers who shoe light horses, as by its use the thinnest shoes can be filed without springing.

CHAPTER XI.

RECIPES AND INSTRUCTIONS.

FOR TREATING DISEASES OF THE HORSE'S FEET AND LEGS.

It seems suitable and convenient as to the general purpose of this book that, after having dwelt somewhat largely upon a review of the principal diseases and injuries which impair the organic soundness of the horse's foot, and treating in detail the efficacy of a safe and scientific mode of shoeing in counteracting such evils, I should devote—in a limited way—a few recipes, such as I have used myself with the most satisfactory results. It is not my intention, however, to advise that the attendance of a regular veterinarian be dispensed with when any serious form of disease exists which calls for medical treatment beyond the reach of the farrier's art. Neither do I desire to appear in a false light with respect to the valid claims of professional veterinary practice. At all times the mechanical work of shoeing is combined more or less with the surgical treatment of the foot, hence the farrier of to-day must be more than a "blacksmith," or a mere worker in iron; and it is for his guidance that I am now writing. Having placed before my readers the undoubted utilities of shoeing for remedial purposes, I likewise submit the following medicaments as useful applications for any of the cases to which they especially refer. Success in the use of these preparations, I may add, depends upon a right understanding of the nature of the trouble in each instance, and then in the proper application of the remedy.

No. 1.

Cleansing the feet.—The importance of cleanliness in keeping the feet of horses free from certain disorders of the skin and other excretory matters that are causative of eruptions can not be overlooked. In prescribing a simple wash for the feet, therefore, it is only a step in the way of preventing disorder in its functions, to which neglect of such precaution may lead. In hot dry weather the extremities of the limbs should be thoroughly scoured at least once a day. Use the best castile soap with a liberal supply of warm water and make a good, stiff lather and apply it with a brush—to rub it in and thus cleanse the skin from all impurities. Then rinse off with clear water and dry with a cloth. This operation should apply to all parts of the ankle and hoof, including the heels, and in this way a clear, healthy condition of skin and elastic, tough, glossy wall will be insured, if the foot is otherwise healthy.

No. 2.

Foot Salve.—Shoemaker's wax, ½ lb.; Beeswax, ½ lb.; Mutton Tallow, for summer use, ¼ lb.; and for winter use, ½ lb. To be melted in an iron pot over a gentle fire, kept constantly stirred until the composition is well dissolved and thoroughly mixed.

This preparation is invaluable for many foot ailments when used according to directions.

For Contraction.—After the foot has been prepared and the shoe fitted, have the salve well warmed and fill the bottom of the foot with it, then cover it with a thin overlay of white cotton or clean oakum, and nail on the shoe with a piece of leather fitted under the web to cover the bottom of the foot to retain the salve in place and protect it from dirt.

For Coronitis.—Warm the salve as before and thoroughly saturate with it several pledgets or thin flat layers of white cotton and cover the coronary band all around with a thick coating of salve, secured with a compress bandage of linen, laid over it to keep it in place, after which rub a warm smoothing iron over the surface from toe to heels, repeating this process once or twice daily for the space of a week or more, being careful not to scorch or burn the bandage in so doing. The application of heat will operate as a tonic to stimulate the circulation throughout the diseased organ, causing it to absorb the salve, which will at once check the ossific tendency and assist the horn secreting powers of the coronary cushion.

For Laminitis and Villitis, or for inflammation and soreness of the villous tissue of the toe and sole of the foot, follow the directions given for treatment and shoeing in Chapter VII, covering such diseases.

For Bruised and Ulcerated Heels.—Have the foot leveled and prepared by removing all the hard, dead, portions of the horny sole around the affected part, then apply the salve and cotton in and around the sore or tender spot. After the shoe is applied, soak the foot in tubs of warm water, as this will act favorably in reducing inflammation and removing soreness.

For Chapped Heels or Dry Skin.—Apply the salve same as above, secured with bandage, and repeat the heating process with warm iron as recommended for Coronitis and all soreness or derangement will quickly disappear.

For Punctured Wounds.—Whenever the foot is wounded by a nail or other sharp body, it will be necessary to immediately open up the injured spot by means of a drawing knife and remove the edges of the wounded parts as deep as the horny tissue extends. The salve is then to be poured into the orifice until the cavity is filled—the foot being held up that the salve may cool and harden. By having it remain there the stimulus which it imparts will soon allay any irritation and bring on a healthy growth.

No. 3.

Liniment for Chronic and Painful Inflammations of Tendons, Coronary Cushion, etc.—Tincture of Aconite Root, 2 oz.; Spirits of Ammonia, 2 oz.; Tincture of Iodine, 4 oz. Mix and shake well before using.

This remedy is applicable to all cases of soreness or inflammation in the tendons and coronary structures, also it operates favorably on bog spavins, wind galls, and chapped hocks. It stimulates the parts affected to healthy action by causing all exudations, whether of the bones or soft parts, to be quickly re-absorbed and the irritations allayed. In applying, saturate and rub the parts affected well once a day, and in severe cases, twice a day, morning and evening, continuing the operation until recovery takes place.

No. 4.

Wash for General Purposes.—The following recipe is a mild caustic, and will result in no injury to the foot if used as directed: Carbolic Acid, 1 ounce; Glycerine, 1 ounce; Distilled Water, 6 ounces. Mix thoroughly.

When used for bruised heels, pare all the dead hard sole from around the bruised parts, thinning the insensitive sole until it will spring under the pressure of the thumb. After having done this, saturate white cotton large enough to cover the affected parts, lay over the bruise, and allow it to remain for fifteen or twenty minutes. Put a few drops of the wash on the cotton occasionally, so as to keep it thoroughly saturated. It sometimes happens that the horse strikes his opposite ankle or shin, cutting it, and quite often proud flesh sets up in the wound. If this happens, take white cotton large enough to cover the wound, thoroughly saturate with the wash and lay over the wound. Bandage the leg to hold the cotton in place, and let it remain on the wound for fifteen or twenty minutes.

This will remove the proud flesh and stimulate a healthy growth. I have used the above wash and it has always produced the best and most satisfactory results.

No. 5.

Witch Hazel Wash, for General Purposes, such as Sprained Tendons, Sore Loins and Soreness of the Muscles.—Witch hazel wash is an old, long-standing remedy, well known to horsemen, and has a well-earned reputation as a relief for the above-named troubles. I have used it myself with the most satisfactory results. Always bear in mind to have the foot properly balanced, and a shoe so constructed and fitted that when nailed to the foot the horse will stand with his foot and leg naturally under the body. In this way the weight of the body is equally distributed to all parts of the foot and leg.

www.ingramcontent.com/pod-product-compliance
Lightning Source LLC
Chambersburg PA
CBHW022104230426
43672CB00008B/1278